Hollon, William Eu-
gene

Frontier vio-
lence; another
look

DATE DUE

Frontier Violence: Another Look

FRONTIER VIOLENCE

Another Look

W. EUGENE HOLLON

New York
OXFORD UNIVERSITY PRESS
1974

Copyright © 1974 by Oxford University Press, Inc.
Library of Congress Catalogue Card Number: 73–87617
Printed in the United States of America

To Ray Allen Billington
Gentleman, Scholar, and Friend

Preface

America has always had a violent past, and the frontier in a way has stood for this country at its most violent. Without exception, the history of every Western state is replete with lawlessness, from the arrival of the early Mountain Men to the appearance of the twentieth-century Minutemen. In between we find a wide range of individual types—claim jumpers, miners, cowboys, cattle rustlers, Indian haters, Border ruffians, Mexican banditti, mule skinners, railroad workers, highwaymen, racial bigots of various colors, professional outlaws, homicidal maniacs, and hired gunslingers. Each group had more than a speaking acquaintance with violence, for the rough life on the frontier prior to 1900 produced scant recognition of the law as law.

In addition, there were the so-called "gentlemen of property and standing"—ranchers, farmers, bankers, town builders, railroad owners, lawyers, doctors, politicians, mine operators and others—who sometimes took the law into their own hands. They generally operated in the West as self-appointed members of mobs formed to apprehend road agents, horse thieves, and murderers. Frequently their victims were Chinese, Negroes, Mexicans, Jews, Indians—any minority group they disliked or distrusted. On the other hand, vigilantes in the East sometimes vented their frustrations on Tories, abolitionists, Mormons, Negroes, Irish, and Catholics.

The frontiersman, often remote from the courts and authorities of established communities, not only had to enforce his own law, he elected which laws should be enforced and which ignored. Payment of debts, for example, might be taken lightly. But stealing horses or cattle was generally punishable by immediate hanging or shooting. In fact, evidence of violence on the Western frontier is so overwhelming that the innumerable examples overshadow the deeper causes. To use a well-worn cliché, it has been difficult at times to see the forest for the trees. Or has it been the other way around?

The distinguished historian James Truslow Adams observed, in an article published in *The Atlantic Monthly* in 1928, that the gang wars of the 1920's were primarily the result of the presence of a frontier for almost 300 years of our history. Two generations later a well-known sociologist and specialist on American violence glibly wrote that "We can report with some assurance that compared to frontier days there has been a significant decrease in crimes of violence in the United States." [1] Such statements, along with the assertion that Canada and Australia evolved from frontier origins with very little corresponding violence, have been repeated so often that they have virtually gone unchallenged.

At the same time, the literature on violence in American history is so extensive that a mere catalogue of books relating directly to the subject fills more than four trays in the Library of Congress card-file index.[2] Approximately eighty of the listed titles were published during the five years between 1967 and 1972. This does not include newspaper and magazine articles, nor, necessarily, all studies on crimes in general. Why then another look at violence at this time, if so much has already been written about it? Is there any point in trying to prove that the frontier was an invitation to violence and that it deserves the primary responsibility for our violent society today, since the idea appears to have widespread acceptance? Is it in-appropriate to ask if we are doing violence to our heritage? Was H. L. Mencken right when he observed that "something which everyone accepts as the gospel truth is inevitably false"? Was the frontier really all that violent, or was there another side of the coin? These are questions which I have asked myself thou-sands of times since beginning this study in 1968.

Before attempting an answer, I first looked briefly at our Pu-ritan tradition of intolerance toward the Indians and religious dissenters. From there I moved on to some of the acts of vio-lence preceding the American Revolution, thence to Jacksonian Democracy and to the series of events that flayed the nation for thirty years before the Civil War. I have placed consider-able emphasis, however, upon the frontiers beyond the Missis-sippi, particularly Texas and California where more than three-fourths of the population of the West resided and where racial bigotry and gun culture achieved a very high level. The pattern of violence established in the gold fields of California spread eastward into the mining camps of Nevada and the Rocky Mountains region, and from Texas it traveled wherever the cattle trails led, into the arid Southwest and throughout the Southern and Northern Plains.

I have also placed major emphasis upon the violence in the West during the last half of the nineteenth century, particu-larly as it related to the Indians, Mexicans, Negroes, and Chi-nese. And I have dealt with the subject of guns, range warfare, professional gunfighters, and legendary heroes. Although Amer-ican cities perhaps experienced considerably more violence, the lawless aspect of Western frontier society has had a much greater appeal to the vicarious reader. Thus, a disproportionate amount of dramatic literature exists on violence in the West in comparison to the material available on the East. This makes it all the more difficult to defend the primary thesis of this study —namely, that frontier lawlessness was primarily the result, rather than the cause, of our violent society. The truth is, our frontier heritage produced much more of what is good in the American character than what is bad. Yet of all the myths that refuse to die, the hardiest concerns the extent of the unmitigated bloodletting that occurred on the Western frontier during the closing decades of the nineteenth century.

Perhaps the real violence of the frontier was related more to anxiety, tension, frustration, and prejudice than to any action by outlaws, Indian fighters, and assorted vigilante groups. Even so, our folklore tends to support the image of Americans as tough, aggressive, and unafraid—real go-getters who tamed the wild frontier and never lost a war. "Winning is not just important, it's everything!" Success depends upon aggressiveness, whether on the football field, in the used-car lot, or behind the desk in the Oval Office of the White House. This may be why the frontier outlaw has endured so long in literature and legend. He went out and got what he wanted with his own two hands, frequently by violent means. His deeds, real and imaginary, have served as a culturally valid metaphor of how we have viewed ourselves.

We are prone to accept prefabricated explanations, but glib generalizations about our bloody heritage do not necessarily explain away our present disorder. In this study I have attempted to synthesize and examine various events relating to frontier violence, and I have taken a look at the other side of the coin. Those who are familiar with Western history will find little here that has not already been said elsewhere—a charge that could be levied against most historical works. But history needs to be rewritten for each succeeding generation, and I hope that my efforts will enable the average reader to appreciate the dilemma we are up against—in ourselves and in our history. Even in the face of the evidence of frontier violence presented in the first nine chapters, I firmly believe that the Western frontier was a far more civilized, more peaceful, and safer place than American society is today.

During the course of my research I spent considerable time

at the National Archives, Library of Congress, and in the Beincke Library at Yale. But the bulk of the material was collected at the Huntington Library at San Marino, California, during the summers of 1969 and 1972. I am especially grateful to the Huntington Library for its financial assistance, which enabled Betty and me to spend some of the most pleasant months of our lives at one of the great research libraries in the world. The Director, Dr. James Thorpe, Senior Research Associate Dr. Ray Allen Billington, Gary F. Kurutz of the Rare Book Department, and the entire staff could not have been more cooperative. I should also like to thank the Huntington Library for the photographs on pages 60, 70, 76, 78, 82, 84, 88, 96 and 97, 138, 142, 144, 164, 176, 180, 181, 198, 199, and 204; the Texas State Library for the photograph on page 38; the Western History Collections, University of Oklahoma Library, for the photograph on page 40; the Kansas State Historical Society for the photograph on page 114; and *The Los Angeles Times* for the cartoon (Copyright © 1973 by *The Los Angeles Times*) on page 120. All of these are used by permission.

Mrs. Martha Manheim of Toledo caught dozens of errors in the galleys that otherwise would have gone undetected. And Mrs. H. C. Peterson of Norman, Oklahoma, did her usual superb job in compiling the index. Once again I had the pleasure of working with Miss Caroline Taylor of the editorial staff of Oxford University Press. Her enthusiasm and cooperation made my task considerably easier. I wish further to express appreciation to my colleague, Dr. Charles Glaab, who read most of the manuscript and offered very constructive criticism. I also am indebted to Michael Tate, John Jameson, and George Schorr for helping out from time to time on proofreading and doing leg work in the University of Toledo Library. Mrs. Lucille Endsley and Miss Sharon Klonowski typed preliminary drafts of individual chapters, and Miss Candy Davis typed the entire manuscript. Unfortunately, I must assume responsibility for all errors.

xii PREFACE

The late Walter Prescott Webb once wrote: "In a Preface the author is supposed to take the reader into his confidence, let him in on a deep and mysterious secret, and tell him the truth. What the author really does is to introduce himself with an air of assumed modesty, try to forestall and fend off the critics, and persuade the reader to go on with the job and buy the book." [3] As much as I would like to fend off the critics, experience has taught me that the task is impossible. In the first place, few people even bother to read the Preface. And many who do, especially if they possess some knowledge of the subject at hand, will not accept the author's explanation of why he did not write the type of book which they feel the subject deserves. All I can say to these latter-day critics is this: "Where were you when I needed you most?"

Toledo, Ohio   W.E.H.
January 1974

Contents

Frontier Violence: Another Look

I

The Colonial Experience

Some psychiatrists believe that a child's personality and character are formed in the first five years of his life. If we apply this analogy to the personality of the nation, then the type of violent society we experience today was determined by our Puritan ancestors. The question then arises, how could a small group, so remote in time and occupying such a limited area of the continent, have had so great an influence on our contemporary life? If there is an answer, it lies outside the realm of the average historian, who is not trained to analyze Freudian behavioral patterns.

"There is little doubt that the myth of the Puritans' influence lives in our minds," Dr. David Abrahamsen observed in *Our Violent Society*. "They are revered and blamed for whatever misfortunes we go through or whatever violence we manifest." Abrahamsen goes on to explain that the Pilgrims and Puritans lived relatively serene lives in England in contrast to what they faced in America. He compared the drastic changes they encountered to that of a newborn baby's experience when it leaves the womb and enters a strange, threatening environment. Realizing that they would not return to England, the signers of the Mayflower Compact felt a com-

pulsive desire to succeed, a desire which intensified their fear
of failure. They resisted any infringement upon their way of
life and suppressed all ideas or beliefs that were alien or
dangerous to their own. Such an attitude was a hallmark of
seventeenth-century European culture. It not only inspired
snobbery, but it also encouraged repression and violence.

The basic instinct for self-preservation manifested itself immediately upon the small party that first set foot on Plymouth
Rock in 1620. William Bradford later described his feelings
and those of his companions as they ventured forth in search of
food and shelter: "For we know not how we should find or
meet with any of the Indians, except it be to do us a mischief."
Since the founders of Plymouth Colony had already resolved
to shoot first and ask questions later, it is not surprising that
it was they, and not the Indians, who committed the initial
act of violence. And so it went.

Dr. Abrahamsen believes that it was not only the reality
of the lives of our Puritan ancestors that shaped the course of
future generations; their experience has also become part of
our national mythology and continues to serve as a powerful
and respected ego-ideal. The founders of Plymouth and Massachusetts Bay Colony have therefore supplied the emotional
function of the "superior" father image with whom millions
of Americans have identified. To carry the analogy of psychoanalysis further, the child identifies with his parents by
unconsciously adopting their ideas and attitudes. If the early
English settlers had to fight against the overwhelming and im-
personal forces of nature to survive, so did the pioneers of each
succeeding frontier. "It was here on the frontier that our
fantasies and dreams were first either transformed into reality
or remained pipedreams." Those who survived—whether they
lived in seventeenth-century New England or nineteenth-century New Mexico—laid down the standards for behavior, rules,
and values for others to follow.

So much for psychoanalysis. For whatever credit or blame

the Puritans deserve, they certainly did not introduce the idea of violence into the New World as a method of problem-solving. Indeed, this continent had been occupied by intelligent humans for at least 25,000 years before the first Europeans arrived. Although we know little of the actual history of these ancient people, sufficient evidence is available to indicate that they constantly battled the elements of nature, as well as one another, and that death and violence were rarely more than a few steps or a few moments away.

Centuries before Columbus, Leif Ericson and his brother Thorvald Karlsefni had already visited the New World. According to Viking sagas, around A.D. 1000 they planted a small colony on the Newfoundland coast, where they immediately encountered a party of nine Indians. The Vikings slaughtered eight of the natives with no more compunction than they would have felt over chopping off the heads of poisonous snakes. Later, Leif's half sister, an Amazon known as Freydis, inveigled her slow-witted husband into murdering her two brothers and several other members of the Vinland colony. When he refused to kill five women in the group, Freydis seized an ax and personally hacked them to pieces. Before returning to their homeland in Greenland, the survivors agreed upon the same story—that the others had chosen to remain behind.

Another 500 years elapsed before the *conquistadores* arrived in North America. Their record of violence is not based upon legend, but upon the records kept by Spanish chroniclers. Hernando de Soto seemed especially fond of killing Indians, and he left a trail of blood from Florida to Tennessee. Coronado's trek from northern Mexico across the Southwest to Kansas, during the same period, likewise was marked by burned villages, raped women, and slaughtered natives. Not all Spaniards, of course, were butchers who killed for sadistic pleasure. Rather, they seem to have believed that the only means of survival in an inhospitable land was by violence. The natives learned quickly to retaliate in kind, sometimes even before being provoked by the intruders.

The record of the early English, Dutch, and French colonizers in the New World was only slightly less violent than that of the Spaniards. The Europeans frequently committed indescribable mayhem against one another, not to mention against the Indians. In the words of Charles Tilly, one of the contributors to *The History of Violence in America* (1969), "Collective violence has flowed regularly out of the central political processes of western countries. . . . The oppressed have struck in the name of justice, the privileged in the name of order, the in-between in the name of fear."

It is not surprising, therefore, that the Pilgrims who survived the voyage on the *Mayflower* did not hesitate to commit atrocities against the Indians. They robbed their graves, stole their food supplies, killed what chiefs and warriors they could find in the area, and made prisoners of the native women. Later, two ships dropped anchor near Plymouth, bringing sixty Protestant men of a different sect. The new arrivals hoped to establish their own colony, but the "Saints" did what they could to make life miserable for their new neighbors. They considered them immoral because they were not "true believers," and, moreover, they suspected them of cohabiting with Indian women. When the heretics refused to conform, they were given the alternative of abandoning their settlement or facing extermination.

The Puritans of Massachusetts Bay also would insist that residents of the colony conform to a strict set of religious dogmas, ideals, and manners. The death penalty was used to punish a wide range of crimes: treason, murder, witchcraft, adultery, rape, sodomy, and arson—among others. Margaret Jones had the dubious honor of being the first "witch" hanged in Boston—in 1648. A few others received similar punishment during the next four or five decades throughout New England and the Middle Colonies. Then witch-hunting suddenly de-

veloped into a mania. Several hundred people were arrested
in Massachusetts during a six-month reign of terror in 1692.
Before it all ended, nineteen so-called witches had been strung
up by the neck. The twelve good and true men on the jury
who had handed down the verdicts later confessed their errors
and asked forgiveness. It is not known if "a higher order"
granted the request, but for all practical purposes the confession marked the end of one of the most senseless and violent
episodes of American history.[1]

Hanging witches might have represented the most bizarre
form of violence in seventeenth-century New England, but
breaking the laws of the mother country was a far more extensive practice. Breaking the law itself does not necessarily
constitute a violent act, but throughout most of American history a general disregard for unpopular laws has led to general
lawlessness and eventually to violence. The founders of Massachusetts Bay Colony, for example, smuggled the company
charter to America and used it as a constitution. To com-
pound their action, the leaders ignored at will various sections
of the charter which gave the British government the right
to control or supervise local governmental affairs.

During the age of great sailing ships, trees suitable for masts
sold at a premium, and England preferred to depend upon
the forests of America rather than upon those of northern
Europe. But the settlers of Massachusetts and other English
colonies believed that it constituted an abridgment of their
rights for the mother country to reserve certain trees for her-
self. They not only ignored the imperial restriction, they cut
down whatever trees they desired for themselves and frequently roughed up the legally appointed "Surveyors of the
Woods." Because the colonists deliberately defied foolish laws
prohibiting the manufacture of woolen goods, nails, and sun-
dry household necessities, they found it easy to ignore more
legitimate measures.

The late seventeenth century was an especially turbulent

period of colonial history. In addition to a series of violent
uprisings by various Indian tribes, which were aimed at re-
gaining lands seized by the white settlers, there were several
rebellious outbreaks among the colonists themselves. The list
is long, but the pattern is consistent. Among them were Bacon's
Rebellion in Virginia (1675–76), Culpepper's Rebellion in
North Carolina (1677–79), Leisler's Rebellion in New York
(1689), Coode's Rebellion in Maryland (1689), and the uprising against Governor Edmund Andros in Massachusetts
(1689). These all resulted from mass dissatisfaction with established authority—the "outs" against the "ins"—and, almost
invariably, they were settled by violence and bloodshed.

The eighteenth century witnessed a steady stream of peti-
tions flowing from the backwoods and frontier regions, from
Vermont to Georgia, to the colonial assemblies or governors'
offices. Small farmers, generally with substantial justification,
complained that they were overtaxed, underrepresented, and
exposed to constant attacks by the Indians. Moreover, they
lived incessantly in the shadows of foreclosure and bankruptcy,
and were treated with contempt by the "Eastern aristocracy."
From time to time they took the law into their own hands,
resisted officials sent to arrest them, tarred and feathered tax
collectors, or marched upon the capital to demand special
legislation.

Domestic violence in the decades before the American Revolution was by no means confined to the frontier. As early as
1712, and again in 1741, New York City witnessed urban riots
involving rebellious slaves and the killing of several blacks.
Newark, Boston, Newport, Philadelphia, and Charleston all
had slave riots during the 1740's. The Boston affair lasted three
days, during which time the Governor fled the city and took
temporary refuge on an island in the bay. The trouble had
started when a royal official tried to impress seamen from the
local dockworks into the British Navy. Fortunately, no one
was killed and the mob rescued most of the impressed men

before the squadron sailed out of the harbor. Action a few years later by similar elements of the Boston population helped bring on the American Revolution.

Meanwhile, the Molasses Act of 1733 and the subsequent Navigation Acts long since had turned most of the reputable merchants of New England into professional smugglers. Their illegal trading with the enemy during the French and Indian Wars undoubtedly prolonged the conflict among the European powers, which were fighting over control of North America. Even after taxes on wine, tea, and other luxury items were reduced to moderate or mere token rates, importers made it their patriotic duty to defy the law and to resort regularly to mob violence.

Certainly one of the most controversial and misunderstood pieces of legislation that Parliament passed during the eighteenth century was the Proclamation Act of 1763, which restricted temporary settlement of the western lands England had recently obtained from France. The policy guaranteed wholesale defiance of authority. Colonials simply could not resist the opportunities offered by the virgin lands beyond the Allegheny-Appalachian ridge, and settlers and traders poured into western Pennsylvania and eastern Kentucky and Tennessee. They ignored not only the laws of Parliament, but those of their own legislatures as well.

The local laws most often flouted by the pioneers concerned the sale of guns and liquor to the Indians or trade with the French and, later, the British occupation forces. Long before the Revolution, Americans were already determined to obey only legislation that they individually approved of or that did not interfere with their own conscience or opportunity for profit. Thus, after a century and a half of lawbreaking following the establishment of Jamestown and Plymouth, disrespect for law as law was fully developed in the colonies. The same contempt or distrust applied to executive officials, royal or otherwise. Citizens of Boston, New York, and elsewhere invariably stood together to protect their friends and neighbors and to thwart governors, judges, and courts whenever possible.[2] This was especially true in cases involving smugglers. Colonial juries would no more convict a merchant for evasion of import duties than a jury of farmers in Missouri would later condemn the James brothers for robbing a bank or a train.

Although a considerable amount of the violence in rural Colonial America was associated with clearing Indians out of the area, widespread disorder was common in the cities from the outset. The urban historian Richard Wade attributes this partly to the fact that most of the young cities were born of commerce, which meant that they invariably contained a large transient population. "At any moment the number of newcomers was large and their attachment to the community slight. Hence when they hit town, there was always some liveliness." Colonial Boston is a particular case in point, in that it had more than its share of seamen, dockworkers, and unemployed laborers looking for excitement. Samuel Adams supplied them with a chance to let off steam under the cloak of patriotism. The Stamp Tax Riots, the Boston Massacre, the burning of the British revenue cutter *Gaspee*, and the Boston Tea Party were all part of a carefully executed campaign of violent politics.

In the Stamp Act Riots, action was directed against those who had been or expected to be stamp distributors or users. Mobs marched through the streets of Boston and other cities shouting slogans of "Liberty, Property, and no Stamps" or "Death to the man who offers a piece of stamped paper to sell." The mobs also destroyed bales of stamps, burned buildings, and tarred and feathered British sympathizers. So effective was the campaign of intimidation that the Stamp Act was already completely meaningless by the time Parliament repealed it. But once open rebellion had begun, it would continue in a series of fitful and violent acts until it reached a climax at Lexington and Concord.

As in all wars, violence in the American Revolution was by no means confined to soldiers on the field of battle. Thomas Jones, a prominent resident of New York, described what was happening in that city during the early years of the Revolution. General Washington had only recently occupied the place in the wake of British evacuation when, in June 1776, a group of "staunch Presbyterians" and leading citizens decided that the time had come to ferret out and punish those who had remained loyal to the Crown.

> . . . When they had taken several of these unhappy victims destined, to the will, the sport, and the caprice, of a bandetti, and the diversion of republicans and rebels, they placed them upon sharp rails with one leg on each side; and each rail was carried upon the shoulders of two tall men, with a man on each side to keep the poor wretch straight and fixed in his seat. In this manner were numbers of people, in danger of their lives from extremity of pain occasioned by this cruel contrivance, paraded through the most public and conspicuous streets in the town, and at every corner a crier made proclamation declaring the offenders to be such and such (mentioning their names), and notorious tories (loyal subjects meaning). The mob then gave three huzzas and the procession went on.[3]

According to Jones, General Israel Putnam accidentally intercepted one of the processions at a street corner, and he was so appalled by the barbarity of the action that he tried to stop it immediately. Whereupon General Washington arrived on the scene and administered a severe reprimand to his subordinate officer. The Commander then declared that to discourage such proceeding was to injure the cause of liberty, which only an enemy of the country would attempt to do. Thus the matter ended, but not before several unhappy victims were forced to endure even more excruciating pain as a result of being bounced up and down on their genitals.

During the war for independence, the Colonies established their own government under the Articles of Confederation, but after the peace old habits proved hard to break. A few months before the Constitutional Convention met in Philadelphia, Daniel Shays and other veterans of the war seized and burned courthouses throughout central and western Massachusetts, intimidated government agents, and destroyed private property. Among other things, Shays and his followers were rebelling against high taxes, voting restrictions, farm foreclosures, and malapportionment in the state legislature. On the occasion of his march to Springfield in 1786 to prevent the state supreme court from meeting, Shays addressed his ragtag troops somewhat as follows: "Men, we're marching to Springfield to fight for our liberty. If you wish to know what liberty is, I'll tell you. It means that every man has the right to do as he pleases, while keeping other people from serving the Devil."

Shays frightened the Eastern propertied men so badly that they hired General Benjamin Lincoln to lead a combined force of militia and federal troops to put down the insurrection. The rebel leader subsequently escaped to New York, but several of his followers were captured and hanged. The disturbance undoubtedly convinced many delegates at the Constitutional Convention of the urgent necessity of establishing a strong central government capable of maintaining law and order.

President Washington was in office for only a brief period before violence similar to that of Shays' Rebellion erupted on the frontier of western Pennsylvania. Thousands of small farmers banded together and refused to pay the new federal excise tax of ten cents per gallon on whiskey. The trouble continued from 1791 to 1794, during which period dozens of tax collectors and certain distillers who complied with the law were tarred and feathered and some were ridden out of town on poles. By the time Washington and some 2000 troops under his leadership had reached the back country, considerable burning and looting of property had taken place. Dozens of leaders were arrested, returned east none too gently for trial, and eventually sentenced to be hanged. In the end the rebellion collapsed, the prisoners were pardoned by the President, and law and order were restored.

Before moving into the early nineteenth century and on to the trans-Appalachian frontier, let us backtrack a bit for a brief examination of another view of the subject. Violence takes many forms, including psychological warfare, violence against a man's psyche or livelihood, or physical aggression against the body. According to the late Professor Arthur Schlesinger, Sr., violence in the form of mob activity in behalf of political ideals was almost unknown in America before 1765. In an article entitled "Political Mobs and the American Revolution, 1765–1776," he divided mob action into two categories—those that are "deliberately engineered" and those that occur as "spontaneous explosions." [4] Examples of the first type include the Stamp Act Riots, the burning of the *Gaspee*, and the Boston Tea Party. In all three instances, leadership was in the hands of men of status and property.

Despite the hounding of the stamp collectors throughout New York and the New England colonies, no lives were lost and surprisingly little property was destroyed. The *Gaspee* affair was organized openly in 1772 by John Brown, one of the leading merchants of Providence, Rhode Island. He and his followers boarded the British revenue cutter, which had run aground near Warwick, captured and bound the crew and put them ashore, and burned the vessel to the water's edge. The property destroyed was English, not American, and it was being employed to enforce the widely disliked Navigation Acts. The mob confined its activities to specific and limited objectives, and, although the identity of its members was known to at least a thousand people, the commission of inquiry set up by the British authorities could find no one willing to testify against them.

The Boston Tea Party provided another clear-cut demonstration of the moderation and respect which the mob exhibited during what is generally considered a turbulent period of American history. Samuel Adams and his followers, some of whom were, in words later used by abolitionist William Lloyd Garrison, "Gentlemen of Property and Standing," limited their objectives to tea alone. They harmed no one aboard the British ships in Boston Harbor, and they were so respectful of private property that they later replaced a padlock which they had broken. The Stamp Act, *Gaspee,* and Tea Party incidents created intense excitement at the time, but they were relatively tame affairs compared to the various "spontaneous explosions" that occurred during the decade of controversy preceding the American Revolution. Professor Schlesinger cites as examples of the second category the ransacking of Lieutenant Governor Hutchinson's house in Boston in 1765, the Battle of Golden Hill in January 1770, and the Boston Massacre a few weeks later.

The fact that only five or six men were killed in these three "explosions"—and they were civilians killed by British troops, not vice versa—would seem to indicate that American patriots rarely if ever resorted to bloodthirsty revenge during moments of great political excitement. This was not necessarily true in the case of English or French mobs throughout the last half of the eighteenth century. Animated by a spirit of uncontrolled fury, they frequently overran their objectives and ended up repudiating or killing their leaders. On the other hand, the mobs in Boston, New York, and elsewhere stopped as soon as they accomplished whatever they had set out to do, and they were never swept up into an irrational destruction of lives and property.

Thus, up to the time of Washington's administration, violence in the United States had, for the most part, been directed against the state, and not against other groups. But, with the exception of the Civil War and Reconstruction, violence would take an entirely different turn throughout the subsequent century. It generally would become more informal and more repressive, more racial, economic, and ethnic; and it would involve citizen against citizen as well as group against group.

II
Melting Pot or Pressure Cooker?

The Colonial period witnessed the formation of the first large-scale vigilante organization in America, the South Carolina Regulators of 1767–69. This group resembled those later associated with San Francisco, the mining camps and cowtowns of the West, and the cattle empires on the open range. Throughout the eighteenth and nineteenth centuries, vigilante committees were formed to establish law and order and to administer immediate "justice" in areas where courts and law officers were either nonexistent, corrupt, or incapable of dealing with the problem at hand. Richard Brown and other authorities on the subject maintain that the early vigilante movements were generally successful in staying within bounds. Yet regardless of the circumstances, vigilantism invariably remained kindred in spirit to outright violence.

Closely associated with the vigilante movements of the Western frontier was the administration of justice by "lynch law." The origin of that term is erroneously ascribed to one John Lynch, founder of Lynchburg, Virginia. The assertion that the expression originated in Galway, Ireland, in 1493, when Mayor John Fitzstephen Lynch ordered the execution of his own son, is likewise erroneous. "Lynch law" seems to have originated from a practice started by Charles Lynch, a Virginia planter who served as a colonel under General Nathanael Greene in the American Revolution.

During the war Virginia had its share of Tories and British sympathizers who harassed the Continentals and plundered and stole their property. In the neutral ground between British and American lines in New York, the marauders came to be known as "cowboys." They proved extremely difficult to control. Further south, in Bedford County, Virginia, the situation got so far out of hand that something had to be done. Because of the high prices that both the British and Americans were willing to pay for horses, stealing them became an extremely lucrative business. The inefficiency, or nonexistence, of local courts made apprehension and punishment out of the question.

Sometime around 1780 Colonel Charles Lynch and his fellow planters formed an organization to punish horse thieves and other criminals. Lynch would order a suspected individual arrested and brought to his home. In the presence of Lynch and three neighbors who served as associate justices, the accused was given the opportunity to face his accusers and to hear the charges against him. He would be permitted to defend himself and to produce witnesses in his behalf. If the court acquitted him of the charges, it usually extended its sincere apologies and sometimes even made reparation. But if it found the victim guilty, punishment followed swiftly and vigorously. The condemned man, almost invariably a Tory, would be tied to a large walnut tree in the Colonel's yard, hung by his thumbs, and given thirty-nine lashes on the back before being banished from the country.

In spite if its illegality, the practice in Bedford County was soon initiated in other parts of Virginia, and it came to be known as Lynch's law and later simply as lynch law. It originally proved highly effective in reducing crime and, under the circumstances, had much in its favor: the government at the time was in a state of paralysis and Virginia was being invaded by hostile forces, the courts were temporarily dispersed, and Governor Thomas Jefferson was unable to carry out his duties. Lynch was a Quaker and an honorable man who had great respect for established authority and was careful to stop short of ordering the death sentence.

Vigilantism and lynch law were often lesser evils than complete lawlessness. This was especially true when the frontier was advancing so rapidly that organized government was unable to keep pace with it, as was the case in the early mining and ranching communities during the nineteenth century. When a man was accused of committing a crime, there were no jails in which to incarcerate him, nor did the community have the patience for a long drawn-out trial. Consequently, some innocent people were hanged. Even so, whatever its obvious faults, the rude system of *ad hoc* government did prove remarkably efficient.

As settlers moved beyond the Appalachian barrier, they took the practice of lynch law with them.

> Vigilantism from 1767 to 1910 produced a total of at least 327 movements or episodes spread over practically all of the trans-Appalachian states and a few of the Atlantic states, especially South Carolina, Virginia and Georgia. Calling themselves "regulators," "vigilantes," "slickers," or other names, these 327 vigilante efforts inflicted at least 737 fatalities and bestowed corporal punishment on thousands more.[1]

In the Appalachian region of the early nineteenth century, and in the South during Reconstruction, vigilantism frequently appeared as a rebellion against too much law, but on the Western frontier it took the form of an opposite response. In California and in the ranching empires of Montana, vigilantes organized to remove lawless elements over which there was no legally sanctioned control.

The difficulty with vigilantism is that it has no stopping place. Men accustomed to taking the law into their own hands continue to do so long after regular judicial processes are established. Moreover, lynch law came to mean much more than merely whipping an individual and banishing him from the country. As the historian Hubert Howe Bancroft wrote:

> Sometimes the most trivial incident would determine whether a culprit would be whipped or hanged. While multitudes of minor offenders suffered capital punishment, no more could be inflicted upon the worst criminals. Lynching for cattle stealing obtained throughout the whole country, and even round San Francisco Bay, as late as 1855. A criminal affair was often made a sort of pastime, which might be prolonged or shortened according to the appetite of the crowd, or the time at their disposal.[2]

In California a victim would frequently be buried with one end of the rope still around his neck and the other trailing out the head of the grave to serve as a warning to others. Also, in the South during Reconstruction, blacks were sometimes castrated before being hanged, and their naked bodies were left dangling from the limb of a tree for several days.

Prior to our entrance into the great conflict in 1917, Woodrow Wilson predicted that our vices would become virtues during wartime, and that it would be painfully difficult to get society back into proper perspective when the conflict ended. The truth of this prophecy was all too evident even long after the "Roaring Twenties" had passed into nostalgic memory. The same had been true after the American Revolution, which had proved, among other things, that violence pays. The lesson learned from the struggle for independence would be applied again and again throughout the nineteenth century, even though the pattern would change.

Aside from the War of 1812, most of the violence from the
end of the Revolution to around 1830 consisted of the informal,
private type committed by citizen against citizen. The Old
Northwest no longer had a serious Indian problem, and the
Old Southwest had yet to experience the various "trails of
tears"—the forced removal by the United States Army of
the Five Civilized Tribes. (These Indians consisted of approximately 100,000 Cherokees, Choctaws, Chickasaws, Creeks, and
Seminoles who lived in Mississippi, Alabama, Georgia, and
Florida. Most of them were eventually driven to the wilderness
frontier of present Oklahoma.) Historians generally agree
that during the first quarter of the nineteenth century the
abundance of land and resources, the absence of class division,
and the rapid expansion of the franchise and development of
democratic institutions had kept American society open and
fluid.

This eyewitness account of the times, which was originally
published in *The New England Weekly Review* and reprinted
in Clark's *Rampaging Frontier* (1964), was written by one
George D. Prentice:

> An election in Kentucky lasts three days, and during
> that period whiskey and apple toddy flow through our
> cities and villages like the Euphrates through ancient
> Babylon. . . . In Frankfort, a place which I had the
> curiosity to visit on the last day of the election, Jack-
> sonianism and drunkenness stalked triumphant—"an
> unclean pair of lubberly giants." A number of runners,
> each with a whiskey bottle poking its long neck from
> his pocket, were busily employed bribing voters, and
> each party kept a dozen bullies under pay, genuine
> specimens of Kentucky alligatorism, to flog every
> poor fellow who should attempt to vote illegally. A
> half a hundred mortar would scarcely fill up the chinks
> of the skulls that were broken on that occasion.

I barely escaped myself. One of the runners came up to me, and slapping me on the shoulder with his right hand, and a whiskey bottle with his left, asked me if I was a voter. "No," said I. "Ah, never mind," quoth the fellow, pulling a corncob out of the neck of the bottle, and shaking it up to the best advantage. "Jest take a swig at the cretur and toss in a vote for Old Hickory's boys—I'll fight for you, damne!" Here was a temptation to be sure; but after looking alternately at the bottle and the bullies who were standing ready with their sledgehammer fists to knock down all interlopers, my fears prevailed and I lost my whiskey.

Shortly after this I witnessed a fight that would have done honor to Mendoza and Big Ben. A great ruffian-looking scoundrel, with arms like a pair of cables knotted at the ends, and a round black head that looked like a forty pound cannon shot, swaggered up to the polls and threw in his bit of paper, and was walking off in triumph. "Stop, friend," exclaimed one of the Salt River Roarers, stepping deliberately up to him. "Are you a voter?" "Yes, by G–d," replied he of the bullet head. "That's a lie," rejoined the Roarer, "and you must prepare yourself to go home an old man, for I'll be damned if I don't knock you into the middle of your ninety-ninth year." . . .

They had now reached an open space, and the Salt River bully, shaking his fist a moment by way of feint, dropped his chin suddenly upon his bosom and pitched headforemost toward the stomach of his gigantic frame. . . . It was a trial of strength, and the combatants tugged and strained and foamed at the mouth and twined like serpents around each other's bodies, till at length the strength of Bullet Head prevailed and his opponent lay struggling beneath him.

"Gouge him!" exclaimed a dozen voices, and the

topmost combatant seized his victim by the hair and
was preparing to follow the advice that was thus
shouted in his ear, when the prostrate man, roused by
desperation and exerting a strength that seemed super-
human, caught his assailant by the throat with a grasp
like that of fate. For a few moments the struggle
seemed to cease, and then the face of the throttled man
turned black, his tongue fell out of his mouth, and he
rolled to the ground as senseless as a dead man. I
turned away a confirmed believer in the doctrine of
total depravity.

It was relatively easy—at least in theory—for the under-
privileged individual to rise above his background, enter the
growing middle class, and be absorbed by the great melting
pot. "The outs had no need for revolutionary violence; the
ins, no need for forceful repression." [3]

Suddenly, near the beginning of the decade of the 1830's,
the picture changed, and a series of racial, economic, and
ethnic disturbances began to flay the nation. It is more than
simple irony that violence involving one group against another
accelerated just when Alexis de Tocqueville was writing his
classic, *Democracy in America*. This young Frenchman's lofty
purpose, according to Henry Steele Commager, was "to prepare men everywhere for the 'providential fact' of equality;
to dissipate fears, quiet excessive hopes, encourage accom-
modation; to lift men above the narrow and selfish and persuade
them to broad and generous views." [4]

"To those for whom the word 'democracy' is synonymous
with disturbance, anarchy, spoliation, and murder," Tocqueville wrote, "I have attempted to show that the government
of democracy may be reconciled with respect for property,
with defense for rights, with safety to freedom, with reverence
to religion; that if democratic government is less favorable
than another to some of the finer points of human nature,

it has also great and noble elements; and that perhaps, after all, it is the will of God to shed a lesser grade of happiness on the totality of mankind, not to combine a greater share of it on a smaller number, or to raise a few to the verge of perfection." [5]

It is doubtful if any book about Jacksonian America has been more durable or more penetrating. In fact, Tocqueville has proven to be uncannily accurate about so many things that it is almost frightening. The same individual who wrote with such Periclean quality would later observe the following:

> I look upon the size of certain American cities, and especially on the nature of their population, as a real danger which threatens the future security of the democratic republics of the New World; and I venture to predict that they will perish from this force, which, while it remains under the control of the majority of the nation, will be independent of the town population, and able to repress its excesses. [6]

The series of disturbances which Tocqueville feared, and which broke out a generation before the Civil War, spread quickly to every corner of the nation. It involved urban communities, the conservative countryside, and the rapidly moving frontier in the West. Violence was unleashed against abolitionists, Catholics, Negroes, Mexicans, Indians, and other ethnic, racial, or ideological minorities. The Nat Turner Rebellion represents an outstanding exception to the general pattern whereby white, Anglo-Saxon Protestants were the aggressors. Turner led a group of sixty or more fellow slaves from plantation to plantation throughout Southampton County, Virginia, in a systematic slaughter. By the time he was captured on October 30, 1831, and summarily hanged, he had slain fifty-seven whites. Their deaths led to the subsequent massacre of approximately one hundred blacks, in retaliation.

The Nat Turner Rebellion had even more disastrous and prolonged effects. It produced a flood of repressive laws and renewed interest in the plan to transport all free Negroes back to Africa. It added to the fear and brutality of the whites and made it impossible for anyone to speak in favor of abolition for fear of being ostracized from Southern white society, or even lynched.

Modern authorities on slavery such as John Hope Franklin, Kenneth Stampp, and Winthrop Jordan maintain that a pathological fear gripped the South in the period surrounding the Nat Turner Rebellion and Prosser's Revolt, which had occurred three decades earlier, in Henrico County, Virginia. Thirty-six slaves were eventually executed and scores of others arrested before the Prosser uprising was put down. Jordan states in his work on American attitudes toward the Negro (*White Over Black,* 1968) that one or two actual revolts such as these caused the fear by whites to magnify a hundredfold. He states that there were just enough instances of Negroes planning revolts, or a deranged slave murdering his master, mistress, or overseer, to give Southerners good reason for constant concern. Moreover, white men concocted a large number of beliefs to prove to themselves the inferiority of the black man and to keep him in his place. Among other things, they believed that his basic instincts were animalistic and that his sexual appetite was enormous. Thus it comes as no great surprise that lynch mobs often mutilated the genitals of black victims.

The three decades before the Civil War also represent the greatest era of urban violence in American history. The development of slums, the arrival of millions of Irish and German immigrants, competition for jobs, and poorly trained police forces contributed to rioting throughout the Northeast.[7] In city after city the story was the same. On August 11, 1834, a mob of lower-class men and boys sacked and burned a convent in Charlestown, Massachusetts, following a series of violent anti-Catholic sermons by the Reverend Lyman Beecher. The mob also burned several Irish shanties and church properties.

There is no evidence that any lives were lost in the Charlestown affair, but it unquestionably helped trigger a generation of religious bigotry and anti-Catholic violence. At least thirty-five major riots occurred in Baltimore, Philadelphia, New York, and Boston between 1834 and 1860. By the time Baltimore had experienced its twelfth riot it had acquired the dubious title of "mob town." That epithet was likewise conferred upon a host of other places far removed from the Atlantic Coast, including Cincinnati, St. Louis, Louisville, and Vicksburg.

From data compiled from the files of *Niles' Weekly Register*, a newspaper that was *The New York Times* of its day, Professor Leonard Richards concludes that urban and rural disturbances between 1812 and 1850 were approximately equal in number. Beginning in the 1830's, "mob violence not only increased markedly but also became a feature of American life—not urban life, or Southern life, or Western life—but American life." While mobs were active throughout New England against Catholics and abolitionists, they also were harassing Catholics and blacks in Philadelphia and Cincinnati, Mormons in rural Missouri and Illinois, Mexicans in Texas, gamblers in Vicksburg, landlords in New York, and prostitutes, foreigners, and assorted outcasts wherever they found them.

In May 1844, Philadelphia experienced three days of violence. Thousands of Protestants roamed the streets looking for Irish Catholics, priests, and nuns. They eventually killed thirteen people, seriously injured fifty others, and destroyed two churches. When natives clashed with immigrant factions during the same decade in New Orleans, four men were killed. In Lawrence, Massachusetts, a mob of approximately 1500 people burned the homes and churches of Irish workers. An election riot in St. Louis in 1854 resulted in the death of ten men and the serious injury of dozens of others. And in Louisville, Kentucky, a Protestant mob marched through the German section, killing twenty men and destroying considerable property.[8]

Rightly or wrongly, mob violence has been identified more with the antebellum South than with any other region of the country. In a study of the subject made in 1942, the Southern historian Clement Eaton observed that mobs and vigilante committees flourished there as powerful instruments in controlling public opinion. He attributes this to a variety of causes, including the fact that the South remained the most poorly policed section of the country, that large numbers of whites went armed with pistols and knives, that jails were few and far between, and that dueling was sanctioned as a proper means for a gentleman to protect his honor. At the same time the South had an abnormally high rate of illiteracy among its native adult, white population—slightly more than 20 per cent, compared to less than half of one per cent in New England. Eaton concluded that an illiterate minority, especially when fortified with corn whiskey, could easily succumb to panics of fear and mob violence.

All of the above conditions combined probably played a less significant role in the causes of Southern violence than the antislavery controversy and the abolitionists' campaigns did. Southerners not only believed that emancipation would disrupt their economic structure, they also felt that it would destroy the entire fabric of their society. As the abolitionists forced them into a more and more defensive position, they became less secure, more sensitive to criticism, and outright paranoid. By 1860 they were so fearful of new Nat Turners and John Browns that they organized miniature armies, and those armies frequently provoked mob violence against blacks, antislavery men, and Northerners traveling below the Mason and Dixon line.[9]

Kansas and Nebraska reached the crisis point in the 1850's, when the growing controversy over whether newly populated

territories would allow slaves or banish them erupted into
violence. These new frontier territories had been created by
the Kansas-Nebraska Act of 1854, legislation which Abraham
Lincoln described as having been "conceived in violence, passed
in violence, maintained in violence, and . . . executed in violence." [10] The bloodshed in Kansas provided an important
ingredient in giving the abolitionists respectability in the
North and turning their movement into a dynamic political
force. It contributed to the inevitability of the Civil War,
provided the breeding ground for hundreds of criminals and
outlaws, and ultimately left a legacy of frontier violence that
lasted for generations.

The abolitionists' struggle to obtain respectability was long
and bloody. Those advocating freedom for the slaves were
almost as unpopular in parts of the Northeast as they were
in the South, where they dared not venture. Throughout the
prewar period, antislavery lecturers were mobbed and tarred
and feathered wherever they went, their homes burned,
and their printing presses destroyed. On one occasion a mob
dragged William Lloyd Garrison, editor of the *Liberator*,
through the streets of Boston. According to Richards, such
acts were not the result of spontaneous outbursts, but "in
nine cases out of ten the mobs involved explicit planning and
organization." [11] Their membership usually included many
prominent, articulate men who had little fear of public indict-
ment or censure and who obviously had the overwhelming
support of the community behind them.

Richards assembled data on membership of anti-abolition
mobs in Utica, New York, in 1835; Cincinnati, Ohio, in 1836;
and New York City in 1834. Utica, unlike the other cities, had
virtually no contact with the South. Yet the composition of
the mob there was very similar to that of the mobs in New
York and Cincinnati. The actual participants in all three cities
came from both the "head and tail" of local society, with

the leadership and financing drawn largely from "high church conservatives." Of the top ranks of the Utica mob, twelve were lawyers by profession, four were bankers, ten were merchants, and one was a prominent physician.

It is fairly easy to understand why the "tail" of society— the lower, less educated classes—would feel threatened by free Negroes, competing for jobs, and would join in the excitement of roughing up those who advocated emancipating the slaves. The reasons why the "head" of society, the men who generally talked most about law and order, reacted the way they did are more complicated.

The "gentlemen of property and standing" in the North did not become concerned about the abolitionist movement until William Lloyd Garrison, Arthur Tappan, and others began to attack the American Colonization Society. Since 1817, this organization, in a campaign to rid the country of the poor and despised blacks, had unsuccessfully promoted the migration of free Negroes back to Africa. As Garrison's *Liberator*, essentially a Negro newspaper, increased its attacks against the Colonization Society, on the ground that it advocated "forceful expulsion," both upper and lower classes in the North became more and more frightened. It seemed clear to them that the alternative to African colonization was "immediate emancipation without expatriation." Slaves represented private property, and property was as sacred to Northerners as it was to Southerners. If the government could expropriate one kind of property, it also could expropriate another. In addition, if free Negroes were not sent back to Africa, then they eventually would be assimilated into American society, an idea that was anathema to most Northerners regardless of background or position.

It must likewise be remembered that the Jim Crow system originated in the North and that integration made little progress anywhere in the United States before the Civil War. "It is five times as hard to get a house in a good location in

Boston or Philadelphia, and it is ten times as difficult for a
colored mechanic to get work here as in Charleston," a Negro
in Boston wrote in 1860.[12] Thus, the heavy limitation and
degradation that segregation placed on Negro life, liberty,
and property contributed to outbreaks of racial violence as
much (or more) in the North as in the antebellum South.

At the very time when the anti-abolitionist movement was
gaining momentum, a disastrous potato famine in Ireland
caused hundreds of thousands of people to flee to the United
States. By the 1840's a network of native societies was publishing hate literature, in the form of books, newspapers, and magazines, in vicious attacks against all foreigners. Out of this
atmosphere eventually emerged a new political party, the
Order of the Star Spangled Banner. Membership remained a
secret; when one asked about the organization's activities and
objective, the inevitable response was "I know nothing." The
Know-Nothings, as they came to be called, scored surprising
victories in the election of 1854–55, when they captured the
governorship of Massachusetts, all other state offices, and an
overwhelming control of the legislature. They also gained
control of seventy-five congressional seats and various state
positions throughout New England, Maryland, Delaware, and
Kentucky.

The great appeal of the Know-Nothing movement was in
its secret ritual and the sincere belief held by a majority of its
members that Catholicism and immigration would ultimately
destroy the country. Their methods, philosophy, and oversimplified solutions bore striking resemblance to those of the
modern John Birch Society—which, incidentally, also realized
its initial success in Massachusetts and still maintains its national headquarters in Boston. Most of the party members
elected to the Massachusetts state legislature in 1854 were
"merchants, laborers, clerks, school-teachers, and ministers
who understood nothing of government process and were ill-
equipped to learn." [13] Fortunately, the party in Massachusetts

was completely discredited when some of the Know-Nothing legislators charged their liquor bills to the state, along with bills for the services of a "lady" in Lowell who answered to the name of Mrs. Patterson.

By the time of the presidential campaign of 1856, the slavery issue had split the Know-Nothing party into warring factions. Its candidate, Millard Fillmore, carried only the state of Maryland. As the election of 1860 approached, Northern members of the party gradually went over to the ranks of the Republicans, while those from the Middle and Southern states disappeared among the ashes of the shattered Democratic party. By then the Irish Catholics were slowly winning the battle of the streets by sheer force of numbers, and they were sometimes even taking the initiative against the Establishment.

What turned out to be America's greatest urban riot began in June 1863, when thousands of Irish workers streamed out of their slums and onto the streets of New York City. Provoked by the efforts of the federal government to draft them into the Union army, they fought hand to hand with local police and, later, with troops rushed in from the battlefield at Gettysburg. The chief victims of the episode were more than a thousand Negroes, with whom the Irish competed for jobs and against whom they vented most of their fury. The whole sordid affair represents a classical example of the assertion, made by Dr. David Abrahamsen, that "frustration is the wet nurse of violence." [14]

Aside from the Indians, who stand in a class by themselves as victims of American aggression, two other groups who tasted the bitter dregs of racism and bigotry during the pre-Civil War period were the Mexicans and the Mormons. American settlers who flocked to Texas after 1821 never hesitated to express their belief that Mexicans were inferior to themselves in every aspect of culture, government, religion, and character. This attitude played a major role in bringing on the war for Texas independence, and the Mexican War a decade later. During the first confrontation, a ragtag army of less than a thousand Texans surprised a much larger Mexican force at San Jacinto in April 1836. They slaughtered the Mexicans by hundreds. What better proof was needed of the superiority of one race over another, especially since the Texans lost only sixteen to twenty men?

The fear that a degenerate, alien race would cause much trouble and could never be assimilated into white society contributed considerably to the reluctance of the United States, in the Treaty of Guadalupe Hidalgo in 1848, from taking all of Mexico. We took instead the sparsely settled Southwest, confident in the knowledge that whites would eventually become the dominant group there.

The discovery of gold in California a short time later hastened the process of Americanization of the former Mexican provinces. When Anglo-Americans swarmed into the Southwest and on to the Pacific Coast, they reduced the Mexicans to a minority. But as long as they remained the dominant ethnic group, the Anglo-Americans generally treated them with respect. As the Anglos became dominant, they began to regard the Mexicans with the same scorn that had once been reserved for the Indians. "The Mexicans are 'aboriginal Indians,'" the New York *Evening Post* editorialized on December 24, 1847, "and they must share the destiny of their race." [15] But an account of Mexican-white relations, particularly in Texas and California, is essentially a part of the story of violence on the trans-Mississippi frontier, and it belongs elsewhere in this book.

Mormons could hardly be classified as "aboriginal" or "alien," since most of the early converts came from Anglo-American Protestant backgrounds. Yet, throughout the first three or four decades following the establishment of the Church of Latter Day Saints by Joseph Smith in western New York in 1830, the story of the Mormons is one of perse-

cution, vituperative attacks, and flight. It is another sorry
chapter in the prolonged nightmare of violent eruptions that
preceded the Civil War. And no group of native-born, white
Americans—including the abolitionists—generated more hatred
or suffered more at the hands of angry mobs than the Mormons did.

In 1831 and 1832, Joseph Smith and most of his followers
migrated to Ohio, where they aroused immediate suspicion.
They were soon being beaten, robbed, and tarred and feathered
by their neighbors. After five or six years the survivors fled
to Missouri, where they again stirred up the wrath of their
fellow Americans, who suspected that Joseph Smith's prophe-
cies that his people someday would inherit the earth really
cloaked a plot to take over the community. More frightening
was the Saints' apparent opposition to slavery, and their alleged invitation to mulattoes and free blacks to settle among
them. In view of the Church's historic doctrine regarding
blacks, these so-called "invitations" doubtless were as exaggerated as was the fear of a Mormon military conspiracy.
Nevertheless, Missouri mobs burned the Mormons' houses,
destroyed their crops, and whipped their Church officials into
unconsciousness. When the Saints organized to defend themselves, they merely provoked their enemies to greater atrocities.

In October 1838, a Missouri mob surrounded the Mormon
settlement at Haun's Mill and killed eighteen residents and
wounded several more. Among those murdered was a small boy
who had taken refuge along with other children in a blacksmith shop. Upon being discovered by a member of the mob
he begged for his life, only to have a gun placed at his head
and his brains blown out. The murderer later boasted of his
performance and apparently was never censured for what he
had done. A short time later the Governor of Missouri issued
the following order: "The Mormons must be treated as enemies, and must be exterminated or driven from the state for
the public peace." [16] The order was followed by the arrest of

Joseph Smith and other Church leaders by the commander of the Missouri militia. Although the victims were sentenced to be shot for treason, they were allowed to escape before the order could be carried out.

By then life was being made so miserable for the Saints that they fled *en masse* to western Illinois. There they prospered, and within five years their new city of Nauvoo, on the banks of the Mississippi, had become the largest center of population in the state. At first the politicians welcomed them, for they held the balance of power between the Whigs and the Democrats. But when Joseph Smith began playing one side against the other, he quickly alienated leaders of both parties. This unpleasantness was compounded by the Prophet's announcement of his candidacy for the presidency of the United States in 1844, and by his excommunication of several prominent members of the sect. When some of the "apostates" established a newspaper in Nauvoo and denounced the leaders, Smith ordered the publication destroyed.

It had long been rumored that a few of the Church leaders practiced free love, and when it became general knowledge that some did have more than one wife, the enemies on the outside were even more morally outraged. The state militia quickly moved in and arrested Joseph and Hyrum Smith. The brothers were housed in the jail at near-by Carthage to await trial, but a mob gathered outside on June 27, 1844, broke through the guard, and murdered the two leaders. The Mormons were now provided with the all-important ingredient that religious movements need in order to survive—dead martyrs. But the nightmare of violence was far from over.

News of the murder of the Smiths brought mobs throughout the area to systematically loot and destroy property until the "Mormon menace" could be erased forever. Brigham Young, the able successor to Joseph Smith, pleaded in vain for the rights of his followers as American citizens. Finally, he agreed to lead all of the survivors—about 15,000—to a new

home beyond the Rockies, as far from Illinois as possible. By
July 1847, he had selected the Valley of the Great Salt Lake
as the place to build a permanent Kingdom of Zion. The trek
westward across more than a thousand miles of plains, deserts,
and mountains represents one of the most heroic accomplish-
ments in the history of the American West. That move, and
the construction of the Mormon capital at Salt Lake City, was
completed by 1850. But another unfortunate and ugly chapter
of Mormon history remained to be written—the Mountain
Meadows Massacre. And this time it was the Mormons who
were responsible. It was one of the most brutal and senseless
massacres in frontier history, and it serves as an excellent example of violence begetting violence.

The Mountain Meadows Massacre took place near Cedar
City, in September 1857. Its victims were 140 immigrants passing through southern Utah en route to California. Most were
respectable farmers, but some were "Missouri Wild Cats" who
created considerable trouble by insulting the Mormons, killing
their livestock, and destroying some of their crops. When a fa-
natical Mormon farmer killed one of the Missourians, his neighbors became fearful that the whole community would be punished for the crime. Consequently, a Mormon mob ambushed
the wagon train and killed every member of it except seventeen small children. Twenty years later, on the spot where the
massacre took place, John D. Lee was executed for his role in
leading the attack against the Missourians.[17]

The settlement of the vast area beyond the Mississippi during the latter half of the nineteenth century made the frontier
West the symbol of the most violent time and place in this
country's history. The realities and the legends of this frontier still live on in our minds—in part because the West is
the most recent in a long procession of frontiers, but mainly
because the theme of violent action associated with it has been
played over and over in films and television stories.

By the time American settlers had moved beyond the Mississippi Valley, they had been well conditioned to violence in all its varied forms. The population, by then heterogeneous, was subjected more to a "pressure cooker" than to a "melting pot" as a result of the interaction of the wide range of their cultural, ethnic, racial, and religious backgrounds.[18] In addition, the struggle over slavery had created a cancer that would persist throughout the remainder of the century. Finally, the lynching of blacks, slaughter of Indians, murder of Mexicans, and denial of civil liberties and civil rights to large groups of individuals had left a brutalizing mark upon society. Too often cruelty to one's fellowman had become the price of survival, and each man was free to set his own limits.

Although the post-Civil War West remained thinly settled and devoid of great urban and industrial centers for many years, the principal themes of social violence experienced by the older section of the country quickly took root in the new environment. It is true, as many historians and specialists on violence have pointed out, that during this same period the western frontiers of Canada and Australia did not produce the level of violence experienced on the western frontier of the United States.[19] It is also true that the eastern frontiers of Canada and Australia did not develop in the same way as ours, nor were the problems associated with their social development compounded by as great a diversity of ethnic, religious, and economic groups.

In 1893 a young historian from Wisconsin named Frederick Jackson Turner revolutionized the teaching of American history with the hypothesis that our frontiers were the most potent force in moulding the character of the American people. Most scholars today still accept the basic premise of the Turner thesis. Even so, it would seem from the scattered events herein examined that the proclivity for violence in the American character was well developed long before large numbers of settlers were ready to move into the Great Plains and the Far West.

III
The Texas
Frontier Heritage

Each Western state went through an initial period of lawlessness, and a corresponding period of mobocracy or vigilante movements designed to bring law and order. Kansas and California, for example, were born in turmoil almost unparalleled in intensity, yet each became reasonably civilized within a decade after statehood. But long after Texas entered the Union and established its leadership as an exporter of cotton and cattle, and, later, of sulphur, oil, and gas (natural and otherwise), violence was still common; indeed, the state's reputation for lawlessness seemed to increase rather than to diminish with economic and political maturity. The question therefore arises as to why Texas maintained a frontier mentality that condoned acts of violence by her citizens until well after the physical frontier had moved on. Perhaps the answer lies in her unique history.

Like every frontier community, Texas attracted many decent, hard-working residents of other states and foreign countries. It also attracted, or produced, more than its fair share of hotheads, professional gamblers, land swindlers, refugees from creditors or law officers or vigilante committees, and, later, professional gunmen. Yet, somehow it worked a curious alchemy with its citizens, educated and untutored alike, and set its own ineffaceable stamp on their souls. "The same process is still working in Texas today," William Ransom Hogan wrote in *The Texas Republic* in 1946.[1] That stamp represents a fighting spirit, which arose not alone from national compulsion, but also from necessity. The immigrants who flocked into the Mexican province west of the Sabine quickly learned how to defend themselves, because they had to—and when they took the offensive they were capable of doing so with unmitigated violence.

Basic to much of the practice of personal and group violence after the Anglo-American phase of Texas history began was race hatred, which was directed against Mexicans, Indians, and, later, Negroes. Violence and racial hatred began almost immediately after the first group of filibusters, led by one Philip Nolan, crossed from United States soil into Texas in the late eighteenth century, ostensibly to capture wild horses. Nolan led several successful invasions, but finally, in 1801, the Spaniards discovered his party encamped near present Waco. In the ensuing fight they killed Nolan and more than a third of his followers. The ten survivors languished in prison in Mexico for several years before they eventually learned their fate. Spanish officials ordered them to roll dice to determine which one would be executed and which of the others would be kept in prison. Only two or three of the original members of the party survived the ordeal of long years of incarceration in Mexican prisons before being allowed to return to the United States.

This harsh treatment did not deter other Anglo adventurers from invading Texas at regular intervals, and each time they did so there was considerable loss of life on both sides. Shortly before Mexico won her independence in 1821, Spain reversed her long-standing restriction and allowed foreigners to enter her northern province. After independence, Mexico continued the policy and even expanded it to allow generous land grants

Border raids by Texas Rangers and Mexican banditti sometimes involved regular troops of the United States Army and irregulars under Mexican revolutionary leaders. These irregulars, commanded by General Emiliano Nafarrate, closed the international bridge at Matamoros, opposite Brownsville, in 1913.

to those who agreed to become citizens of Mexico and converts
to the Catholic Church.

At first the two groups got along reasonably well, considering the antipathy that they held for each other. But it was
inevitable that as soon as the Anglos felt strong enough they
would be more open in expressing their true feelings toward
Mexican customs and officials, and more determined to have
their own way. The Mexican-American historian Rodolfo
Acuña recently wrote: "There is ample evidence that Anglo-
Americans arriving in the Southwest believed that they were
racially superior to the swarthy Mexicans, whom they considered a mongrel race of Indian halfbreeds." [2] When Mexico,
in 1830, attempted to restrict further immigration into Texas
from the United States, she acted too late. The new law made
the wilderness region more enticing than ever, especially to
the adventurous and raffish elements of Tennessee, Kentucky,
Louisiana, and other bordering regions. Their departure frequently improved conditions in the communities they abandoned, though it did not necessarily improve them in the parts
of Texas where they resettled.

The later arrivals were more contemptuous of authority than
the earlier Anglo immigrants had been, and they generally
ignored laws that did not suit them. In the words of a Mexican
official, "each one carried his political constitution in his pocket
[and] assumed that he was a sovereign in his own right." [3] Such
an arrogant attitude naturally produced a reaction and hastened
the process of revolution. The climax came on April 22, 1836,
at San Jacinto, where the Texans won a decisive victory and
avenged the "massacres" at the Alamo and Goliad.[4] But the war
between the Texans and the Mexicans was far from over, as
both sides continued to raid back and forth across the Rio
Grande. The subsequent conflict between the United States
and her southern neighbor (1846–48) in behalf of Manifest
Destiny hardened the contempt that "gringos" and "greasers"
held for one another.

The Texas Rangers had a reputation among the Anglos as unswerving defenders of law and order, but to Mexicans on both sides of the international boundary they possessed all the sensitivities of rattlesnakes.

The various armies that invaded Mexico in 1846–47 consisted of large numbers of Texans and volunteers from throughout the United States, thousands of whom were a disgrace to the human race. General Winfield Scott admitted that the Americans had "committed atrocities to make Heaven weep and every American of Christian morals blush for his country. Murder, robbery and rape of mothers and daughters in the presence of tied-up males of the families have been common all along the Rio Grande." And Lieutenant George C. Meade later compared the volunteers to "a set of Goths and Vandals without discipline." These men were capable of fighting and dying gallantly, but at times they defied all of the laws of civilized behavior. Mexican newspaper editors called them "vandals and monsters" who had been vomited from hell and were "thirsty with desire to appropriate our riches and our beautiful damsels." [5]

For sixty years after the United States had annexed more than half of their territory, Mexican nationals continued raiding isolated ranches and border settlements north of the Rio Grande. In the best frontier tradition, the Texas Rangers pursued the enemy, ignoring international boundaries in the process. Each side referred to the other as bandits. "I can maintain a better stomach at the killing of a Mexican than at the crushing of a body louse," a former Texas Ranger boasted in 1856.[6] Undoubtedly, many Mexicans felt the same way toward their gringo adversaries.

The Rangers were organized during the early days of the Texas Republic, and they quickly developed a reputation as efficient Indian fighters. They considered Mexicans their natural enemies and seldom gave them the benefit of the doubt. These frontier law officers played a major role as scouts with the army of General Zachary Taylor when he invaded Mexico via Monterrey and, later, when General Winfield Scott marched via Vera Cruz to Mexico City. "Take them all together," a private in Taylor's army recorded in his diary,

"with their uncouth costumes, bearded faces, lean and bronze
forms, fierce eyes and swaggering manners, they were fit representatives of the outlaws who made up the population of the
Lone Star State." [7] It is no wonder the Texans struck terror
into the hearts of Mexican peons who had the misfortune to
get in their way.

In the early days, the Ranger went armed with a rifle, one or
two Colt revolvers, and a bowie knife. He was an excellent
horseman, used an American version of the Mexican saddle,
and carried a rawhide riata and a lariat for roping horses—or
"stretching necks." With a Mexican blanket tied behind his
saddle, one small pouch for salt and another for ammunition,
and some parched corn and tobacco in his pockets, he was
equipped for months. Game abounded throughout early Texas,
so food was rarely a problem. Thus unencumbered by baggage
wagons or pack trains, a small body of Rangers could travel
lightly and efficiently in pursuit of Indians or Mexican outlaws.

The Texas Ranger's reputation as an unswerving defender of
law and order has been enhanced to the point of mythology
on one side of the international boundary, but to the Mexicans
on both sides he possessed all the sensitivity of a rattlesnake.
That opinion has not been completely dissipated today, especially among "Chicanos," Mexicans of American birth, who
vociferously demand that the Rangers be abolished. They com-
pare the famous law enforcement group to the Ku Klux Klan
and maintain that the Rangers delight in harassing, intimidating,
and jailing Chicanos on the flimsiest of charges.[8]

It is unfair to say that the Rangers were a major cause of
the turmoil that Texas experienced during the past century
and a half, although they unquestionably were a contributing
factor, and in the process they came to symbolize the "high-
noon syndrome" that many associate with the state of Texas.
"They may now patrol in automobiles instead of upon horses
and may carry the most effective modern weapons, but, un-

fortunately, their minds still seem to work in a rigid nineteenth-century mode," one critic recently observed. "The
times have passed them by, and they still believe that enforcement by fear and at the pistol point is good police practice." [9]

One reason the heritage of the Texas frontier has survived
so late into the twentieth century is that the physical frontier
survived there perhaps longer than in any other region. Texas
spent more than half a century trying to solve its Indian problem, while most frontier states took only a decade or two to
do so. Unlike the placid Diggers, who were quickly and easily
eliminated as a threat to undisputed white possession of California, the Comanches, Kiowas, and Apaches were formidable
warriors and superb horsemen. Long after they had been
rounded up from throughout the Southern Plains region and
settled on reservations in present Oklahoma, they considered
settlers of western Texas fair game, and they practiced upon
them "an eye for an eye and a tooth for a tooth." During the
Civil War they pushed the frontier line of settlements back a
hundred miles or more in parts of western Texas. The settlers
retaliated, and more often than not the victims on both sides
were the innocent, rather than the perpetrators of the crime.

Sam Houston was genuinely sympathetic with the Indians'
position in Texas, and soon after he became the first elected
president of the Republic in 1836, he initiated a policy of
peace, friendship, and trade. His successor, Mirabeau B. Lamar,
believed that the only solution to the Indian problem was total
extermination or expulsion. He repudiated earlier treaties and
used the army and Rangers against various tribes with impul-
sive regularity. It was also during Lamar's administration that
the Council House Fight occurred, an event which completely
destroyed the waning confidence of the Indians in the government of Texas and absolutely guaranteed violent and prolonged warfare on the frontier.

On March 19, 1840, representatives of the Texas government met in San Antonio with a small delegation of Comanche Indians headed by Muguara, chief of a band disposed to be friendly toward the whites. The Texas delegation had, in the meantime, worked out a secret plan to seize and hold Muguara, and the twelve warriors who accompanied him to the council deliberations, until the band surrendered all of its white captives. Muguara maintained that the only captive he had was Matilda Lockhard, whom he had brought to San Antonio along with several dozen Indian women, children, and old men. The girl promptly disputed the statement and asserted that her captors planned to bring in others one at a time for high ransom. The comment provided the excuse that the Texas negotiators needed, and they immediately surrounded the Indians with three companies of infantry who had been stationed close by.

When the warriors suddenly realized that they had been led into a trap, they refused to be taken alive. In the ensuing fight forty-three Indians were killed and a handful of prisoners taken. Seven white soldiers died and eight others received serious injuries. The Council House Fight proved to be one of the stupidest blunders the Lamar administration could have committed.[10]

The people of Texas believed that, once annexation was achieved, the United States would put an end to their Indian problems. They were to be sadly disappointed, in spite of constant efforts by state militia, frontier citizens, Texas Ranger companies, and federal troops. Upon the close of the Mexican War in 1848, the United States army began constructing a chain of forts extending from present Fort Worth to Eagle Pass, with the idea of keeping the Indians of the South Plains and western Texas well beyond the line of frontier settlements. But even before the Civil War, white settlers began moving on to lands reserved for the Indians, thus making conflict inevitable. Later, white hunters took over the Indians' favorite hunting grounds and slaughtered buffalo by the thousands.

By the Treaty of Medicine Lodge (October 1867), Comanches, Kiowas, Arapahos, and Cheyennes were assigned
reservations in present southwestern Oklahoma. But they refused to stay put, and, determined to keep the whites off their
lands, they began hitting isolated settlements along the Texas
frontier and the borders of Kansas, Colorado, and New Mexico.
Finally, in August 1874, some 3000 federal troops, divided into
five separate commands, converged upon Indian encampments
in the Texas Panhandle. More than fourteen pitched battles
were fought before all of the remaining warriors agreed to
return to their reservations. The last bedraggled band of once-
proud Comanches surrendered to federal authorities at Fort
Sill, Oklahoma, in 1875 and agreed to leave Texas to the
Texans. The promise was kept for the simple reason that
most of the young men had by now joined General Sheridan's
legion of good Indians—dead ones. The remainder were less
fortunate: they were forced to idle away their time on the
reservation, finding solace in alcohol or peyote.

Until the eve of the Civil War, Texans were too concerned
with Indians and Mexicans to worry much about another
minority group in their midst—the Negroes. Indeed, at first
they did not hate blacks in the same sense that they hated
Indians and Mexicans. Rather, the feeling in the 1840's was
more or less one of benevolent amusement. "It is said by
many as a serious fact that if a Negro child be kept clean and
well clothed, it will pine and die," William Bollaert wrote
during his travels in Texas in 1843, "but if allowed to roll and
play about in the dirt there is no fear of [for] its thriving." [11]
    The total slave population of Texas in 1836, after fifteen
years of colonization, was something like a thousand or less.
There were also a few free Negroes who had been attracted
to the province by the promise of cheap land and the chance
to begin a new life. Among these was Greenbury Logan, who
arrived in 1831 and would soon write to friends and relatives

in the North that he "loved the country" and felt "more a
free man than in the States." Logan fought in several battles
as a volunteer in the war for independence and received
serious injuries at San Jacinto which left him permanently
disabled. Some Negro slaves also participated in the final
engagement and won their freedom for bravery on the battlefield.

Soon after independence from Mexico, Texas quickly developed into a major slaveholding region, and just as quickly
it forgot its Negro patriots. Logan, for example, was denied
tax exemption on his farm, even though he was too disabled to
work the land—which he had received as a bonus for services
in the Texas army. Other free Negroes also found their rights
greatly restricted and their presence no longer welcome in the
land they had helped defend. According to the census of 1850,
free Negroes in Texas numbered 397, while there were 58,161
slaves and 154,034 whites. Ten years later the population of
the state had jumped to 604,215, of which 182,921 were listed
as Negroes, but with no distinction made between those who
were free and those who were slaves.[12]

Most foreign observers during the pre-Civil War years
maintained that slaves were well treated and not overworked
or ill-used by their masters. "In the eastern counties," Bollaert
wrote, "they are principally family Negroes or brought up by
their owners, and when they get old are kept upon the plantation and not sold to an indifferent master." [13] Most owners
allowed their field hands to do as they wished on Saturday
afternoons and Sundays, and let them maintain a small plot of
ground back of their cabin for raising a vegetable garden and
keeping pigs and chickens. If they chose to pick cotton during
their leisure time they were paid for it or else allowed to keep
for themselves all that they could gather in half a day.

This situation changed drastically as the war approached.
During a four- or five-week period in July and August of
1860, some slaves "confessed" that they had been participants

in a grand plot to sweep across Texas, systematically destroying towns, stores, mills, corn cribs, and various other properties, and poisoning wells and springs. The Negroes supposedly were to be led by abolitionists, or "Lincolnites," and when news of the uprising spread throughout north Texas it was rumored that thousands of white women and children had fled their homes in terror, hiding out in the woods or seeking shelter with friends and relatives.

Militia companies and vigilante committees were formed almost overnight in practically every section in the state. A resident of Harrison County wrote to a friend on August 12, 1860, that at least half the men in Texas were doing constant patrol duty. "Judge Lynch has had the honor to preside only in ten cases of whites (northern Lincolnites) and about sixty-five negroes, all of whom were hung or burnt, as to the degree of their implication in the rebellion and burning." The writer claimed that the Northern churches were responsible for the hysteria that had broken out, and he accused them of fomenting trouble in revenge for the expulsion of several Methodist ministers "for preaching and teaching Abolition incendiarism to the negroes."

> Unless the churches send out new recruits of John Browns, I fear the boys will have nothing to do this winter (as they have hung all that can be found), the school boys have become so excited by the sport in hanging Abolitionists, that the schools are completely deserted, they have formed companies, and will go seventy-five or one hundred miles on horseback to participate in a single execution of the sentence of Judge Lynch's Court.[14]

The existence of an insurrection plot by abolitionist agents in Texas in 1860 is well supported by documentary evidence.[15] The plot failed because it was inadequately organized, poorly executed, and covered too vast a territory. In addition to the loss of life, at least two million dollars' worth of property damage resulted from various acts of violence committed by both blacks and whites in urban and frontier communities. The plot and its discovery encouraged harsher discipline of slaves and intensification of sentiment for secession throughout Texas.

Four years of war and a much longer period of Reconstruction continued to fan the flames of racial hatred and fear and to scar the souls of thousands of Texans. The freedmen were the chief beneficiaries of Reconstruction, and in some sections of the South whites seemed unable to comprehend that they no longer had the right to exercise the old controls over them. General W. Swayne reported to Congress in 1872 that at least two-thirds of the Negroes in east Texas counties to whom he had talked had not received one cent for their labor in the cotton and cane fields. A few had been promised something at the end of each year, but instances in which these promises had been kept were rare indeed. Swayne further declared that many field hands did not even know that they were free until he told them they were.[16]

Prior to General Swayne's tour of inspection, a special Committee on Lawlessness and Violence had submitted an even more devastating report to E. J. Davis, president of the convention to construct a new constitution for the state of Texas.[17] According to the committee, a "war of races" had taken place in the forty selected Texas counties which they had visited. Between June 1865 and June 1868, at least 373 Negro freedmen had been lynched by mobs or shot down in cold blood by individuals with no provocation—"except for the fact that men naturally hate those whom they have wronged." Among the several dozen examples cited were the following: In Panola County, a party of whites rode up to a cabin wherein several Negroes were singing and dancing. The visitors hesitated only long enough to fire point blank into the cabin, killing three men and one woman and seriously injuring several others. In Dewitt County, in 1867, a white killed a black man merely because he observed him carrying a buggy whip in his hand. A short time later, in Fort Bend County, a white rode by the local Freedman's Bureau, saw a Negro standing on the steps, and promptly drew his revolver and killed him. In Newton County, a white met a Negro driving a team of mules. After pulling alongside, he stopped, ordered the Negro to get out of the wagon, and then riddled his body with bullets.

Bad as conditions were in Texas during the Reconstruction period, the state emerged in much better economic condition than any other member of the Confederacy. Relatively few military engagements had been fought on Texas soil, her railroads generally had been left intact, and there were hundreds of thousands of longhorn cattle available for the hungry Northern markets. Some returning veterans quickly realized the opportunities for tremendous profits in the cattle industry, and they soon employed hundreds of young men on their vast ranches or on the long trail drives to the Missouri and Kansas cowtowns. At the same time, thousands of residents of the Old South flocked into the state, attracted by the millions of acres of virgin land on the Texas frontier and impelled by the hope of getting a new start. Their former lives and fortunes had been ruined by the war, and for this they held the Negroes primarily responsible. Their bitterness soon reinforced the racial hatred that had already built up among native Texans.

Comanche County, on the extreme western edge of the Upper Cross Timbers, offers an excellent example of how an attitude of racial arrogance could easily turn into senseless violence.[18] The census of 1880 gave the total population of the country as 8529 whites and 79 Negroes. Although the frontier by then had moved well beyond the region, it had left in its wake a vigilante tradition of organized groups pursuing outlaws and trailing parties of raiding Indians. Back in 1875, a

Negro resident of the county had become deranged, and he
had killed two young black girls and two white boys before
a vigilante committee ended his life with a rope. At the time,
the talk of "chasing all Niggers" out of the region amounted
to no more than excess braggadocio by a few hotheads.

By the middle of the next decade the bitter memories of
Reconstruction had faded considerably, but a difficult period
still lay ahead. A series of summer droughts and winter blizzards started in western Texas and soon spread throughout the
Great Plains and prairie states. The year 1886 was a particularly difficult one for Comanche County because of crop
failures, bankruptcies, and political disturbances. Various reform movements of the day were creating almost as much
heat as the blistering Texas sun. Rash actions became the
rule instead of the exception as more and more groups made
their particular views felt by night rides and mob force. The
explosion came on July 24, 1886, when an eighteen-year-old
Negro shot and killed the wife of a white farmer. As the news
spread throughout the county, hundreds of men and boys from
the towns and rural areas joined in a search for the youth.
When captured the next day he readily confessed that he had
shot the woman "just for meanness."

Because it was Sunday, and also to provide time for more
people to assemble and enjoy the most exciting event in
years, the posse postponed execution until the following Mon-
day. The hanging provided an emotional outlet for thousands
of witnesses, but the leaders of the mob were not yet ready
to settle down and go back to their jobs. They first rounded
up several Negroes in the immediate area and ordered them
to bury what had been left of the corpse after souvenir hunters had cut off toes, fingers, and other parts of the body. Later
that day members of the mob visited every Negro shack in
the county and ordered the occupants to "pack up and get
out within ten days or be killed."

In spite of efforts by a few responsible people to protect

various Negro friends and employees from the violence, every single Negro had fled the area long before the deadline expired. Within a month the only reminder of the July incident was a sign at the public well in the county seat of Comanche County which read: "Nigger, don't let the sun go down on you in this town." (Similar warnings were not uncommon on the outskirts of small, drab West Texas towns prior to World War II.)[19]

Texans of the late nineteenth century were fairly typical of all Southerners in their attitude toward Negroes, in that their feelings ranged from affection and amused superiority to extreme fear and outright hatred. To be called a "Nigger lover" was worse than the earlier epithet of "Indian lover" and could create as much violent response as a suggestion that one possessed canine ancestry. Official statistics on the number of lynchings of blacks during Reconstruction days in Texas are unreliable, but they are reasonably accurate after 1889, when the *Chicago Tribune* began keeping score of public lynchings. According to the *Tribune*, some 3224 individuals were killed by lynch mobs in the United States between 1889 and 1927. Only 702 of these were whites; 2522 were blacks.[20]

The Southern states claimed the largest number of victims, 2834, while the North had 219 and the West 156. Georgia led the states with 386 lynchings, followed closely by Mississippi with 373 and Texas with 335 for the thirty-eight-year period. However, after 1918 Texas assumed the lead, and it averaged more than five mob lynchings per year throughout the next decade. Of the fifty-five people lynched in Texas between 1918 and 1927, most were Negroes or Mexicans. In eleven cases, the victims were burned alive, in three instances their bodies were burned after death, while two individuals were killed by public beatings. The others were hanged publicly.[21]

The most common cause for lynching Negroes in Texas

during this period was assault upon a white woman. In many cases the evidence was clear-cut, but in others it rested upon no more solid ground than the entering of a white woman's room, or merely brushing against her on the sidewalk. But once a mob formed there was rarely any stopping it until its leaders had tasted blood. The following item appeared in the *Chicago Tribune* on November 22, 1895: "News has been received of the lynching of a Negro in this part of Madison County [Texas] on Tuesday night. He was accused of riding his horse over a little white girl and inflicting serious injuries on her. Later developments go to show that the mob got hold of the wrong negro. The guilty one made his escape." [22] There was much more than frivolity to H. L. Mencken's observation that public lynchings often took the place of the merry-go-round, the theater, the symphony orchestra, and other diversions common to large communities.

Negroes were not the only victims of violent hatred and general lawlessness during the post-Civil War period. According to the report submitted to the State Constitutional Convention in 1868, a total of 1035 killings occurred in Texas during the first three years after the Civil War. More than half of these were committed by whites against whites—some for political reasons. Yet in spite of the large number of homicides, only 279 individuals were indicted. Five of these were eventually convicted, but the only person who was executed was a Negro resident of Harris County.[23] In 1870 Texas registered 323 deaths from homicide, 195 more than the second-ranking state. In that same year local officers in 108 counties reported 2790 criminals at large, a figure that would almost double by 1887.[24]

As on all frontiers, widespread homicide engendered the customary vigilante movement. According to Richard Brown, Texas also had the dubious distinction of having experienced fifty-two such movements before the end of the nineteenth century—considerably more than any other state.[25] One of the most infamous vigilante episodes in American history started in Shelby County, in east Texas near the Louisiana boundary, during the days of the Republic. By 1839 the county had come under the control of a loosely organized gang of horse thieves, counterfeiters, murderers, and fraudulent land speculators. Local vigilantes organized under the name of "Regulators" in an effort to restore order and destroy the power of the "Moderators," the name that the gang later adopted. Bad elements soon infiltrated the Regulators, and their excesses in crime later rivaled those of the Moderators. The situation evolved into a complexity of personal and family feuds, and complete anarchy existed until 1844. In that year President Sam Houston restored a semblance of order by placing the county under martial law, but by then eighteen men had been murdered and many more had been seriously wounded. The forces of hatred that the survivors passed on to their descendants was still evident half a century later.[26]

Between 1865 and 1890, certainly the most prolonged, turbulent period of Texas history, twenty-seven vigilante movements took place in the Lone Star State. Many of the movements were related directly to Reconstruction, while others started as family feuds or fights over land or water rights, barbed-wire fencing, or cattle rustling. Outlaw gangs took full advantage of the social disorganization and of the lack of resources available to support constables, policemen, and sheriffs, or even to construct jails. "If you want distinction in this lawless country," a visitor to Texas wrote during the period, "kill somebody." [27] The observation was far from facetious. Vigilante groups often formed to pursue notorious gunmen in the region, men such as John Wesley Hardin or Ben Thompson. These were two of the best known individuals that Texas produced during the nineteenth century, and either one would have made Billy the Kid look like a Boy Scout.

Hardin was born in 1853 at Bonham, a small north Texas

town later to become known as the birthplace of Sam Rayburn, Speaker of the U.S. House of Representatives. How
many men Hardin killed before he himself was murdered (in
1895) is undetermined. At the age of nine he possessed a
reputation for deadly accuracy with a six-shooter, which he
carried at all times. This was not unusual in pre-Civil War
Texas. The *Southern Intelligencer*, published in Austin, commented on October 13, 1858, that "It is a common thing here
to see boys from 10 to 14 years of age carrying about their
persons Bowie knives and pistols." At age eleven Hardin
killed his first man, and by the time he was eighteen the number had increased to twenty-seven. To some he was the most
feared and hated man in Texas, but to others he was a full-
blown hero. An admirer who watched him shoot down five
armed opponents in less than a minute said later that "with
either hand or both hands at the same time, that boy can handle
a pistol faster than a frog can lick flies." [28] The comment was
widely quoted, and it did nothing to detract from Hardin's
reputation as a man with steel nerves, a cool head, and a
lightning-fast draw—qualities that Americans greatly admired
throughout the frontier period.

Ben Thompson also shot his way to fame, although he started
his career as an expert pistoleer a few years later in life than
John Wesley Hardin did. To tangle with him was regarded
as suicide, and by the time he was twenty he had one notch on
his gun for each year of his life. "He possessed the qualities required for a top-notch [no pun intended] gunfighter," according to one of his many biographers. "He was fearless, pro-
ficient in the use of a pistol, cool and resourceful under trying
circumstances. He had the steadiest of nerves, and could shoot
a human being with the same precision he shot at a target.
. . . Few men have crowded more excitement into forty-
three years of life [1842–85] than did Ben Thompson . . . a
man who never failed to go 'all out' for a friend." [29]

The John Wesley Hardins and Ben Thompsons were products of their time and place, just as were most men who lived by violence. Their careers perhaps offered a vicarious escape for many Texans who suffered the frustrations of poverty or the endless routine of drab small towns and rural areas. Yet, even though the majority might have taken pride in the belief that such men represented a special breed, it did not follow that they all accepted the idea that the quickest solution to a problem required the aid of a gun, bowie knife, or a rope. For, along with its outlaws and homicidal maniacs, the Texas wilderness also produced an astonishing number of intelligent, hard-working, law-abiding, and even urbane citizens.

Although the growth of cities in the twentieth century has added significant new dimensions to the character and extent of violence in America, the image of frontier Texas as the most violent of lands is still difficult to erase. To deny that lawlessness existed in wholesale quantities throughout much of the state's history would be as foolish as to pretend that snow is not characteristic of Alaskan winters. The sons and daughters of the Lone Star State have to live with the bad residue of their heritage as well as with the good. The fact that one's life was probably much safer on the Texas frontier a hundred years ago than it is on the streets of most American cities today is irrelevant. The same is true of the assertion that on any given day, more violent crimes are committed in a ten-square-mile area of Philadelphia or New York City than in the entire 267,339 square miles that constitute the present state of Texas.

IV
Golden California: For Anglos Only

"Take a sprinkling of sober-eyed, earnest, shrewd, energetic New England-business-men: mingle with them a number of rollicking sailors, a dark band of Australian convicts and cutthroats, a dash of Mexican and frontier desperadoes, a group of hardy backwoodsmen, some professional gamblers, whiskey-dealers, general swindlers . . . and having thrown in a promiscuous crowd of broken-down merchants, disappointed lovers, black sheep, unfledged dry-goods clerks, professional miners from all parts of the world, and Adullamites generally, stir up the mixture, season strongly with gold-fever, bad liquors, faro, monte, rouge-et-noir, quarrels, oaths, pistols, knives, dancing, and digging, and you have something approximating California society in early days." [1]

This description of early California is duplicated, in substance, in thousands of letters, diaries, and memoirs left by the forty-niners. And, however enlightened and tolerant the residents of the Golden State have since become (with major exceptions, of course), California's record for unprovoked violence and uncivilized treatment of nonwhite groups is a formidable one indeed. The turmoil produced by the state of nature that characterized the mining camps and cities probably would have turned Jean-Jacques Rousseau into a political Tory. Hubert Howe Bancroft, in his massive, two-volume *Popular Tribunals* (1887), documents many of the acts of violence committed by individuals and by vigilante groups during the first seven years after California was wrested from Mexico. Considerable new evidence has been uncovered since Bancroft's work, but it all tells very much the same story of human depravity.

The discovery of gold on the American River in January 1848 touched off a rush to the Pacific Coast that was unprecedented in the history of the world. Within two years more than a hundred thousand people had reached "the promised land." Like the raw Texas frontier a generation earlier, California attracted many decent residents from all parts of the United States and several foreign countries. It also attracted riffraff in wholesale quantity, and the influx of good and bad people was simply too swift for order and justice to keep pace. The Golden State would become reasonably civilized within a decade or two after admission into the Union, particularly so in its northern counties. In the meantime, it crowded more violence into a briefer period than any other American frontier did—including Texas. Once again, the basis for much of the unjust exercise of force related directly to the prejudices against non-white groups which the gold seekers brought with them.

In the mid-nineteenth century, the average American frontiersman assumed that all dark-skinned peoples were born inferior and therefore were not entitled to the equal protection of the law. The inhuman treatment of minority groups a century ago in California seems incredible. Voices of protest and influence would be raised today against the killing of Indians, Orientals, blacks, or members of any other ethnic group, or at least millions of Americans would be outraged, and some of the perpetrators of the crime would be brought to trial.[2] But in the Gold Rush days, few objected and no one was tried—much less condemned.

Anglo-Americans in California possessed no monopoly on prejudice against Indians. Spanish soldiers at the various *presidios*, and priests at the missions, had frequently looked upon the lowly Diggers and Mission Indians as subhumans and treated them accordingly. "The Indians of California may be compared to a species of monkey," wrote the Franciscan missionary Geronimo Boscana at San Juan Capistrano in 1825. "The truth is not in him," the friar continued, "unless to the injury of another, and he is exceedingly false." [3] Many priests and soldiers frequently compared the California Indians to a much lower form of animal than the monkey.

Time after time priests ordered neophytes—women as well as men—stripped and flogged for minor or imaginary offenses. The most common crime committed by the Mission Indian was running away to escape the incessant labor, inadequate food, and miserable lodging. The pioneer California historian Hittell wrote in 1885 that on such occasions, and they were frequent, men, women, and children "were hunted down and punished with tenfold rigor." [4] When an Indian wept over the death of his wife and child at Mission Dolores (San Francisco) in 1797, Father Antonio Danti ordered him whipped five times. Another went in search of food, and when he returned—voluntarily—he received twenty-five lashes.

Soldiers sent out to round up large parties of fugitives sometimes killed their prisoners rather than return them to the mission. But, they carefully gave each victim the opportunity to accept the baptismal rite of having his head doused with water before being shot. The American fur trapper Joseph Walker witnessed an example of what he called "Spanish justice" in 1833, when he and his party of mountain men came upon a company of Spaniards (Mexicans) in the San Joaquin Valley. The pursuers were following the trail of several hundred neophytes who had run away from San Jose Mission with 300 horses, and he and some of his men joined in the chase. When they eventually discovered the Indian camp, most of the animals had already been slaughtered for food, and the younger and stronger refugees had escaped into the mountains.

So furious were the Spaniards that they indiscriminately slaughtered the feeble old men and women and small children who had been left behind. In some cases they cut off the ears of the victims and then shot them in the shoulder in order to prolong the agony of death. Some were driven into brush huts and burned alive. This was too much for the Americans, hardened as they were. Some of them intervened and released a group of prisoners about to be burned, only to have the Spaniards "dispatch them as if they were dogs" as they tried to escape.[5]

The process of secularizing the California missions began in 1831. Some neophytes were then allowed to return to their native ways or to work on the large ranchos owned by American or Spanish grandees. For all practical purposes, their lot was far from improved, for many were simply taken over by the new owners of the mission lands, along with the cattle and sheep. They were frequently traded or sold like any other property. Captain John A. Sutter, upon whose land gold was discovered in 1848, owned 600 to 800 Indians, whom he kept in a complete state of slavery. According to a visitor to Sutter's Fort, near present Sacramento, the natives were fed once a day, like swine, in ten or fifteen troughs three to four feet long. The food was brought out in buckets, and once the troughs were filled the men, women, and children were allowed to fend for themselves.[6]

Historians generally estimate the number of Indians in California in 1769, the year that the first Spanish mission was constructed (near present San Diego), at 300,000. Three-quarters of a century later, as the period of Mexican control came to an end and the American period began, no more than

Helen Hunt Jackson's famous novel *Ramona* (1884) was based upon real characters. It is the story of a girl of Scottish and Indian ancestry who eloped with Alessandro, a Mission Indian. He was driven mad and died because of persecution. In this rare photograph, Ramona is standing beside Alessandro's grave.

100,000 natives remained. (There is considerable confusion about the classification of the various tribes of California Indians, especially since they represented a wide variety of linguistic stocks. Those who were more or less kept in a condition of peonage or slavery at the various missions were generally called "Mission Indians." The term "Digger" or "Root-Eater" was applied to most natives living among the mountains and deserts of the West. The Diggers were usually of Shoshonean linguistic stock.) By the time secularization had been completed and the Americans had arrived in large numbers, little distinction existed between the Mission Indians and the Diggers, and the miners generally referred to all of them by the latter name.

The fate of the California Indians constitutes one of the darkest chapters in American history. The Diggers lived in small, defenseless communities, and when they got in the way the miners fell upon them with savage fury, drove them from their homes, burned their villages, raped their women, and enslaved or murdered their men. "If an Indian dared attempt a defense of his wife or sister," a forty-niner wrote, "he was fortunate indeed if he escaped a shot or stab in connection with a sound beating." The same writer also tells of a young boy who threw a rock among some peaceful Indians and instantly killed a baby that hung in a basket on its mother's back. "It was the expressed opinion that he was a bad boy, but no complaint was made; probably his parents never even heard of the circumstances." [7]

No one seems to have had a kind word for the Diggers. An Easterner named William Perkins spent three years in California and kept an extraordinarily interesting journal of his observations of life in the mining camps. His characterization of the Diggers as the most wretched of all North American Indians appears in writings of hundreds of others, including Mark Twain's frequently quoted *Roughing It* (1871). Perkins wrote:

They are about four feet high, with very large heads
and huge shocks of hair, coarse and black. Their limbs
are very small; their legs are no larger than the arm of
a moderate size man. . . . They go strictly naked
even in the severe region in which they reside, and
subsist on roots, acorns, berries and small edible parts
of the pine cone, which is found in great abundance
in all the mountains of California.[8]

The fact that the Diggers also ate insects, vermin, reptiles,
lizards, or anything that crawled doubtless helped salve the
consciences of various white men who allegedly shot them for
sport. A California pioneer recalled years later that in 1871
some ranchers in the Sacramento Valley found a steer that
had been wounded by Indians. They trailed the Diggers with
dogs and finally cornered them in a cave. There were about
thirty Indians, including several women and children. The
children were saved until the last because "Kingsley could not
bear to kill them with his 56-calibre Spencer rifle. 'It tore
them up so bad.' So he did it with his 38-calibre Smith and
Wesson revolver." [9]

Within twenty-five years after the conquest of California,
more than three-fourths of the local Indians had been destroyed by outright violence, starvation, disease, and alcohol.
According to a pioneer resident of Napa Valley, many tribes
"become so desperate that they took to murdering their off-
springs at birth, otherwise they would come into life diseased
and are born only to suffer and die." [10] Most modern authorities on Indian history, the majority of whom are sympathetic
to the red man's cause, maintain that there was never an
organized campaign of genocide conducted during the past
two centuries of Indian-white relationship in the United States.
This may be technically correct, but the fate of the California
Indians amounted to the same thing.

Again we return to William Perkins' journal for a description of an expedition to hunt down and punish a party of Indians accused of stealing seven mules from one of the settlements near Sonora. On February 1, 1850, Perkins and seventeen American companions joined a dozen Mexicans in pursuit of the Indians high into the mountains. Although the trail was well marked as a result of recent snows, climbing was extremely difficult, and several days passed before the party came upon the Indian camp. Perkins is vague on the number killed in the brutal attack that followed, but he carefully points out that he and his fellow Americans avoided shooting the women and children. The Mexicans, he asserted, had no such qualms. Later the entire Indians' possessions were piled and burned, and Perkins admitted that he was not entirely satisfied with himself.

> After the excitement of the fray had subsided, I could not help asking myself the question, as to how far we were warranted in destroying life and property to such an extent; for although the value of property destroyed did not amount to much, still it was the whole amount of worldly goods possessed by the tribe. The houses, we may readily believe, have as great a value, comparatively speaking, to their owners, as ours in Sonora. Their baskets, and above all their supply of provisions, may certainly be placed on a par with our household goods. And we had invaded and destroyed the lives and property of these poor, miserable people, to chastise what in their eyes is no crime.[11]

When Mexico won her independence from Spain in 1821, the Spanish nationals who remained there automatically became Mexican citizens. Later, according to the Treaty of Guadalupe Hidalgo (1848), Mexican residents of California were to be accorded the full rights and privileges enjoyed

by any other American citizen. This "guarantee" was honored
for an even briefer period than were the usual treaties between
the federal government and various Indian tribes.

Less than two years after the Treaty of Guadalupe Hidalgo,
the population of California approximated 80,000 Anglos,
8000 Mexicans, and 5000 South Americans—mostly from Chile
and Peru. Many of the Mexicans were native born, and they
preferred to call themselves *Californios*. At first the Americans
seemed to treat them as equals, particularly the more prosperous rancheros with Spanish blood. But as news of the discovery of gold spread southward, thousands of nationals from
Mexico, Chile, and Peru came to California, and they quickly
outnumbered the *Californios*. Soon all Latins were being
lumped together as "greasers," and were treated by the
Yankees with the same contempt they conferred upon the
Indians. Even though many *Californios* were well educated,
held title to vast tracts of land, and ranked higher in the social
structure than the Mexicans and Chileans, most white miners
came to consider them, at best, as "half-civilized black men."

The *Californios* soon withdrew from the field and left gold
mining to the Yankees. Leonard Pitts' story of their disintegra-
tion is another explicit description of the shattering effect of
Anglo-Saxon violence upon a non-white society.[12] Their
collapse was so rapid that in northern California they became a
small minority almost overnight. Although some held their
own in the southern part of the state for another twenty years,
they could not compete with the aggressive Yankees, who
took their lands and cattle under the pious clichés of "the
Californios are culturally unsuited to the new order," "they
brought it on themselves," and "the race goes to the strong."
Many eventually repatriated to Mexico, and all but a handful
of the rest were absorbed into the main population stream before the end of the century.

The treatment of the Mexican, Chilean, and Peruvian gold
seekers represented a more physical and direct form of violence

than that which was practiced against the *Californios*. It would be impossible at this late date to catalogue the number of hangings, brandings, whippings, ear croppings, and banishments of Latins by white miners. Judging from the examples cited in Bancroft's *Popular Tribunals*, the figures would be substantial indeed. The fact that the Mexicans were both experienced and successful in the early days of the gold strikes made the Yankees all the more resentful. Soon most mining camps passed *ad hoc* regulations that forbade foreigners from holding claims or carrying on mining activities on their own. In 1850, the California state legislature passed the Foreigners' Mining Tax, which more or less legalized the prohibition by requiring foreigners to pay twenty dollars per month for the right to work in the mines, either for themselves or for others.[13]

This tax, combined with the crude race hatred of all "greasers," contributed to considerable violence and lynch law in the mines. The greatest number of incidents occurred in the southern regions of California, where white gold-seekers from the South and Southwest predominated. Charles Howard Shinn, in his study of the development of government in the mining camps, concluded that the tendency to despise, abuse, and override the Spanish groups in California ranks alongside the treatment of the Indians as perhaps the darkest thread in the fabric of American frontier government.[14]

In some areas where the potential taxpayers were particularly strong in numbers, printed posters appeared which denounced the mine tax and called for its repeal. On May 12, 1850, some 4000 non-Yankees, mostly Mexicans, held a mass meeting near Sonora, California, and flatly declared that they would not pay the exorbitant sum, although they would be willing to accept a reasonable fee of approximately three to five dollars per month. When the tax collectors held their ground (they were backed up by several hundred fellow Americans who had accompanied them to the scene), most of the foreigners lost their nerve and immediately dispersed. One

Mexican refused to be intimidated and remained behind, but he was quickly stabbed to death by a bystander with a bowie knife. News of the incident spread to near-by camps, and white miners stopped work and rushed to the "defense" of the town of Sonora.

By the following day some 400 armed Americans marched to the camps of the foreigners, chased away those who could not pay the tax, and sternly warned them not to return. "The posse then liquored up for the road, hoisted the Stars and Stripes to the top of a pine tree, fired off a salute, and headed for home." [15] The celebration proved a bit premature: a few days later there was a series of robberies and violent killings in which all the victims were Yankees. The miners assembled once again and drew up resolutions to cleanse the hillsides completely of every "greaser" in southern California except those "respectable characters" who could purchase "permits of good conduct." The results this time were very effective, judging from the fact that some 15,000 Mexicans, Chileans, Peruvians, and other minorities scattered in all directions. Those who paid the twenty-dollar fee and received certificates of good conduct soon found that they had purchased very little protection.

Fear and hatred of the Latins created an atmosphere so hostile that their harassment and even murder became a patriotic ritual in some regions of southern California. According to Hittell, lynch-law proceedings sometimes allowed heinous crimes to be committed in the name of American justice. A forty-niner named Clarence King told of an incident that occurred in a mining town in the early 1850's. It seems that when a well-known miner discovered that two of his donkeys and a horse were missing, he charged the theft to the first Mexican he sighted. A crowd gathered immediately, seized the suspect, and was ready to hang him on the spot until someone persuaded them to "Give 'em a fair jury trial, and rope 'em with all the majesty of the law. That's the cure." [16]

A jury was quickly selected in the street, and, despite a refusal at first by some to serve, the crowd locked them in a back room of the local saloon until they could reach a verdict. Meanwhile, the occasion called for a celebration, and while the jury deliberated the crowd got uproariously drunk. When the verdict of "not guilty" was announced, the jury was once again locked up and informed that it "would have to do better than that." Half an hour later some well-armed citizens entered the jury room to ascertain how the deliberations were proceeding. When informed that the verdict was "guilty," the chief spokesman responded: "Correct! You can come out. We hung him an hour ago." Later that evening, after the festivities were over and the mob had dispersed, the bartender observed the missing animals resting in the shade of an oak tree behind his saloon. He suddenly remembered that he had seen them there earlier in the day, but in the rush of business at the bar he had forgotten to inform his customers.[17]

It is doubtful if many of those who participated in this disgusting affair experienced much guilt about hanging an innocent man, for they probably rationalized that the Mexican deserved the sentence anyway for other crimes that he had actually committed. "The 'Greaser' has all of the characteristic vices of the Spaniard; jealous, revengeful and treacherous, with an absorbing passion for gambling; and he has a still greater likeness to the inferior tribes of Indians; the same apathetic indolence; the same lounging, thieving propensity; never caring for the morrow, and alike regardless of the past or the future." [18] The author of this comment later observed that "the summary execution of a few Mexicans has had a more wonderful effect than could be anticipated." [19]

More than three-fourths of the Spanish-speaking miners had been driven out of the gold fields of southern California before the end of 1850. Many returned to Mexico or to South America, but large numbers settled in the village of Los Angeles, where they remained a majority group until the

1870's. Others took to the roads and countryside to seek revenge against the hated "gringos." According to Pitts, the general alarm against Mexican badmen was first sounded in 1850, after the foreign miners' tax was imposed.

Not all of the bandits were Mexicans, but the Anglos took it for granted that all Mexicans encountered on the roads were bandits. Some riders, upon seeing a Mexican approaching on foot or on horseback, immediately leveled a rifle or pistol on the stranger and ordered him to keep his hands over his head until he had continued on past for several hundred feet and well out of range. All of the roads around southern California soon became extremely dangerous for travel. Individuals and small parties were robbed, herds of longhorns being driven to market from the ranchos were rustled, and scarcely a day passed without a murderous atrocity being committed. "It is next to impossible to say who are the guilty parties in the various cold-blooded murders we have had lately," Perkins wrote. "Most likely they are Mexicans, for I do not think white men could be so bloodthirsty. . . . The Mexicans are actually fond of butchering the white men . . . they show no mercy, but butcher with all the savage cruelty of wild beasts." [20]

It was during this period that the phantom-like Joaquin Murieta became California's most famous folk hero. To many he represented the archetypal leader of a small gang of *bandidos* who held up stagecoaches, murdered lonely mail riders and teamsters, stole or destroyed everything valuable, left no witnesses, and never stopped to fight. At first the gang seemed to specialize in killing Chinese, whom the Mexicans for some reason hated as much as they did the "gringos." The leader's real identity has become clouded, and most probably there were several Joaquins who terrorized the southern counties throughout the 1850's. There is little doubt that the "Joaquin scare" was real, whether the individual was or not. As the killings and robberies continued, the miners formed vigilante committees and ranger companies "to exterminate the Mexican race from the country."

In 1853, the California legislature posted a reward for the capture of Joaquin, created a company of twenty men, veterans of the wars in Texas and Mexico who modeled their troop after the Texas Rangers, and gave them three months to finish the job. Obviously, the reward would not go unclaimed. A few days after the expiration of the time period, the company killed two "suspicious looking characters" in a running gun battle and promptly identified one as Joaquin and the other as three-fingered Jack Garcia, his chief lieutenant. The rangers cut off the head of one and the hand of the other and bottled them in whiskey. They later collected a reward of $5000 from the appreciative legislature.

There are many versions of the life, adventure, and final capture of Joaquin, most of which are highly romanticized. Some historians have maintained that he never existed, others that he was not captured until 1856, and still others that he eventually died of old age. Even so, the head of the man alleged to be the real Joaquin became a prized trophy, was taken on a world tour, and eventually ended up as a popular attraction in a San Francisco saloon. Fortunately, it vanished from sight in the 1906 earthquake.

The voluminous accounts of life in early California tell a similar story of how indifferent the forty-niners became to the presence of violence and bloodshed. The daily brawls and murders came to be looked upon with a callousness of feeling, even though one man's life was in as much danger as another's. Most of the evidence seems to confirm the stereotype of the average forty-niner as a hard-drinking man with a quick trigger finger. Robert Glass Cleland states that the unrestrained sale of adulterated, and often poisoned, liquor resulted in an appalling amount of crime. On Saturday nights the streets of Los Angeles would be filled with intoxicated mobs, and when

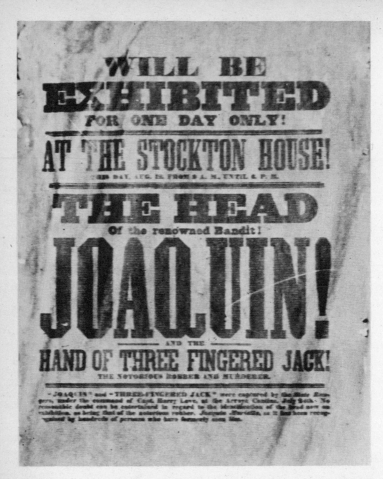

The head of a man alleged to be the real Joaquin became a prized trophy, was taken on a world tour, and eventually ended up as a popular attraction in a San Francisco saloon. Fortunately, it vanished in the 1906 earthquake.

the police made their regular Sunday morning rounds of the alleyways and gutters, "it was taken for granted that they would find a few stabbed or bullet-ridden corpses among the night's debauch." [21]

"Yesterday was an exciting day and long to be remembered," A. C. Sweetser wrote from Sacramento City on February 26, 1851. Sweetser then described, in considerable detail, a fight that had broken out at a monte table between a gambler named Frederick J. Roe and a miner. While Roe and a companion were beating the miner unmercifully (he died a few days later, leaving a wife and five children in Ohio), a peaceful citizen named Myers attempted to part them, urging fair play and not two against one. Roe then shot Myers in the head and killed him instantly. "In eight hours time [after] the man [was] shot, the prisoner [was] arrested, and the jury appointed, the prisoner [was] tried and strung up by the neck; and this is California speed in bringing culprits to Justice." [22]

Even more bizarre is a story of violence attributed to Hinton Helper. Not because it could not have happened, given the conditions that existed in California at the time, but Helper's later use of questionable statistics in his famous *The Impending Crisis of the South* (1857) has caused many historians to question almost everything he ever wrote. Be that as it may, Helper recorded in his *Land of Gold* (1855) an incident involving Ned, the nine-year-old son of the landlord of the hotel wherein Helper resided for a brief period. The youth joined the men at their nightly card game and quickly demonstrated his ability to deal the cards like a veteran. When one of the players accused him of "shifting" the cards, young Ned stood up and shouted: "God damn you, I'll shoot you." Bedlam followed, and everyone started firing away. When a bystander was mortally wounded, the crowd immediately seized the man believed to have fired the shot, hauled him off to the nearest tree, and hanged him without a trial. Apparently nothing happened to Ned, who had touched off the whole fracas.[23]

Civilization was slow in reaching the southern counties. The *San Bernardino Semi-Weekly News* observed, on January 8, 1864, that "a horde of the worst kind of characters now infest the lower portion of the State, and there is little or no safety for travellers, when a murder . . . can be committed in broad daylight, on a frequently travelled road, and within a short distance from town." From other sources it appears evident that lawlessness and violence continued almost unchecked in the region until after 1870. Cleland attributes this to the inevitable result of a "backwash" from the mines and the bitter resentment of the *Californios* and Mexican immigrants over the loss of their land or the right to mine gold. In addition, southern California attracted an unusually large number of drifters and professional outlaws from the southwestern frontier of Texas, New Mexico, and Arizona.

Northern California had its share of violence also, and before 1856 the use of lynch law there was as common as it was in the south, where more Spanish-speaking people lived. San Francisco, for example, attracted a vast army of thieves and riffraff from all parts of the world, especially from Australia and other British penal colonies in the South Pacific. According to Hittell, thefts, robberies, burglaries, arson, and assassinations were daily occurrences, and no one's life was secure. By the spring of 1851 conditions had become so intolerable that the regular courts of law were helpless in combating crime and violence. Even the police did not dare enter certain precincts of the city.

Thus, in June 1851, there arose out of the unsettled conditions of San Francisco the Committee of Vigilance—its constitution and by-laws signed by approximately 200 of the leading citizens and published prominently in all of the local newspapers. Hittell and Bancroft devote considerable attention to the San Francisco movement of 1851 and its even more extensive and more famous successor, which was organized five years later. This second organization, incidentally, claimed somewhere between 5000 and 8000 members and was perhaps the most effective vigilante committee in American history. Both pioneer California historians agree that it was necessary, orderly, and semi-legal, under the conditions that existed. But vigilantism in the past had left so much anarchy and chaos in its wake that by the time of the California Gold Rush the idea was repugnant to most law-abiding citizens. For, as we have seen, men accustomed to taking law in their own hands are loath to give up the practice after regular judicial processes and governments are constituted.

Richard Brown and Barton Olsen, among others, generally agree with Bancroft and Hittell that the San Francisco vigilante movements of 1851 and 1856 were exceptions to the rule, in that the results were more beneficial than bad. Both movements were directed by men of property and standing—bankers, merchants, importers, lawyers, and doctors. In 1851 they broke up a gang of Australian cutthroats, and five years later they turned their wrath on gamblers, machine politicians, ballot-box stuffers, and so-called "shoulder strickers" (bullies). They hanged a total of eight and expelled or frightened away hundreds of known criminals. Even the *New-York Tribune*, which usually equated mob action and lynch law with barbarism, applauded the action of the San Francisco committees.[24]

Although virtually every town and coastal city in California has its story of its own vigilantes during the 1850's, San Francisco was unique in that its committees gave each victim a formal and fair trial, they worked with the established police and courts, and they disbanded before the leadership and the original objectives of the movements got out of control.

But vigilantism is still vigilantism, and one of its most revolting aspects, regardless of how deserving of capital punishment the victim might have been, was the behavior of the crowd. One English visitor wrote:

When a criminal was due to be hanged, the sandhills of San Francisco swarmed with human beings. They seemed to cluster together like bees on a tree branch, and for the purpose of seeing a criminal convulsed and writhing in the agonies of violent death! This desire seemed to pervade all classes of Americans in the city.

As sheriff and victim trudged through the streets, the bystanders rapidly snowballed behind them into a dense crowd. People in nearby houses leaned far out of second-story windows. In the clearing around the gibbet, the silent audience massed, quietly jockeying for the best place while priest, sheriff, and star performer played out the inexorable last act.

After a while the body hung limp, no longer kicking, swaying gently in the wind from the Bay. The show was over. Back to the city romped the mob in holiday mood, led by the Marion Rifles. When they reached the business district the militia band concluded the entertainment by going through a snappy drill on the plaza.

Lively music and quick steppers in peacock uniforms—you can't deny Californians had a natural flair for executions. Truly the Argonaut bore little resemblance to his remote forebearer, the austere and pious pioneer of Plymouth Rock. But this he and the Pilgrim had in common; both loved a duel, a dogfight, or a hanging day.[25]

Bancroft describes a public execution in San Francisco—probably the same event witnessed by the English visitor. The sarcasm of his comments is biting:

It was a happy sight, I say, this hanging of the moneyless, friendless Spanish stranger; it set so splendid an example to other poor friendless strangers of every nationality. Of course, to wealthy and respectable criminals, the spectacle taught nothing; but they did not dislike it. Sweet to those who escape just punishment is the just punishment of others. It was a gala day in San Francisco, this 10th of December 1852.[26]

That the first decade of the Americanization of California represents the nadir of racial prejudice, lawlessness, and unrestrained frontier violence would be difficult to dispute. How many individuals lost their lives as a result can only be estimated. For what it is worth, Hinton Helper, in his *Land of Gold*, put the total figure of deaths by murder, hanging, suicide, accident, starvation, and attack by Indians at 16,400 for the years 1849–54. Bancroft, who studied the criminal records for 1855 for California, states that 583 persons met death by violence during the twelve month period. Of these, 373 were whites, 133 Indians, 32 Chinese, and 3 Negroes. He admits that the killing of additional hundreds of Digger and Mission Indians went unrecorded.

The official records for 1855 indicate that 47 people were executed by mobs, 9 by legal tribunals, 10 by sheriffs or police officers, and 6 by collectors of foreign miners' licenses. Most of the remainder of deaths of miners resulted from claims or gambling disputes. These figures for 1855 represent an improvement over previous years. The district attorney for San Francisco, for example, asserted that, between 1850 and 1853, 1200 murders took place in that city alone.[27]

It is true that the California experience brought out the basic qualities of decency and humanitarianism in many of the forty-niners. But in others it brought out greed, racial prejudice, and homicidal cruelty. It is the second group that has attracted a disproportionate amount of attention. Some were professional outlaws and scoundrels who ended up on the gallows, were shot down in barroom brawls, or were driven out of the community by vigilante committees. For the most

A wedding, funeral, and camp meeting combined did not create as much excitement and entertainment—nor draw as large a crowd—as a public hanging on the frontier. When a criminal was to be hanged, the sandhills of San Francisco swarmed with human beings. The star attraction at this scene was one Michael G. Lachenais, who was hanged October 4, 1871.

part, these criminals were Anglos from the older states and Western territories and from the British penal colonies, and they deserve little of our sympathy.

The great majority of the forty-niners, however, must be held responsible for the treatment of the various unassimilable ethnic groups in early California. It is difficult to say who got the worst deal, but it probably was the Indians. The Spanish-speaking groups did not fare very well either. As for Negroes, from the very beginning they were most unwelcome in California, and few of them ever reached the gold fields. There were one or two instances of blacks being lynched in early California, but their small numbers and their reluctance to raise their voices afforded them a degree of protection, however uncertain, from senseless, physical violence. Nevertheless, they suffered discrimination in various forms, including being denied the right to testify in court against whites. There were also small numbers of Polynesians, Filipinos, and Frenchmen who were held in contempt by the Anglos.

Jews also came to the gold fields and within a few years each mining town and city had a sizable representation. "On a first arrival in our city," a San Francisco resident wrote in 1861, "it becomes a matter of astonishment to all who see the large number of mercantile houses conducted by Israelites, being much greater, in proportion to the commerce, than in any other city in America. Every line of business is engaged by them, with credit to themselves and honor to the community." [28] Jews blended into the Establishment with surprising ease. A recent examination of virtually every newspaper published in mid-nineteenth-century California by Professor Robert Levinson of San Jose State College turned up very little evidence of violence involving Jewish residents.[29]

Perhaps the main reasons that so small an amount of aggression and prejudice was practiced against the Jews in California is that they rarely engaged in mining in competition with their fellow Americans. Moreover, they provided the miners with

There were few Negroes in the Far West, but among the most famous characters in San Francisco in the 1880's and 1890's was Peter "Nigger" Johnson—shown here preaching a sermon on the streets of Chinatown. Johnson also dabbled in politics and raised hogs.

essential services and goods—especially clothing, hardware, and banking facilities. Jewish merchants and peddlers developed a reputation for prudence and honesty. They worked hard, disposed of their stock in a short time at minimum profits, and their so-called "cheap-stores" quickly became popular establishments in each community.[30]

V
"Not a Chinaman's Chance"

The opening stanza of a popular song of the Gold Rush period is a mild understatement of the attitude that Californians held toward the Chinese in the mid-1850's:

> "John Chinaman, John Chinaman
> But five short years ago,
> I welcomed you from Canton, John—
> But wish I hadn't though"

Much that has been written about the Chinese in the Far West since then is poignant, a recent example being Gunther Barth's *Bitter Strength* (1964), a phrase which, in Chinese, is *k'u-li*. The Chinese began migrating in large numbers to the Pacific Coast soon after the discovery of gold in California. For the promise of a few hundred dollars, they willingly endured with *k'u-li* the years of hardship at the hands of their own countrymen, who exploited them, and the American "barbarians," who despised them. The wages they earned were just enough to perpetuate their dreams of success, yet small enough to secure their continuing dependence, or state of peonage.

According to a series of newspaper articles reprinted in the *Sacramento Bee* on January 21, 1886, the first Chinese immigrant arrived in San Francisco in 1847. He was a Cantonese named Chum Ming, and apparently he became very successful in the mines during the early months of the Gold Rush. Some twenty-five others landed at the San Francisco wharf the next year. They came via Peru. Most had worked aboard ship for their passage, while the remainder arrived as stowaways. This pioneer group formed the nucleus of an Oriental population which would soon grow to several thousand and bring the hatred and persecution usually reserved for non-whites in America throughout the nineteenth century. And, whereas the Californians referred to the local Indians and Mexicans of the period as "Diggers" and "greasers," their derogatory terms for the Chinese covered a much wider range: "chinks," "celestials," "heathens," "coolies," "slant-eyes," and "moon faces," to name only a few.

Statistics on the number of Chinese in California are very inconsistent before 1860, when the federal census began taking a careful count. David DuFault says there were 660 in the state in 1850, approximately 35,000 in 1860, and almost 50,000 ten years later.[1] The peak came in 1880 with 75,000, and the Exclusion Act followed, two years later. Sooner or later, practically every city in California passed ordinances restricting the civil rights of Chinese or reacted to their presence by burning down their houses and buildings. The Chinese, along with the Japanese, who came later, represent the only foreign nationals ever to be excluded from migration to the United States by federal legislation. And, in spite of the brutal treatment they received, they never retaliated in organized fashion against the whites, as did the Indians, Mexicans, and, in a few instances, the Negro slaves. Indeed, it was their misfortune to arrive in the United States when the attention of the whole country was focused on the question of slavery. But it probably would not have made much difference, for all minority groups suffered the same persecution when they became too visible.

In the beginning the Chinese were looked on with favor by

Practically all of the business houses along this street in Chinatown in Old San Francisco were gambling establishments. The Chinese were inveterate gamblers, but they seemed no worse for the habit than the Anglos in the far western towns and mining camps.

the people of San Francisco, who hired them at low wages as household servants or for other menial work because of their intelligence, dependability, and industry. In May 1851, a leading California newspaper commented editorially: "Under our laws and with the treatment they will receive here they will be valuable citizens and we shall be pleased to see large additions during the coming years to this class of population. We congratulate our farmers on the prospects of obtaining that description of labor of which the country is so much in need." [2]

The Anglos were not long in discovering that the Chinese were "heathen" who brought more evil than good. Within one year after the above comment appeared, the same newspaper published an article warning that the "tawny serfs" from Asia would soon be covering the land like the locusts of Egypt. "They will meet our brothers and relatives in the rich mining regions—laying claims to mining locations to the exclusion of our own people." The writer went on to predict that disputes would arise, blood would flow, and that the Chinese "coolies" would be driven from the state by violence instead of law. "This can now be prevented by the passage of statutory laws, prohibiting this class of foreigners from occupying the mines." [3]

According to an article printed in the *San Francisco Alta* on May 16, 1852, opposition to the presence of Chinese laborers in the mines throughout the northern counties was reaching such intensity that mass meetings were being called in practically every town in the state. The article estimated that the number of Chinese had already reached 12,000, only seven of whom were women. The fear of increasing hordes was already causing the Americans to drive many Orientals from their mining claims. "The Chinese are of mild character," the writer concluded, "and should the Americans push matters to the extreme, it is not anticipated that much, if any, bloodshed will ensue." [4]

His predictions generally proved correct. The Chinese were simply driven away from place after place. They were only

The Chinese in the California gold fields were only allowed to work the tailings and poorer diggings that would not pay enough for the white miners to fool with.

allowed to work the tailings and poorer diggings that would not pay enough for the white miners to fool with. By the time of the Civil War, the majority lived in cities, and inflamed passions against them seem to have temporarily subsided. "The laundry business affords those who live in San Francisco, and other cities, the most steady and lucrative employment," Hinton Helper wrote. "Catching and drying fish is another business in which they engage . . . others are engaged in mercantile pursuits; and here and there you will find one in a public house, filling the place of a cook or a waiter." [5]

Since the Chinese were forbidden to testify in court, many crimes committed against them went unpunished. Forced to take care of themselves, they often found some strength and security in their kinship organizations and district companies. The most famous of these were the Six Companies of San Francisco, originally the agents of the Chinese firms that had established the "coolie" trade from Hong Kong to San Francisco. According to Richard Dillon, there was never any deliberate mystery about the Six Companies, but the American press and public persisted in ascribing to them all manner of evil and dictatorial powers. In truth, in the 1850's the companies were "little more than benevolent societies whose principal object was to assist Chinese to come to California or return to China, to minister to the sick, to bury the dead, and return their corpses to the homeland." [6]

By 1868 the Six Companies claimed a total membership of approximately 60,000 and had, more or less, merged into a loose confederation. Its members looked to their leaders for guidance and protection, particularly in dealing with the many legal restrictions placed upon their activities. By this time anti-Chinese agitation had heated up again, and the issue was being taken over by organized labor. It reached a peak during the economic depression a few years later, and thereafter Denis Kearney and his "sand-lot crusaders" continuously threatened to burn down all the Chinatowns in California and drive the

"heathens" into the sea. "During the years of Kearneyism,"
Professor May Coolidge wrote, "it is a wonder that any Chinese remained alive in the United States." [7]

An original letter in the Manuscripts Division of the Huntington Library, written in 1876 and addressed "To the President and Members, Six Chinese Companies," furnishes an
excellent example of the limitless anti-Chinese feeling of the
period. In an obvious attempt at harassment, the author of the
unsigned correspondence warned of consequences that would
soon befall the Chinese community of San Francisco. He continued:

> I will inform you for your welfare [that] you are
> mistaken in the Boys with whom you are dealing.
> We are not a small gang of shouters who have made
> themselves conspicuous at the corners of streets and
> on the platform of every Public Hall—But Boys
> whose ancestors fought for the independence of this
> great and glorious country and some of our Principal
> members fought and Bled resenting the insolence of
> your moon eyed Pig faced Monsters in 1857 and who
> mean to show you what white men and Christians can
> do. . . . ours is a secret organization until the day of
> action then *Woe be to Him or they who molest us*
> when we shall care for no authorities, but defy them,
> and do now. We are aware of the fact of your having
> friends . . . but they are *Powerless*.

Not only did the Company have to face bigotry and threats
from outsiders, it also struggled for fifty years in an effort to
keep order among its various fraternal lodges and lawless tongs.
Newspapers referred to the encounters between the hostile
groups as "the Chinese Wars," and whites for their own amusement eagerly played one side off against the other. In the early
days, more than one such incident ended in tragedy. In Trinity
County, in 1854, the Hong Kong and the Canton clans had

trouble, and when one of the leaders of the Cantons was killed,
the other side issued a challenge for an open confrontation.
The white miners were delighted. They cooperated in every
possible way by supplying rifles, knives, and revolvers to both
sides as substitutes for the traditional spears, pike poles, brush
scythes, and bamboo shields.

Every day, for three weeks before the battle, there were
public parades and drills with flying dragon banners in the
streets of the mining towns throughout the district. Excitement mounted and thousands of spectators gathered as the date
for the pitched battle approached. When the Cantons and
Hong Kongs eventually met on the battlefield, instead of commencing the fight immediately, they preferred to stand and
hurl insults at one another across a neutral zone. But the
Anglos had not come to witness a war of words; they wanted
to see blood. By three o'clock in the afternoon it was obvious
that nothing was going to happen without forceful encouragement on the part of the spectators. Consequently, they
swarmed onto the field and literally pushed the two sides together, at which time a drunken Swede began firing into the
crowd. Another white man immediately killed the Swede. In
the general melee that followed, the Hong Kongs suffered
eight dead, while the Cantons lost two of their members.
Twelve others later died of wounds. Had the spectators exhibited the "coolness and courage" of the Chinese, no one
would have been killed. (Some later admitted to being ashamed
of their role in the affair.)[8]

Another brawl, which occurred two years later, had the
same elements of an *opéra bouffe* and likewise ended in tragedy. It took place in Toulumne County and involved approximately 2500 "warriors." One side expended over $40,000, buy-
ing muskets and bayonets and hiring whites, at ten dollars per
day plus their meals and all the whiskey they could drink, to
instruct them on how to use the weapons. The other side spent
$20,000. The battle started on schedule, and when it became

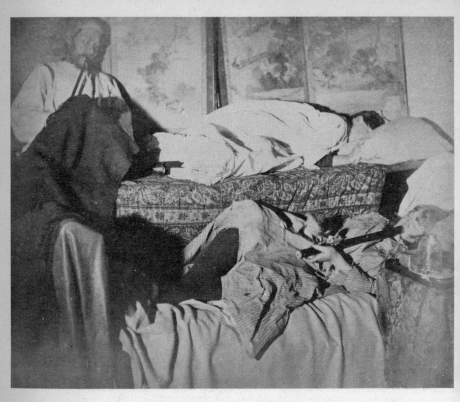

Among the common charges against the Chinese were that they lived in filth and squalor, corrupted the morals of Americans, were addicted to opium, and could never become citizens or Christians. As to the opium charge, the women here are white.

obvious that both sides merely planned to bruise, and not to kill, the white instructors joined the fight and mortally wounded two Chinese. Both companies then beat a hasty retreat from the field.[9]

There were other skirmishes between warring clans in the mining towns and coastal cities throughout the next few years. It is probable that very few people would have been killed in these affairs if it had not been for the encouragement of the white spectators. At the same time, credit belongs to some local sheriffs, who frequently prevented bloodshed by arresting the leaders and breaking up the conflict before it could get out of hand.

Throughout the West, wherever the Chinese went, prejudice and violence followed. Among the common charges against them were that they lived in filth and squalor, defied the laws of the land, kept up the manners and customs of China, were addicted to opium, and could never become citizens or Christians. Some of these points obviously were true: the Chinese rarely drank alcohol, but they did enjoy smoking opium, and most of their women in the early days were harlots. But authorities generally agree that the Chinese were able to exercise better control over opium than most white miners could over whiskey, and that they seemed no better or worse for the habit.

There were prostitutes of every nationality in California in the early days, but the Chinese professionals experienced no shortage of white customers. And, as for living in filth and squalor, some unbiased observers maintained that the Chinese generally were more careful about personal cleanliness than the Anglos were. Furthermore, nearly all agreed that, whatever faults the Orientals might have had, they were steady and dependable workers. "A disorderly Chinaman is rare and a lazy one does not exist," Mark Twain wrote in *Roughing It*.

The Chinese had no opportunity to become Americanized until the twentieth century, for whenever they reached siz-

able numbers in any Western community they became the victims of flagrant discrimination. In 1879, Robert Louis Stevenson crossed the American continent on the Union Pacific's
third-class immigrant cars. He was appalled at the attitude of
the Americans toward the Chinese passengers, who were seg-
regated in a separate car. "Of all the stupid ill-feeling, the
sentiment of fellow Caucasians toward our companions in the
Chinese car was the most stupid and the worst. They seemed
never to have looked at them, listened to them or thought of
them, but hated them *a priori*." [10] Little wonder the Chinese
found it difficult, if not impossible, to assimilate the Anglos'
ideas of citizenship or religion.

Armies of Protestant missionaries failed miserably in their
efforts to Christianize the "heathens," for the Chinese maintained their own temples and shrines wherever they settled.
"They were unable to distinguish between our mobs and our
Christian workers and could not be expected to favor or tolerate our religion," one missionary complained. "They had no
way of knowing that Christianity was a religion of love, not
one of bowie knife, insult, and the worst oppression the world
has yet seen." [11] Henry Ward Beecher put it more sarcastically:
"We have clubbed them, stoned them, burned their houses and
murdered some of them; yet they refuse to be converted. I do
not know any way, except to blow them up with nitroglyc-
erin, if we are ever to get them to Heaven." [12]

More basic to the development of anti-Chinese feeling which
contributed to several senseless massacres was "the cruel and
treacherous battlefield of money," as Robert Louis Stevenson
put it. An official spokesman for the city of San Francisco
summed it all up before a Special Committee of Congress in
1876:

> The burden of our accusation against them is that
> they come in conflict with our labor interest; that
> they can never assimilate with us; that they were a

perpetual, unchanging, and unchangeable alien element . . . a degraded labor class, without desire for
citizenship, without education, and without interest
in the country it inhabits, is an element both demoral-
izing and dangerous to the community within which
it exists.[13]

The Chinese sometimes were charged with robbing the
sluice boxes of the other miners, who administered twenty-five
to fifty lashes upon the accused and sometimes cut off their
queues, or pigtails. The latter was a supreme punishment, for
the average Oriental treasured his pigtail and groomed it with
considerable care. So many observers have testified to his pa-
tient and law-abiding qualities that many of the charges of
theft and other crimes levied against him are highly suspect.
In the letters and diaries of the forty-niners one reads over
and over of Chinese workers being robbed, beaten, and even
killed by whites, and of the sheriff and other elected officials
taking little or no trouble to ascertain the particulars of such
cases.

"Not having a Chinaman's chance" quickly took on a grim,
literal meaning, and derogatory jokes about "chinks" became part of the folklore of the West. Even J. Frank Dobie,
a humanist and fighter for civil rights in Texas during a generation when it took real courage to be one, regularly told the
story, to his classes in Southwestern literature, about a Texan
who shot and killed a Chinese worker on the Southern Pacific
Railroad in 1883 near Langtry, Texas, and who was brought
to trial before Judge Roy Bean, the self-appointed "Law West
of the Pecos." Judge Bean looked through two or three dilapi-
dated law books before remarking that he'd be damned if he
could find any law against killing a Chinaman. He then discharged the prisoner on condition that he pay for the "Chink's"
burial—and that he buy drinks for the house.

If Chinese workers were allowed to remain in an area dom-

inated by whites, they could expect to be the butt of frequent
practical jokes. Sometimes the jokes were sadistic, like one
at a mining camp near present Butte, Montana, in 1868, when
the miners got drunk and celebrated the occasion by hanging
one of the Chinese workers. "It was not a judicial execution,"
the *Anaconda Standard* explained many years later. "It was
simply the cool, premeditated act of disheartened, yet patriotic
and Fourth of July conscious miners who hanged the Chinaman to a cottonwood tree just for the devilment and in hopes
that it might bring luck." [14] Obviously, the victim did not appreciate either the humor or the patriotic fervor of the occasion.

How many innocent Chinese were strung up by exuberant
mobs throughout the mining frontier is impossible to determine
at this date. In the cemetery at Florence, Idaho, these words
appear on the gravestone of a former Chinese resident: "Hung
by mistake." The victim may or may not have been the inspira-
tion for a popular ballad written sometime before 1900 and
still sung by folksingers through the Northwest:

Old John Martin Duffy was judge of the court
In a small mining town in the West;
Although he knew nothing about rules of the law,
At judging he was one of the best.

One night in the winter a murder occurred,
And the blacksmith was accused of the crime;
We caught him red-handed and give him three trials,
But the verdict was "guilty" each time.

Now he was the only good blacksmith we had
And we wanted to spare him his life,
So Duffy stood up in the court like a lord
And with these words he settled the strife:

"I move we dismiss him, he's needed in town";
Then he spoke out these words which have gained him renown:

"We've got two Chinese laundrymen, everyone knows;
Why not save the poor blacksmith and hang one of those?"

What most California historians refer to as one of the most
violent and barbaric episodes in the history of the state began
on October 24, 1871. It originated among the Chinese themselves, in the Chinatown district of Los Angeles. The Mexicans
had originally named the area "Calle de los Negros," but it
eventually became known by the less elegant name of "Nigger
Alley." [15] In the 1860's and 1870's the Chinese who concen-
trated along Calle de los Negros usually settled their disputes
without benefit of legal procedure, and murder was not uncommon. The tragedy of 1871 started with the threat of a tong
war. A young, attractive Chinese woman had run away from
her master, and she soon came into the possession of a rival
company. The original owner regained possession of his chattel
through legal procedure, only to have her stolen away again.
This time Yo Hing, the wealthy and respected leader of the
company who had lost the decision of the court, married the
Chinese woman in order to strengthen his otherwise illegal title
to her. Whereupon the rival company offered a reward of
$1000 for Yo Hing's scalp.

On the morning of October 23, two shots were fired at Yo
Hing as he passed along Calle de los Negros. The attempted as-
sassins were soon arrested, along with their intended victim,
but all three got out on bail immediately. Both sides then prepared for open conflict, and when the police officer heard
shooting near Chinatown the next afternoon and approached
the scene of action, he too was fired upon. The officer then
called for help. After reinforcements had arrived, along with a
crowd of spectators, he attempted to enter a Chinese place of
business. A bullet, fired through the door, struck him in the
head, and he died one hour later. Two others among the crowd
received minor injuries from additional shots fired from inside
the building. By then the crowd had grown to a mob of 500

"Angels," practically all of whom were equipped with rifles, bowie knives, or pistols.

This enraged "scum and dregs of the city," as Professor Cleland described them, stormed through the Alley, broke down doors and windows of the houses, and beat or stabbed all of the hapless Chinese they could find. One who was flushed from his hiding place and attempted to run away was shot down in the street. Another was chased down by the crowd, dragged through the streets to a near-by corral and strung up by the neck. The rope broke the first time, but the second attempt proved successful. A third man was captured and dragged over the cobbled stones of the street with a rope around his neck until all signs of life were gone. The total number of victims hanged, shot, or beaten to death by the mob is estimated from twenty to twenty-five. One of them was a doctor named Gene Tong, an inoffensive old man who had pleaded for his life in Spanish and English and is said to have offered his captors several thousand dollars in exchange for his life. The mob strung him up anyway, then ripped off his trousers to obtain his money more readily. As he was choking to death, someone in the crowd rushed up and severed a finger from his hand with a bowie knife to get a large diamond ring that would not slip off easily.[16]

While these murders were taking place, other members of the mob were robbing and looting every room, trunk, and box in the Alley. Estimates of the loss of property vary from $3000 to $70,000. "Of all the Chinamen murdered, it is not believed that a single one of them was in any way involved in the shoot- ing, except Ah Cloy. The leaders, Yo Hing and his gang, all fled to the country when the fight commenced." [17] The grand jury which investigated the affair a month later condemned the rabble for "disgracing our city," and criticized the law officials for not performing their duty properly. But the jury failed to indict and bring to trial a single individual associated with the crime. Nine years later, A. J. Wilson, a poet-historian, wrote that "American 'hoodlums' and Mexican Greasers, Irish 'tramps' and French communists—all joined to murder and dispatch the foe. He who did not shoot, could shout; who feared to stab, could steal; there was work for all." [18]

The overwhelming majority of the citizens of Los Angeles deplored the massacre of 1871, and the anti-Chinese movement did not gain expression there again until 1876. In that year "Anti-Coolie Clubs" began to spring up throughout the state, primarily as a result of agitation by Denis Kearney and the rising influence and power of his Workingmen's party. An increase in Chinese immigration in the early 1870's coincided with a deterioration of economic conditions and provided Kearney with considerable ammunition in his campaign "to tax, boycott, and exile all Chinese from the borders of the state." But California would never experience another massacre of its Chinese residents similar to the Los Angeles affair of 1871. Although verbal and legislative harassment continued for several years, the Workingman's party suffered a series of defeats after 1877. The signing of a bill, on May 6, 1882, by President Arthur, which provided for the suspension of Chinese immigration for ten years, helped take some of the pressure off of those already here. But Orientals still had a long way to go before they would be accepted into the mainstream of American society.

The murder of Orientals became such a commonplace occurrence throughout the second half of the nineteenth century that newspapers seldom printed the story. But an event took place in Rock Springs, Wyoming Territory, in September 1885 which attracted nationwide attention, for it proved to be even more of an outrage than the massacre in Los Angeles fourteen years earlier. Many Chinese laborers had settled in the Union Pacific town following the completion of the main line of the railroad in 1869. Most of them worked in the coal mines, which were owned and operated by the company, despite the strong opposition of white workers. A strike against

Seven thousand Chinese workers literally hacked out the right-of-way through the Sierras for the tracks of the Central Pacific Rail-

road. "A disorderly Chinaman is rare and a lazy one does not exist," Mark Twain wrote in *Roughing It*.

the mine owners called by the Knights of Labor ultimately resulted in a lockout and the bringing in of additional Chinese.
The Union Pacific rehired some of the white miners when the
labor organization lost its fight, but white resentment of the
Chinese continued—because the Orientals were better workers,
and because, by 1885, they outnumbered the white miners,
326 to 155. This situation set the stage for trouble, and matters
were further compounded by an increase in unemployment
within the white community.

On the afternoon of September 2, 1885, a man named White-
house came to work and found two Chinese in possession of
what he considered his "room" in the mine. He ordered them
out, and, when they refused to leave, a fight erupted. Other
miners, both whites and Chinese, rushed in, and during the
ensuing fight three Orientals were badly injured and a fourth
was killed outright. When word of the fight reached the outside, a heavily armed mob assembled at once for a systematic
march on Chinatown.

The defenseless Chinese were taken by complete surprise by
the angry mobs, who routed them out of their shacks and dug-
outs. Years later, a white who had been a foreman at the mines
described the scene: "Bullets followed the fleeing Chinese and
sixteen of them were killed brutally, while the other casualties
met an even more horrible fate the same evening when some of
the citizens satisfied their murderous instincts and inhumanly
slew the few remaining Chinese for the money which their
victims had hidden on their persons, after setting fire to the
buildings to hide the crimes." Chinatown was burned to the
ground, and "the smell that arose from the smoking ruins was
horribly suggestive of burning flesh." [19] The total number who
were killed in one manner or the other is generally estimated at
fifty, or 10 per cent of all the Chinese in town.

The *Rock Springs Independent*, which was in sympathy
with the anti-Chinese feeling, put out an extra the next day,
September 3. It commended the saloonkeepers for closing

down during the action, and it observed: "It cannot be said that a 'drunken mob' drove out the Chinamen. Everyone was sober, and we did not see a case of drunkness. All of the stores in town were closed, and men, women and children were out watching the hurried exit of John Chinaman and everyone seemed glad to see them on the wing."

News of the massacre spread quickly throughout Wyoming and the nation. The Union Pacific immediately closed down its mining operation at Evanston, on the main line in the southwestern corner of Wyoming Territory, and advised its Chinese workers there to leave before another massacre could take place. Meanwhile, the company requested federal troops to protect its property at Rock Springs, as well as to rush provisions and help to the destitute Chinese refugees in the countryside. The troops arrived a few days later, much to the chagrin of many of the townspeople, and began the job of rounding up and protecting the frightened and half-starved refugees.

According to a story in *The Nation*, published on September 24, 1885, the Chinese had by that date gone back to work at all of the Union Pacific mines in Wyoming. The white men who had formerly been employed at the Rock Springs mine and who were known to have participated in the massacre were subsequently paid off, issued railroad tickets, and "urged" by the commander of the federal troops to leave the territory. (No one was ever indicted for the murders, which is not too surprising.) The company was threatened with strikes all along its line and in all departments, but by December the situation at Rock Springs had eased considerably. Of the total number of workers back in the mines, 457 were Chinese and 85 were white. Federal troops remained in the area until the outbreak of the Spanish-American War in 1898.[20]

Newspaper and magazine editors across the country overwhelmingly condemned the "wild and lawless characters of Rock Springs." *Frank Leslie's Illustrated Newspaper* stated, on October 3, 1885: "With them the pistol is the arbitrator of all

disputes, and the restraint of law and morality are always sec-
ondary to the gratification of personal rancor." In its next
weekly issue, dated October 10, the same publication referred
to the men responsible for the riot as "the worst of our European immigrants: degraded Poles, ignorant and besotted Hungarians, and lazy Italian convicts, determined to drive honest
workers out of the mines, and so compel employers to hire
them at their own terms." Practically all publications that reported the Rock Springs incident agreed that "not one single
person concerned in the massacre was a native born American."

"Such men," the October 1885 issue of the *Overland
Monthly* observed, "never doubt that, with all their coarse ig-
norance and brutality, they are by divine right superior to the
most learned and virtuous Chinaman or Japanese that ever
spent his days and nights in study, or sacrificed his whole fortune to a scruple of honor, or an impulse of patriotism." A
subsequent grand jury investigation, incidentally, revealed that
practically all of the non-Chinese participants in the massacre
were *not* Italians, Hungarians, and Poles, but Irish, English,
Scotch, and Welsh, plus a handful of Swedes and Danes. The
general assertion that none of these men were citizens likewise
proved false.

The incident at Rock Springs inspired similar outrages in
various parts of the West. "The anti-Chinese craze on the
Pacific Coast has reached its limits of insane folly," *The Nation*
declared on November 19, 1885. The editor attributed the
cause of much of the trouble to the *San Francisco Post*, which,
having played a major role in the campaign to get the Exclusion Act of 1882 passed, was now advocating the return to
China of those nationals already here. The *Post* also had been
less than indignant over the Rock Springs affair, a position
which doubtless reflected the attitude of the majority of Californians at the time. But the *Overland Monthly*, which was
published in the same city, took a far more civilized view. "Our
State . . . has cause for deep humiliation that this monstrous

occurrence has received only lukewarm condemnation among us," the editor stated. He further reminded his readers that they "should remember that generations go by, and policies are settled, and evils removed, but a stain of this kind never fades." [21]

A few days after the Rock Springs affair, some white men were arrested at Seattle, Washington Territory, and charged with killing several Chinese hop pickers while they were asleep in their tents. An anti-Chinese group assembled shortly thereafter and adopted a manifesto that all Chinese inhabitants in the area should be compelled to depart. It also appointed committees of fifteen local inhabitants for each of the larger centers of population, such as Seattle and Tacoma, and nine-member committees for less important communities. Each committee was instructed to personally warn all the Chinese residents in its district to leave on or before November 1, 1885.

Two days after the expiration date, a Tacoma mob, armed with clubs and estimated at approximately 300 members, marched in semi-military formation to Chinatown and began routing the frightened Orientals out of their quarters. They gave them half an hour to gather up a few belongings before being escorted out of town. The sick and the aged, along with a few of the heavier bundles, were loaded onto wagons assembled for the purpose. Although the night was cold and rainy, the mob marched to the outskirts of Tacoma, unloaded the wagons, and warned the Chinese not to return. The next day every item of value left behind was expropriated by the mob and every structure in Chinatown was burned to the ground. The Tacoma Committee of Fifteen, which included women as well as men, later boasted that the action they had taken was not one of violence, but of "peaceful expulsion." (This is not much different from a current phrase—"protective reaction.") They then called upon committees in the near-by smaller towns to emulate this "splendid example," a request which was quickly complied with in half a dozen counties. Meanwhile, federal troops were rushed to the area, and later they assisted many of the refugees in obtaining rail passage to Portland, Oregon.

Events did not work out as smoothly for the Committee of Fifteen in Seattle. For one thing, the local mayor and sheriff were opposed to the forceful expulsion of the Chinese who had settled there following completion of the Northern Pacific Railroad. And before the anti-Chinese leaders could act, federal troops arrived to help local officials maintain order and to arrest members of the Committee of Fifteen for violation of the Civil Rights Act of 1868. A subsequent trial dragged on, but it ended in mid-January 1886 without a single conviction. Three weeks later the Committee called a mass meeting in a local theater and agreed upon a plan of action—namely, a thorough inspection of Chinatown for violation of the sanitary laws of the city.

Among the inspection teams sent out was the acting chief of police and his entire force, all of whom were in sympathy with the real objectives of the Committee. Several hours before daylight on Sunday morning, February 7, 1886, well-armed teams invaded the homes of the Chinese on the pretense of ascertaining whether the "Cubic Air Ordinance" was being respected. Once inside, the "inspectors" ordered the occupants to pack up at once and to march to the wharf under guard. There they were to be put aboard the steamer *Queen of the Pacific* for shipment to San Francisco.

By the time the sheriff learned what was going on, some 300 to 400 Chinese already had been assembled for debarkation. What followed was total confusion. The sheriff and various forces in Seattle which were willing to cooperate with him eventually gained control of the docks, but not before the *Queen* was filled to capacity with approximately 200 passengers. It sailed away a few hours later, leaving another 200 Chinese behind. Federal troops arrived on February 9; martial law went into effect; and leaders of the mob were arrested, locked up in jail, and then released on bail. A federal judge informed the Chinese of their rights under the law, but granted them permission to leave the city if they wished. Only fifteen chose to remain.

No other steamer was scheduled to arrive in Seattle before February 14, and until then the Chinese had to be constantly protected against heavily armed mobs. The lawless element soon drifted out of town or went back to whatever they were doing before the disturbance began. Again, no one was ever convicted for the violence perpetrated against the Chinese. Yet, but for the courage of a few determined citizens of Seattle, dozens of lives would have been lost. As it was, only one person was killed.[22]

At about the time of the outbreak of violence in Washington Territory, Pierce City, Idaho Territory, was experiencing some excitement of its own. The good citizens of this once booming mining and supply center were horror-stricken on the morning of September 10 to discover the body of D. M. Frazier, "chopped to pieces in his own store." Frazier was an old resident of the community and the operator of one of the town's principal mercantile establishments. A mob quickly formed, and it lost little time in deciding that the murderers could be no other than a couple of Chinese merchants who operated a store in competition with the deceased. Vigilantes arrested the partners and tortured each into accusing the other of having perpetrated the foul deed before deciding that both men should be hanged. In the process, the vigilantes agreed that they might as well get rid of three other "undesirables" of the Chinese community, a "hard featured" barber, a gambler, and a "parasite"—a local camp prostitute.[23]

At this point, the more responsible leaders of the vigilantes persuaded the group to turn the five prisoners over to the local deputy sheriff, who promised to deliver them to the county seat at Murray for a formal trial before the hanging. The deputy then swore in a posse of six men and set out, with the pris-

oners bound together in a wagon, for the five-day journey over
the Bitterroot Mountains. They did not get far. A few miles
along the road, a large assemblage of masked men relieved them
of their prisoners and ordered the deputy and his posse back
to town. The vigilantes then tied one end of a rope around the
neck of each Oriental and the other to a pole placed between
the forks of two pine trees. When the wagon was driven forward, the weight of the five victims broke the ridgepole and the
job had to be done over again. "Whether intentionally or not,
the Chinese suffered a death nearly as horrible as the hatchet
murder for which they had been summarily convicted and
executed." [24]

News of the lynching soon reached the outside world, and
the Chinese government demanded that the State Department
in Washington, D.C., investigate the matter thoroughly. In the
meantime, groups in other Idaho towns began setting deadlines
for the local Chinese to leave the territory. An editorial published in the Idaho City *World*, on October 23, 1885, urged
everyone to refuse employment to them and to ostracize them
completely, otherwise "The Mongolians will become a fixture
. . . and remain a menace and a nightmare to civilization."

The Idaho Territorial official did not receive orders from the
Secretary of State for an on-the-spot investigation and full report of the Pierce City incident until six months later. Governor E. A. Stevenson eventually journeyed to the area for
"a full investigation," during which time he talked only to
those known to be unfriendly toward the Chinese. He subsequently wrote to Washington that he had been unable to ascertain the names of any of the men who had participated in the
hanging.

He also expressed regret for the vigilante action, but said he
was convinced that "the Chinese hanged were the identical
parties, who so cruelly, shockingly and brutally murdered
without the least provocation (except jealousy) one of the
best citizens of Idaho." Governor Stevenson did not try to

disguise his belief that the only solution to the Chinese problem was deportation. The reason, he explained, was because "their low, filthy habits, their high-binder piratical societies, together with their low dens of infamy, prostitution and opium smoking, have disgusted our people." [25]

Just as it seemed that the campaign for federal legislation to deport all Chinese nationals out of the country might possibly bear fruit, Japanese immigrants began arriving on the West Coast in large numbers. Fortunately for the first group, the old racial prejudices and the body of discriminatory legislation shifted to the second. The "Japs" never became the victims of bloody massacres and public hangings by vigilante groups, but the story of their verbal and legal harassment and their relocation in concentration camps during World War II is equally shameful.[26] The unhappy story of the anti-Japanese movement belongs largely to the twentieth century, but it represents a clear-cut example of the perpetuation of a frontier attitude into a modern industrial society. Not until the operations of humanitarian sentiment and American ideology could exert sufficient strength were both the Chinese and Japanese allowed to participate in the promise of American life.

VI
Gun Culture
and Cowboy Mentality

Throughout the last half of the nineteenth century, parts of the Western frontier were ruled by mobs of gunmen who were called outlaws or posses—depending upon one's point of view. "There is more law in a Colt Six Gun than in all the law books," was a common expression of the period. Along the same line is the venerable anecdote about a famous pioneer judge in Texas who was known as "Three Legged Willie" because he walked with the aid of a peg leg strapped to one knee. While trying a man accused of assault and battery, the judge began quoting the law from the Revised Statutes of the State of Texas. Whereupon the accused unsheathed a large bowie knife, laid it on the table, and replied, "Here's the law of Texas." Judge Willie calmly pulled out a six-shooter, placed it alongside of the knife, and responded, "Yes, and by God here's the constitution of Texas."

The story may be apocryphal, but there seems to be little doubt that America has long been a gun culture. Indeed, every aspect of violence in our history, from Indian wars to presidential assassinations, has been exacerbated by that fact—which is without parallel among the industrial nations of the world.

"In some measure, our gun culture owes its origin to the need of an agrarian society and to dangers and terrors of the frontier," Richard Hofstadter wrote, shortly before his death in 1971, "but to us the central question must be why it has survived into an age in which 5% of the population makes its living from farming, and from which the frontier has long since gone." [1]

At the beginning of English settlement of the New World, this wild continent abounded with game, without which the pioneer settlers surely would not have survived. Moreover, as Hofstadter points out, the common man, for the first time since the beginning of feudalism, was free to roam wherever he wished without fear of arrest for poaching. The better the gun he owned and the more accurate his aim, the more food he was able to put on the table for his family. And he needed a gun to protect his crops, garden, and livestock from wild vermin and predatory animals. There also were the Indians, and men, women, and children throughout some two and a half centuries of frontier history generally felt safer with a loaded rifle close at hand, just in case any Indians—friendly or otherwise—paid a visit. "A well grown boy at the age of twelve or thirteen years was furnished with a small rifle and shot-pouch. He then became a fort soldier, and had his port-hole assigned him," the Reverend Joseph Doddridge remarked, in reminiscing about his years on the Virginia frontier.[2]

Testifying before a Senate subcommittee in 1968, Franklin Orth, executive vice-president of the National Rifle Association, stated that "there is a very special relationship between a man and his gun—an atavistic relation with its roots deep in prehistory, when the primitive man's personal weapon, so often his only effective defense and food provider, was nearly as precious to him as one of his own limbs." [3] But what began as a necessity of the frontier soon took hold as perhaps America's most popular sport, and it remained so until the rise of the spectator games performed by professional and amateur athletes. Gun collecting, target shooting, and hunting are still very much a part of our popular culture.

It is the six-shooter, not the rifle or the shotgun, that the general public associates in its mind with the conquest and settlement of the frontier beyond the Mississippi. During the 1950's, when the valedictorian of one of the graduating classes at the University of Oklahoma referred to his native state as "shaped like a heavy-handled pistol pointing West," he received an immediate, spontaneous ovation. In reporting the incident the following day, the *Norman Transcript* observed that the figure of speech contained a Shakespearean quality that made the audience of some 20,000 parents, relatives, and friends of the graduating seniors suddenly realize the "true meaning of Oklahoma's glorious heritage."

Without a gun hanging low on his hip, a visiting cowboy would have felt half naked as he swaggered down the streets of Dodge City, Kansas, during its heyday as a cattle town. Stanley Vestal, in his history of Dodge, wrote that the people there during the 1870's and 1880's felt about guns as Americans now feel about their automobiles—"they kill and maim far too many people, but we cannot get along without them." According to Vestal, "if all the killers in Dodge had been brought to trial, Ford County would still be paying off the debt." [4] The statement is an obvious exaggeration, but the victims who reside in the local boot hill today constitute Dodge City's principal tourist attraction.

Walter Prescott Webb pointed out many years ago that, whereas the ax, boat, and rifle were the principal instruments and agencies that enabled the pioneer to conquer the frontier east of the ninety-eighth meridian, the first two were unimportant in the settlement of vast stretches of the West, which had few trees and little water. As for the long rifle, it was unsuited to the needs of a man on horseback; his favorite weapon was the six-shooter. And whatever sins it may have to answer for, Webb maintains that this weapon stands as the first adaptation made by the American people when they emerged from the timber and met a new set of needs in the open country of the Far West.[5] The six-shooter constituted the most dramatic revolution in firepower since the invention of the musket. It enabled the white man to fight the Plains Indian on horseback. It also made a little man feel ten feet tall. According to Joseph G. Rosa, the six-shooter created the Western "gunfighters," some of whom would become the most deadly single engines of extermination that the world had seen until then.[6]

Before the modern revolver made its appearance in 1835,[7] the knife and the bludgeon were the common weapons of the homicidal criminal and ruffian. The dueling pistol was the instrument for gentlemen who wished to settle differences in accordance with their code of honor. The clumsy horse pistol could be used on horseback, but a rider could not carry more than two of them, and if his arsenal of weapons also included a rifle, he still had only three shots. Even under the best of conditions, it took a full minute to load and prime a horse pistol or a Kentucky rifle—time enough for an Indian warrior to fire off more than two or three dozen arrows. Then, thanks to the mechanical ingenuity of Samuel Colt, the revolver was invented. It made shooting easier, for it could be loaded with six shots in a few seconds and needed no priming. It was first used as an effective war weapon in the Texas struggle for independence against Mexico, and it quickly found its way into the hands of the Texas Rangers, the men most in need of it for chasing bandits and Indians.

By 1848 the revolver had been refined into a cheaper, handier, and more accurate weapon than the one first used by the Rangers. Reduced in size to fit the capacity of an ordinary pocket, it could be concealed easily and drawn for use in an instant. (According to legend, the hip pocket was invented specifically for that purpose.) The revolver attained a national reputation during the Mexican War, for it was then worn and used effectively by Jack Hays and his Texas Rangers, who served as spies and scouts for General Zachary Taylor's army of invasion. Every soldier who saw the wonderful Colt wanted one for himself.

Most Western historians maintain that the war with Mexico demoralized and changed the habits and conduct of thousands of men who through it had become familiar with scenes of slaughter and blood and suffering. Some became reckless of life and hardened to death. This was particularly true on the already wild and lawless frontier of Texas. In personal quarrels, the "word and a blow" all too frequently changed to the "word and a shot," and instead of the knockdown, there came the death wound. Practically every man who went to California during the Gold Rush, from Texas or from New York, carried a six-shooter in his belt or hip pocket. Later the weapon became as much a part of the paraphernalia of the cowboy as the wide-brimmed hat and the high-heeled boots. And the reputation for having "killed his man" became a passport to general recognition and respect.

For the individual on the frontier who felt insecure or inferior, the six-shooter became "the great equalizer," "the difference." The professional outlaw-killer, as Rosa points out, almost invariably was a drifter, an antisocial misfit who was unable to settle his personal problems or achieve fame except through violence. In the process he helped create a climate of barbaric lawlessness. To "die with one's boots on" was proof of one's game quality; to "have a man for breakfast" was an ambition that inspired every bully in the gold fields.

Some Freudians argue that the gun is "an obvious phallic symbol, conferring on its owner a feeling of potency and masculinity." [8] Hofstadter dismisses this oversimplified generalization, but he admits that there is the Walter Mitty in all of us, and that every American male has had his moment when he is Gary Cooper, stalking the streets in *High Noon* with his gun at the ready: "D. H. Lawrence may have had something after all when he made his characteristically bold, impressionistic, and unflattering judgment that the essential American soul is hard, isolate, stoic, and a killer." [9]

"We not only tolerate violence," Dr. Karl Menninger recently observed, "we love it. We put it on the front page of our newspapers. One-third or one-fourth of our television programs use it for the amusement of our children." The noted psychiatrist went on to proclaim that two of our most popular team sports, football and hockey, are so violent as to verge on savagery. Perhaps this helps to explain why the likes of Billy the Kid and Lieutenant William Calley are more hero than villain to large numbers of people. Perhaps it also explains why John Wayne has remained one of America's most popular motion picture stars for more than three decades.

In a movie called *The Cowboys*, made in 1972, Wayne plays the role of Will Andersen, a tough trail boss who is deserted by his hired hands when they learn about the gold strike in California. Andersen is stuck with a large herd of cattle which he has to get to market, and in desperation he signs on eleven adolescents who barely know the difference between a horse and a cow. Will's job is to teach them a little about riding and roping, and a lot more about cussing and shooting. After a few weeks on the trail the kids become bona fide cowboys, and when a gang of desperadoes attacks the herd and kills the boss, they vow revenge.

The moral of the movie comes across loud and clear near the end—a child is not a man until he has killed someone. Naturally, the youngsters dispose of the villains, and, in some of the most chilling scenes ever filmed, savagery becomes heroism. The Motion Picture Association of America gave *The Cowboys* a rating of GP—suitable for viewers of all ages. John Wayne pronounced it a "lesson in patriotism," and Warner Brothers advertised it as "a swell movie for the whole family." Like literally thousands of motion pictures, TV productions, and stories about the Western frontier, the principal social

problem depicted in *The Cowboys* is uncomplicated. It is
simply a conflict between good and evil. Depraved individuals
can never be reasoned with; you must shoot it out with them
and, when confronted with superior force, lay your body on
the line and go down fighting.

But let us return to the real world of the nineteenth century.
Bancroft, in his *Popular Tribunals*, makes frequent references
to the fact that during the early years of the California Gold
Rush every man carried "glittering implements for the losing
of human life, [and] it was taken for granted that no life was
safe without such implements." [10] He deplored the lack of
common sense that the forty-niners displayed by going armed
to the teeth with bowie knives and six-shooters and thus openly
inviting violence. Except in extraordinary cases, even in the
rough communities of the gold field the man who went unarmed was less likely to be attacked, and thus far less in danger
of losing his life, than the man who was armed.

Bancroft estimated that, by 1855, more than ten million dollars' worth of gold taken from the mines of California went to
pay for six-shooters and other instruments "with which the
people might butcher each other, and without which all would
have been better off." On the one hand, the historian believed
that perhaps no man on the face of the earth was more honest
or less tolerant of petty thievery than the average forty-niner.
On the other, the freedom of life, the absence of social restrictions, the stimulation of whiskey, and the invigorating climate
contributed to the release of passions. "Hence it was in the
earlier stages of arbitrary justice that the thief was hanged
while the murderer was left to run at large." [11]

The California Gold Rush created a tremendous demand for
six-shooters, and soon reliable and improved models of Colt
revolvers were arriving by the thousands. The lightweight and
excellently balanced .36 caliber Naval pistol eventually became

the most popular, and, according to William B. Edwards, in *The Story of the Colt Revolver* (1953), among the gold seekers it was featured in more duels and homicides than any other model. The struggle in Kansas over slavery brought a still greater demand for the Colt revolver before the end of the decade. On one side were the Border Ruffians, who invaded the territory from Missouri, first to vote to make Kansas a slave state, later to destroy the homes, crops, and other possessions of the Free Staters, and finally to commit cold-blooded murder. Allied against them were the Jayhawkers,[12] whose acts of violence in the course of retribution became indistinguishable from those of their adversaries. The war in Kansas, which began in 1855, continued until it merged into the larger conflict between North and South six years later.

No major battles fought on Kansas soil involved regular Confederate and Union forces. Yet some of the most brutal acts of violence of the Civil War were committed there. They involved guerrillas, many of whom were hotheads and irresponsible individuals. The most famous leader of all the various guerrilla bands was William Clarke Quantrill, a native of Ohio who came to Kansas in 1857 as a young schoolteacher and soon threw in his lot with the Southern states. Somewhere along the way Quantrill and his band of approximately 450 Southern guerrilla soldiers crossed the line and became depraved murderers. The same could be said of their opponents, the Jayhawkers.

One authority on frontier outlaws describes Quantrill as "probably the worst all-time bad man this country will ever know." On August 21, 1863, he and his cutthroat ruffians ransacked and burned the town of Lawrence, Kansas, and killed an estimated 150 to 185 men, women, and children. "He was a past-master instructor for men like Jesse and Frank James in the art and science of outlawry. He must have been thoroughly evil—all through and through. . . . He wrote his name in flam-

Colt Single Action .45 with a 4¾ inch barrel, the so-called "gun that won the West." This was the six-shooter favored by most cowboys, famous gunfighters of the frontier, and more recently by those who engage in the Fast-Draw sport.

ing red across the crime-stained history of this country and inflicted more terror in Kansas, Missouri, and other central states than ever known before or since his time." [13]

The roster of Quantrill's guerrillas reads like a *Who's Who* of bad men of the West. In addition to the James brothers, there were the Dalton brothers, Frank and Kit; the four Younger brothers, Cole, James, John, and Robert; Dick Burns; Ike Flannery; Thomas Little; and a host of others. (The Jayhawkers had their distinguished alumni too, the most famous of whom were William F. Cody, Theodore Bartles, and Wild Bill Hickok.) Some of these men eventually settled down to peaceful and prosperous lives after the Civil War, but Carl W. Breiham estimated that fully half of the 296 guerrillas whom he was able to identify as having ridden with Quantrill later pursued criminal careers, served prison sentences, were shot by peace officers or other outlaws, or were executed by state authorities or lynched by mobs.[14]

Each guerrilla, whether Ruffian or Jayhawker, carried from two to four six-shooters at all times and engaged in target practice every day that he was not otherwise occupied with the profession of outlawry. By 1861 there were plenty of revolvers available on the frontier, the most popular of which was the Colt .44 caliber Army or Navy special. The Colt Company manufactured 130,000 of these models during the Civil War, while the Remington and other companies made unspecified numbers and types of revolvers. In addition, several Southern manufacturers were turning out copies of Colt and Remington weapons by the thousands—and at a time when the war was producing a generation of men accustomed to violence and equipped with the skills to use them. The four years of official homicide ended at Appomattox, but out of the dislocation of the war grew a wave of lawlessness that "transcended all expectations in which it perpetuated itself as a noteworthy dynasty of outlawry." [15] In every state in the Union, the number of cases of manslaughter and assault with intent to kill increased ten- to twentyfold over that in prewar years. In most of the crimes of blood, whether on the raw frontier or in the crowded city slums, the revolver was the weapon of death.

In the South the Klan rose to power and met the violence of Reconstruction with even more savage violence. It was also during this period that labor and capital in the North began their bloody wars which were to continue throughout the remainder of the century. Few Americans today remember, or have ever even heard of, the Mollie Maguires, the Homestead Steel strike, or Eugene V. Debs, who was charged with responsibility for violence resulting from the Pullman strike. Yet who has not heard of Billy the Kid, Doc Holliday, Wyatt Earp, Bat Masterson, John Wesley Hardin, Ben Thompson, and Wild Bill Hickok? These individuals were men of the gun who have been idolized and thoroughly enshrined into the valhalla of heroes. Scholars who have attempted to debunk the gunmen's heroic exploits have generally lost out to the hack writers, motion picture producers, and TV serials. No matter how many times the real Wild Bill Hickoks are revealed for what they actually were—psychopathic killers—the myth of their righteousness overshadows the reality of their depravity.

It is common knowledge, for example, that President Dwight D. Eisenhower was extremely fond of books relating to the exploits of Wild Bill Hickok, his childhood hero. In a nationwide television address in 1953, the President of the United States referred to the former marshal of Abilene, Kansas, Eisenhower's home town, as an example of courage and devotion to duty that all Americans might well emulate. The facts about the real Hickok have been revealed so many times that some listeners were shocked that he would be used as a model of American manhood. Hickok's marksmanship was far superior to his character, and throughout his adult life he possessed many of the qualities of a mad dog.

Wild Bill served as marshal of Abilene from April 15 to December 13, 1871, during which time he added greatly to the town's notorious reputation. The general picture we have of him in his prime is that of a man of approximately 175 pounds, slightly more than six feet tall, with long wavy blond hair worn shoulder length, a yellow moustache, an aquiline nose, small hands and feet, a low voice, and a sinuous and graceful form. In a carefully studied attempt to attract attention, Hickok generally dressed in the fashion of the river gambler—in black and white broadcloth, fancy vest embroidered with flowers, expensive high-heeled boots which were always polished, checkered pants, Prince Albert coat, pleated white shirt, and two ivory-handled pistols. He was mean but memorable, and "beyond a shadow of a doubt . . . the most fearless and perhaps the most dangerous man . . . on the frontier." [16]

Almost in every respect the physical opposite of Hickok was Billy the Kid, whose reputation as a killer is based upon his record as an out-and-out badman and not as a so-called peace officer. During the past century, Billy has been the subject of approximately 500 books and articles, few of which have been objective. But, just as in the case of Hickok, several misguided admirers excuse or tacitly approve of many of the acts of violence which Billy committed during his brief career on the New Mexico frontier. At least some of his victims were armed at the time they were murdered, unlike Lieutenant William Calley's at My Lai.[17] This latter-day American hero, incidentally, has much in common with Billy, even though the two lived and performed a century apart. In addition to having the same first name, both were approximately the same age when they achieved fame, as well as the same pint-size. But a man's height, or lack of it, means nothing as long as he is equipped with a "great equalizer," whether the double-action Colt .45 which the Kid made famous, or its offspring used by Calley, the submachine gun.

Billy the Kid has been described as a "first-rate killer and a fourth-rate cowboy." Not by any stretch of the imagination could a majority of the cowboys of the post-Civil War decades

be called gunfighters, but certainly most of the famous gunmen of the period were in one way or the other associated
with the cattleman's frontier—as professional gamblers, saloonkeepers, or law officers in the cattle towns. There were also
the cattle rustlers, horse thieves, and general outlaws who hid
out in caves, river bottoms, lost canyons, or on the wide open
and fenceless spaces of the rolling Plains.

Many outlaws who used the forested, hilly area of the Indian
Territory, now eastern Oklahoma, as a refuge were sometimes
cowboys by occupation and horse thieves, cattle rustlers, and
bank robbers by avocation. But regardless of whether they ever
punched cattle or rustled them, the men (and at least one
woman, the infamous Belle Starr) who gave the territory its
reputation for violence wore the traditional garb and six-
shooter of the typical cowboy. The vast no-man's-land on the
edge of the great cattle kingdom from which they operated
was for a time under the jurisdiction of Judge Isaac Parker's
federal court at Fort Smith, Arkansas. During his twenty-one
years on the bench (1875–96), Judge Parker tried 13,500 cases,
most of which involved outlaws brought in from Indian Territory. Of the 9500 who were convicted or pleaded guilty, 344
had committed crimes punishable by death. Judge Parker sentenced 172 of these to be hanged, a record which earned him
the title of "the Hanging Judge."

In America, the word "cowboy" was applied to a member
of a Tory guerrilla band that operated between the American
and British lines near New York City during the American
Revolution. It naturally acquired a bad connotation. When the
word returned to general use as the cattle industry began to
spread beyond the borders of Texas on the eve of the Civil
War, "cowboy" and "outlaw" came more and more to be considered by many people as synonymous terms. For one thing,
the cowboy was easy game for the gamblers, pimps, peace
officers, and prostitutes who frequented the cow towns, and

his only recourse was his gun. The cowboy also found the Colt six-shooter the ideal tool for killing rattlesnakes and predatory animals, chasing rustlers, fighting Indians, turning a rampaging herd of longhorns, signaling the start of a horse race, or just letting off steam at the end of the trail. He wore a holster at his side as naturally as he wore a wide-brimmed hat pulled low over his forehead.

He cut a dashing figure, on horseback or sauntering down the dusty street of a Kansas cattle town, and he delighted in appearing more rough than he was. His ever-present six-gun excited the imagination of every boy or man who saw it. It unquestionably played a major role in painting him as a lawless frontiersman, a reputation which he less than half deserved.

Somehow the cowboy symbolizes all that was violent about the Western frontier, and, at the same time, all that was good. Call it mythology, Freudian, or whatnot, children of all ages in most of the countries of the world have a love affair with the American cowboy and are enthralled by the mystique of his six-shooter. The reasons for this have been analyzed and expounded over and over again, but so far no one has explained the phenomenon with complete satisfaction.

It may be argued that the cowboy was neither the typical Westerner, as Walter Prescott Webb once described him, nor was he, typically, lawless.[18] Yet even the most objective student of the West has to admit that there was considerable violence associated with him and the cattle industry in the vast region beyond the ninety-eighth meridian throughout the frontier period. An important consideration is the fact that the laws the people brought with them simply did not fit the immediate needs of the new country. Each man had to defend himself and protect his life and property by the force of his character and by his courage and skill at arms. All men went armed, and they moved over vast areas among other armed men. Under such circumstances, the six-shooter became the final arbitrator and the court of last resort for a man whose life was at stake.

Senate Bans 'Saturday Night Special' — News Item

An American today is thirty-five times more likely to be murdered by a hand gun than is any Briton, Dane, German, or Swede. Each day an average of 21 Americans are killed with a gun, 150 are assaulted with a gun, and 200 are robbed with a gun.

Without it he could not have been a cowboy, a forty-niner, or a peace officer.

For all his faults and virtues, the cowboy, rather than the more deserving plowboy, would become the ultimate symbol of the land's lost innocence and the hardy pioneers who tamed it. He remains the indestructible legend, the folk hero. Perhaps the cowboy and his ever-ready six-shooter evoke fascination because modern society has found in myths and Western movies a code which it tries to apply to current problems. The cowboy therefore serves as an escape from today's reality, but he also provides the source of much of our dilemma. To many Americans over forty, the very mention of the word "cowboy" conjures up a vision of John Wayne when he was a young cowboy hero, on horseback, in Monument Valley. It is a picture of a proud figure, in a bright and clear landscape, which recedes from us.

Americans have not known a true frontier for more than three generations, yet we refuse to grow out of our cowboy mentality and our love for guns. What started out as a necessity for survival has become part of our national culture. We are not the only people with a frontier history, but we can offer our citizens a greater choice of guns than any other country in the world. There are snub guns that fit in a woman's handbag, semiautomatics that fire eight bullets almost simultaneously, thirty-eights that can hit a man at fifty feet, forty-fives that can knock a man three or four yards and leave a hole in him as big as a fist, and very light twenty-twos that a six-year-old child can fire. How many of these instruments of violence do we have in the United States? No one can be sure, since we do not have a national gun registration law. *Time* magazine estimated that there are in America somewhere between 50 million and 200 million pistols, revolvers, shotguns, rifles, machineguns, bazookas, mortars, and even antitank guns. In addition, more than three million new hand guns are sold to civilians each year.

Since 1900, approximately 800,000 Americans have been killed by guns—considerably more than have died in battle in all our wars since the Revolution. According to former United States Senator Joseph Tydings, who was defeated for re-election in 1970 primarily because of his efforts to push effective gun-control legislation through Congress, every American today is thirty-five times more likely to be murdered by a hand gun than is any Briton, Dane, German, or Swede. Each day an average of 21 Americans are murdered with a gun, 150 are assaulted with a gun, and 200 are robbed with a gun. In 1967 there were more than 7000 murders and homicides, 3000 accidental deaths, 10,000 suicides, and 100,000 people wounded in the United States—all by gunfire. Indeed, guns are used in 65 per cent of all killings in this country, while only 20 per cent of the victims are dispatched by knives and most of the remainder are done in by poison or bludgeons of one type or another.[19]

An article published in the *Los Angeles Times* on August 20, 1972, stated that London was the safest city in the world and that there were recorded only 77 cases of murder there in the whole of the previous year—while there were 58 in a typical week in New York City. In 1895 there were approximately 500,000 convictions for offenses of all kinds in London, and six decades later the number remained about the same even though the population had more than doubled. Criminologists attribute the low murder rate and the generally not-so-violent nature of British society to the country's strong anti-gun laws, which make it difficult for private individuals to buy firearms.

Modern American society is violent, but not simply because guns are available. The slogan of the National Rifle Association, "guns don't kill, people do," is as oversimplified as the assertion by Congressman John M. Murphy that "gun nuts think their weapons are an extension of their penises." [20] In any case, thanks to our pioneer heritage, the casual wearing or possession of hand guns long after the traditional dangers of the frontier have disappeared makes easier the job of settling personal problems. It also contributes to homicidal violence. Obviously, it was quicker and less messy to dispose of an adversary in Dodge City in 1880 with a Colt .45, for example, than to stone him to death with marshmallows or cow dung—the latter doubtless being in much greater supply there at the time than the former.

VII
Genocide—or Manifest Destiny?

Few people were as good at fighting against professional soldiers or won as many battles as the American Indians, yet they won no wars. The late Fred Allen once observed, with as much bitter truth as humor, that "all books and movies about the Indians are the same—the redskins invariably get it in the end." Estimates of the number of Indians massacred in the United States since 1789 vary from 4000 to 10,000. Thousands more have been killed by alcohol, smallpox, chickenpox, measles, and other diseases against which the victims had little or no immunity. In addition, the whites have suppressed or practically destroyed their culture and religion. And not one of the 370 treaties made with the Indians since 1789 has been kept by the federal government (at least, not one that I have discovered).

The allegations made by some modern observers that there never was an organized campaign of genocide against the Indians may be correct, but it is difficult to describe the slaughter of the peaceful Diggers in California in any other terms. This tragic example may not represent a microcosm of 300 years of Indian-white relationships, but it is a fact that whenever the Indian got in the white man's way, the consequences were violent. A special commission reported to President Grant as early as 1869 that "The history of the border white man's connection with the Indian is a sickening record of murder, outrage, robbing, and wrongs committed by the former, as the rule, and occasional savage outbreaks and unspeakable barbarous deeds of retaliation by the latter, as the exception." [1]

Hatred of the Indian began before the first English settler reached American soil. Governor William Bradford, in his history of Plymouth Colony, wrote that the passengers on the *Mayflower* in 1620 were aware of the "perills & dangers" that faced them. English fishermen who had been to the New World warned that the settlers would be liable to famine and that "the chang of aire, diate, & drinking of water, would infecte their bodies with some sickness, and greevous diseases." Those who escaped or overcame these difficulties would "yet be in continuall danger of ye salvage people, who are cruell, barbarous, & most treacherous, being most furious in their rage, and merciles when they overcome; not being contente only to kill & take away life, but delight to torment men in ye most bloodie maner that may be; fleaing some alive with ye shells of fishes, cutting of ye members & joynts of other peesmeale, and broiling on ye coles, eat ye collops of their flesh in their sight wilst they live; with other cruelties horrible to be related." [2]

The small party that went ashore soon after the *Mayflower* dropped anchor off the Massachusetts coast quickly encountered a group of natives, chased them inland for several miles, and looted their stone houses of their grain. Yet, in spite of their initial fears, the newcomers soon found it necessary to live peacefully side by side with their neighbors, but only as long as they were weak and the Indians were strong. The Pilgrims even paid for the stolen grain, and Squanto and others later taught them how to fish, plant corn, and survive in the harsh new surroundings. It is a fact that everywhere in the New World the Indians greeted the first settlers with friendship. Columbus, for example, informed the King and Queen of Spain that the people on the island of San Salvador treated him and

his men with honor. "So tractable, so peaceful, are these people," he wrote, "that I swear to your Majesties that there is
not in the world a better nation . . . and though it is true that
they are naked, yet their manners are decorous and praise-
worthy." [3]

The captain of the *Discovery*, one of the three ships that
brought the initial settlers to Jamestown in 1607, wrote that
the natives of Virginia were supposed to be treacherous, "how-
beit we could not find it in o'r travell up the river [James], but
rather a most kind and loving people." [4] But attitudes often
change quickly. The newcomers saw in Indian society only
what they wanted to see—that people whose cultures were different from those of Christian men and women were obviously
uncivilized. Such groups could not be reasoned with or trusted,
especially when they possessed what the Europeans had come
thousands of miles to obtain—land. Thus, by seeing the original owners merely as "lazy savages," white men could easily
justify their overkill. The task of making the Indian the enemy
and eventually dehumanizing him began early in the seventeenth century.

For almost 300 years, pioneer settlers pressed westward in
their insatiable greed for more land. Every man (white man)
was entitled to his fair share, and if the Indian stood in the way,
then he violated the basic law of nature. Had not God ordained
that Americans were destined to extend their superior institutions to the less fortunate peoples of the continent—even if
they had to kill them in the process? By 1845 that ordination
had been refined and broadened to include Mexicans and any
others who dared challenge "the manifest design of Providence." Soon the cry of "Manifest Destiny" could be heard
throughout the land. [5]

This power of rationalization is still very active in the American psyche. There is little difference, for instance, in the way
some feel about our role in the world today from the way

political leaders of an earlier age talked about taming the Western wilderness. Indeed, the following sentences from candidate Richard Nixon's 1960 election eve speech could have been delivered by John L. O'Sullivan in 1845, or Senator Albert J. Beveridge in 1898, or President Richard Nixon in 1972: "My friends, it is because we are on the side of right, it is because we are on God's side, that America will meet this challenge and that we will build a better America at home and that better America will lead the forces of freedom in building a new world."

Transforming the Indian into a savage made it easier to hate him, and "Indian hating . . . no doubt will continue to exist as long as Indians do," Herman Melville wrote in 1857. In an essay entitled "The Metaphysics of Indian Hating," Melville explained why the frontiersman of his day regarded the red man in much the same spirit that a jury regarded a murderer, or a trapper a wildcat—"a creature, in whose behalf mercy were not wisdom; truce is vain; he must be executed." [6] Speaking through a fictitious character called "The Judge," Melville describes how one becomes thoroughly grounded in the subject of Indian depravity from the time he is born until he reaches manhood: A father tells his son in indelicate language what an Indian is and what he must expect from him. If the lad is inclined toward knowledge, he learns from his schoolmaster and from books about the Indian's proclivity toward lying, stealing, double-dealing, lack of conscience, diabolism, and bloodthirstiness. "The instinct of antipathy against an Indian grows in the backwoodsman with the sense of good and bad, right and wrong," the Judge continues. "In one breath he learns that a brother is to be loved, and an Indian to be hated." [7]

The assumption that the red man constituted an obstacle to progress made it difficult for the New England Puritans and the early Virginia settlers to recognize Indian virtues. The fact that the Puritans saw their life in the New World as part of a preordained plan and the unfolding of God's will reinforced their prejudices. The Indians were merely part of the hostile environment, even though some had been most generous in helping the early settlers survive. "In a sense," Professor Wilbur Jacobs writes, "the colonists overcame a feeling of guilt by anticipating hostile, violent, brutish savages who would resent white encroachment on their land." [8] As time passed, each group found less and less in the other's character to admire.

The first major all-out effort to exterminate an entire tribe occurred in the Pequot War of 1637. Atrocities committed by both Indians and whites set the stage for the general court of the recently settled River Towns of Connecticut to declare war on the Pequots on May 1, 1637. A few days later, Captain John Mason led a party of several hundred men from Massachusetts and Connecticut, plus a number of Mohegans (Mohicans) and Narragansett Indians, in a surprise attack against the Pequots, who had sought sanctuary in their fort at Mystic. Mason and his Indian allies surrounded the fort and took the enemy by complete surprise. No one could escape.

Many Pequots were killed in the initial assault, and the attackers then set fire to the various buildings and homes inside the palisade. Governor Bradford described the event:

> All was quickly on a flame, and thereby more were burnte to death then was otherwise slain; it burnte their bowstrings, and made them unserviceable. Those y^t scaped ye fire were slaine with ye sword; some hewed to peeces, others rune through with their reapiers, so as they quickly dispatchte, and very few escaped. It was conceived they thus destroyed about 400. at this time. It was a fearfull sight to see them thus frying in ye fyer, and ye streams of blood quenching ye same, and horrible was ye stinck & sente ther of; but ye victory seemed a sweete sacrifice, and they gave the prays therof to God, who had wrought so

wonderful for them, thus to inclose their enemise in their hands, and give them so speedy a victory over so prud & insulting an enimie.[9]

From the Pequot War in Colonial New England to the massacre at Wounded Knee in South Dakota on December 29, 1890, the twin strains—civilization and extermination—marched side by side through American history. The Pequots ceased to exist as a separate tribe within two decades after the founding of Plymouth Colony in 1620, the Narragansetts were destroyed in King Philip's War in 1675, the Mohicans were gone by the middle of the next century. And so it went. "Where today are the Pequot? Where are the Narragansett, the Mohican, the Pokanoket, and many other once powerful tribes of our people?" the great Shawnee chief Tecumseh asked in 1811. "They have vanished before the avarice and oppression of the white man, as snow before a summer sun." [10]

The history of Indian-white relations is not a simple story to tell—with or without its violent connotations. Once the pattern was set, it was repeated over and over, with only minor variations, until the westward movement had erased the physical frontier. "It was we," said Lenape, one of the last of the Mohican chiefs, "who so kindly received them on their first arrival into our country. We took them by the hand, and bid them welcome to sit down by our side and live with us as brothers; but how did they requite our kindness?" [11] The chief then answered his own question with a long and dismal oration about ingratitude and treachery: The white man at first asked for only a little land to raise food for his family and pasture his cattle, and the Indian gave freely. He soon wanted more, and his request was granted. He then saw the game in the forest which the Great Spirit had put there for the Indian, and he wanted that too. As he moved further westward in search of more game and discovered plots of land which pleased him, he took them. Finally, when the Indian was loath to part with

any more of his land, the white man drove him far from his
ancestral home.

Many other chiefs, before and after Lenape, recited the
same litany of wrongs that the white man had perpetuated
against the Indians. Some whites listened and were ashamed, but
not enough really cared until it was too late. In 1881 Helen
Hunt Jackson, a minor poet and novelist, published a book
describing the callous disregard of Indian rights. Historians
generally have dismissed it as a one-sided and emotional tract
that hardly should be taken as a fair appraisal of Indian-white
relationships. Yet who can deny the validity of the following
charge: "So long as there remains in our frontier one square
mile of land occupied by a weak and helpless owner, there will
be an unscrupulous frontiersman ready to seize it, and a weak
and unscrupulous politician, who can be hired for a vote or for
money to back him." [12]

On occasion, when the white man attempted to purchase
land rather than take it by force, he signed a treaty or entered
into a legal contract on the assumption that the Indian's institutions were mere imitations of his own. Nineteenth-century
Americans held firmly to the philosophy of John Locke on
"the rights of man" and "life, liberty, and property." Their
concept of ownership was total, while the Indian believed that
the water in the streams and the air overhead were impossible
to own. Land, like the fish, birds, and animals, belonged to the
Great Spirit, and the white man was a fool to pay money for it.
So the Indian often moved back on hunting grounds he had
sold, an act which proved that he was a savage and an enemy
who could not be trusted. Rarely did either side understand
the other's point of view, and each took advantage of his opponent's "stupidity."

It has frequently been said that the Indians who sold Man-
hattan for twenty-four dollars were like the man who sold the
Brooklyn Bridge for ten dollars. They did not own the island,

but chanced to be there, on a fishing trip, at the right time. It has also been said that most treaties were deliberately broken by the white man before the ink became dry. In Arthur Kopit's popular play, *Indians*, the following dialogue takes place between a Blackfoot Sioux and a group of Senators who are members of a United States Peace Commission:

JOHN GRASS At Fort Laramie, Fort Lyon, and Fort Rice we signed treaties, part of which have never been fulfilled.

SENATOR DAWES Which parts have never been fulfilled?

JOHN GRASS At Fort Rice the Government advised us to be at peace, and said that if we did so, we would have a span of horses, five bulls, ten chickens, and a wagon!

SENATOR LOGAN You . . . really believed . . . these things were in the treaty?

JOHN GRASS We were told they were.

SENATOR LOGAN You . . . saw them written?

JOHN GRASS We cannot read very well, but we were told they were!
(*The Senators glance sadly at one another. John Grass grows confused. Pause.*)
We were also . . . promised a Steamboat.

SENATOR MORGAN A Steamboat!

SENATOR DAWES What in God's name were you supposed to do with a steamboat in the middle of the plains?
(*He laughs.*)

JOHN GRASS I don't know.

Perhaps nothing in the development of the American West has created more interest or has been the subject of more writing than the Indians. Most of the popular works, as well as the scholarly ones, emphasize the violence of Indian-white relationships, and for seventy or eighty years university students have referred to courses in Western history as "Cowboys and Indians" or "Cavalry and Indians." The accounts of battles generally have been written by white historians from official army records. There were barbaric acts committed by both sides, of course, but since the Indians did not keep written documents, their side of the story too often has been ignored or given short shrift.

Alexis de Tocqueville observed in the 1830's that it was unfortunate that the Indian was brought into contact with the citizens of the most grasping nation on the globe while they were still semi-barbarians. But it would have been an historical impossibility for the Indian to have kept his land. "You cannot stop the locomotive any more than you can stop the sun or moon, and you must submit and do the best you can," General William T. Sherman told an assemblage of Indians at Medicine Lodge, Kansas, in 1869. "Our people East hardly think of what you call war here, but if they make up their minds to fight you, they will come out as thick as a herd of buffalo, and if you continue fighting you will be killed. . . . This commission is not only a Peace Commission, but it is a War Commission also." [13]

Chiefs Black Kettle, Satank, Crazy Horse, Mangus Coloradas, and their like might have been savage killers to the white settlers, soldiers, and some writers, but to the Indians they were great patriots. They fought in defense of their people, and they insisted that their treaties be honored and their sacred hunting grounds protected from greedy land grabbers and gold-seekers. Because they could not be reasoned with or trusted, because they frustrated and embarrassed the military time and time again, naturally they had to be "wasted."

The assertion made by one historian that a mere listing of battles between whites and Indians would cover more than a hundred pages in 6-point type is more hyperbole than fact. Indeed, the exact number of engagements that occurred between the early seventeenth century and the end of the nineteenth century is difficult to determine. But Don Russell has documented 1243 skirmishes between United States troops and Indians from the beginning of the Republic, in 1789, until the last encounter took place at Leech Lake, Minnesota, in 1898. In addition, there were hundreds of fights between bands of Indians and state troopers, posses, and Texas Rangers. It would appear that there was almost constant warfare on the American frontier, but it must be remembered that most of the skirmishes were small affairs and involved only a company or two of men.[14]

The period that witnessed the largest number of conflicts occurred between 1860 and 1890. The theater was a vast one; it extended from Minnesota to the Pacific Coast, and from the Canadian border to Mexico. During these three decades the once great Cheyenne were brought to ruin—along with the Ute, Sioux, Apache, Comanche, Kiowa, Nez Percé, and all of the other tribes that stood in the way of what Senator Beveridge called "The March of Empire." The fundamental cause of the trouble was the overrunning of Indian lands by white settlers. With the outbreak of the Civil War and the withdrawal or reduction of regular troops at the far-flung frontier garrisons, Indians throughout the Great Plains and Southwest took to the warpath to pillage wagon trains and raid isolated settlements, in efforts to reclaim their hunting grounds.

The Navajo were the first to declare full-scale war, and United States troops and New Mexico militia finally subdued them after three years of almost constant fighting. By mid-July 1864 some 2000 men, women, and children had died of starvation or had been killed by soldiers. Another 8000 had been rounded up and placed on the small Bosque Redondo reservation in eastern New Mexico. Meanwhile, the Navajos' hogans had been destroyed, their livestock stolen or killed, and their food supplies depleted.

Life was not easy for the captives. The soil at Bosque Redondo was too poor to grow crops, the water unbearable, and wood extremely scarce. By 1868 the federal government finally realized that the only way the Navajo could be held in that God-forsaken region was through force, and that the wisest thing to do was to let them return to their canyons and mesas of northeastern Arizona. Some 7000 men, women, and children eventually survived the "long walk" back to their beloved homeland. Since their return the Navajo tribal council has kept the promise to remain at peace. Even though the struggle has been far from easy, their ordeal was brief and less severe than that of any other Western tribe.

The turn for the Cheyenne, Arapaho, Sioux, Crow, and other natives of the Great Plains came next. In 1851 these tribes allowed the federal government to build military roads and a chain of forts across their hunting grounds. Soon stagecoach lines, wagon trains, soldiers, and miners were driving wedges through the tribal land, and they were followed by settlers staking out ranches and farms. Up to that time, the Cheyenne especially had always remained friendly toward the whites, but as they witnessed their buffalo herds decimated, treaties ignored, and land expropriated, their attitude changed drastically. For the next two and a half decades they remained almost constantly at war with militia or federal troops. By 1880, "the fighting Cheyenne" were too weak to resist any longer, having suffered perhaps more casualties in actual combat than any other Plains tribe.

Among the great Cheyenne warrior chiefs were Roman Nose, Black Kettle, and Dull Knife. Black Kettle especially deserves to be remembered, for he had the misfortune of being present at two of the most infamous massacres in the history of Plains warfare—at Sand Creek in southeastern Colorado and at the Washita River in Western Oklahoma. In 1864 his band received permission from the Commander at Fort Lyons to camp for the winter at near-by Sand Creek, alongside a few hundred Arapaho. The Commander assured them that as long as they displayed the United States flag over their tepees, they would be safe from attack.

Earlier that summer several companies of volunteers had been organized in Colorado and sent out, under the command of a Methodist minister named Chivington, in search of Indians. According to George Bird Grinnell, it was well known in Denver that the Colonel's orders to his troops were to kill all Indians they encountered, "little and big, friendly or not." Upon his arrival at Fort Lyons in late November, Chivington learned that Black Kettle and a large band of peaceful Cheyenne were camped near by. Some of the officers at the fort tried to persuade the Colorado troops that a surprise attack upon friendly Indians would be plain murder. Chivington remained adamant, and one of his trusted officers confessed years later that "When we came upon the camp on Sand Creek, we did not care whether the particular Indians were friendly or not." [15]

The Cheyenne and Arapaho had been so confident that they were safe that they had not bothered to post sentries around their camps at night. Also, many of the young men were away on buffalo hunts at the time of Chivington's arrival. The attack came early on November 29, when 600 volunteers and another 100 regular troops from Fort Lyons swept down on the sleeping women, children, and old men. The fighting lasted three or four hours, but the number of Indians killed is unknown. Chivington later claimed 500, but Grinnell believes that George Bent, who was married to a Cheyenne woman and was present at the time, came closer to the actual figure with his estimate of "over 150." At any rate, it would be difficult to read an objective account of the affair without having a feeling of guilt.

When Chivington's men returned to Denver with their scalps, trophies, and stolen horses they were received as conquering heroes by a grateful citizenry. Meanwhile, Black Kettle and other Cheyenne and Arapaho survivors were to be kept under close army surveillance until a permanent disposition of them could be made. On October 14, 1865, at the mouth of the Little Arkansas River, the old Chief, Little Raven, and other head men of the Southern Cheyenne and Arapaho tribes signed a treaty with United States Commissioners. They agreed to give up all claim to eastern Colorado and live south of the Arkansas on lands belonging to the Kiowas, in present Oklahoma. But many of the young braves refused to be restricted by the terms of the treaty, and they left the barren reservation at will. The results were inevitable.

In the early hours of November 27, 1868, General George Armstrong Custer and four detachments of his famed Seventh Cavalry attacked Black Kettle's camp on the Washita River. Within ten minutes the troopers were in possession of the village, but the Cheyenne warriors fought desperately in hand-to-hand combat to save their women and children. If it were not for the large number of Arapaho, Kiowa, Comanche, and Kiowa-Apache camped in the vicinity, Custer undoubtedly would have killed every Cheyenne in Black Kettle's camp before he ordered the hasty withdrawal. As it was, he claimed to have destroyed 51 lodges and to have captured 900 horses and large quantities of skins, food, and arms. In addition, he placed the Indian casualties, including Black Kettle and his wife, at 103 killed and 51 captured. His own casualties amounted to thirty-five killed or wounded.[16]

The second half of the decade of the 1860's also witnessed the negotiation of numerous treaties between the United States and most of the Western tribes. At Medicine Lodge, at Fort Laramie, at the mouth of the Little Arkansas, and elsewhere, chiefs of the Cheyenne, Arapaho, Comanche, Kiowa, Sioux, Modoc, Nez Percé, and Bannock "touched the pen" or "put their mark" on treaties that they either did not understand or had no alternative but to accept. In every case they agreed to cede portions of their lands and to restrict their hunting and farming activities to the small reservation allotted to them. And without exception they were to find it difficult if not impossible to make a living by traditional means. Commanders at army posts throughout the West were charged with keeping them in line, a task made easier by a cruel and effective ally— starvation.

For centuries the Plains Indians' existence and much of their culture had depended upon the buffalo. But at about the time their hunting grounds were reduced and their movements restricted, white buffalo hunters moved onto the Plains and indulged in a systematic slaughter of the gregarious beasts. Unfortunately for the animal's future existence, his bones, hide, and meat all possessed commercial value. His ultimate extinction would leave the Indians with a choice between complete surrender to military control over their lives or outright starvation.

The army realized the vital role of the buffalo to the Plains Indians and actually encouraged its destruction. "Instead of stopping the hunters," General Philip Sheridan told a congressional committee, "you ought to give each hunter a medal of bronze with a dead buffalo on one side and a discouraged Indian on the other. . . . Send them powder and lead, if you will, but for the sake of peace, let them kill, skin, and sell until the buffalo are exterminated. Then your prairies can be covered with cattle and the cowboy, who follow the hunter as a second forerunner of an advanced civilization." [17] Ironically, General Sheridan's philosophy has been memorialized more widely than he possibly could have imagined; hundreds of millions of United States coins long carried the imprint of a buffalo on one side and that of a Plains Indian on the other.

Throughout the post-Civil War decades, most of the hardest fought battles of the West occurred between the army and the desperate "Reservation Indians." Some conflicts resulted from wide-ranging hunting and foraging expeditions made by young

"Instead of stopping the buffalo hunters," General Philip Sheridan told a congressional committee, "you ought to give each a medal of bronze with a dead buffalo on one side and a discouraged Indian on the other. . . . let them kill, skin, and sell until the buffalo are exterminated."

braves off the reservation, others took place because white hunters and settlers invaded Indian lands, and still others came about when troops surprised the Indians in their winter camp. The most famous battle between Indian and United States troops occurred in June 1876, when the glory-seeking General George Armstrong Custer and 260 mounted soldiers were killed by several thousand Sioux and Northern Cheyenne at Little Big Horn in southwestern Montana Territory. The details of this engagement are well known to professional and amateur historians of the West. Recently the massacres of Southern Cheyenne at Sand Creek and Washita have received widespread popular coverage through Dee Brown's *Bury My Heart at Wounded Knee* and the highly successful movie *Little Big Man*.[18]

In the mountains, on the Great Plains, and in the desert the Indians fought desperately to hold on to their hunting grounds. By 1874 most of the Kiowa chiefs, among them Big Tree, Satanta, and Satank, had been captured or killed and their people rounded up by the army and confined to a small reservation in southwestern Oklahoma. There they have remained at peace ever since, but the price they have paid for "following the white man's road" has been wretched poverty. The same has been true of their neighbors, the Comanche. The last of the great Comanche chiefs, Quanah Parker, surrendered in 1876 when the so-called Red River War finally ended and he and his band returned to the reservation. Also by this time, all of the Apache except Geronimo's small band of Chiricahua had been settled on reservations in New Mexico and Arizona.

Not until 1886 were troops successful in taking Geronimo prisoner and bringing the last of the wars of the Southwest to a close. The overwhelming number of soldiers and settlers had made existence off the reservation, however temporary, too dangerous. By this time the Navajo and Pueblo had long since returned to their dreams and ceremonies, and the Southern Cheyenne, Arapaho, Kiowa, and Comanche were too reduced in number and too beaten in spirit to offer further resistance. As for the smaller desert tribes such as the Pima, Yuma, Papago, Havasupai, and Hopi, they had found that the job of taming the formidable environment left them little time or inclination for anything else. Besides, their reservations consisted of lands that had been their traditional homes for centuries and, fortunately, were too poor and isolated for the white man to bother with.

Before the Indians in the Southern Plains and the desert Southwest had been killed or "civilized," the army had its problems with the tribes of the north. The Homestead Act of 1862 sent wave after wave of farmers, or "nesters," onto the Northern Plains. These pioneers, combined with the ranchers and miners, paved the way for a showdown over control of the last major frontier region of the West. Meanwhile, in the mid-1860's, whites tried to open the Bozeman Trail, which drove through the center of the Indian hunting grounds of Wyoming to the mining fields of western Montana. The great Sioux Chief Red Cloud made life so hazardous for the travelers on the road that the army built a chain of forts to protect them. But when small companies of troopers ventured beyond the garrisons, they frequently ran into ambushes and were lucky to escape annihilation. Because of the determined efforts of Red Cloud's people, the army eventually abandoned the trail—in one of the rare occasions of Indian victory over the whites. But not for long.

Further west, in Oregon, the federal government tried to deprive some of the tribes of their reservation, but General O. O. Howard found in the principal Chief of the Nez Percé an amazingly formidable opponent. Against overwhelming odds, Chief Joseph repeatedly defeated or thwarted the army before retreating over the Bitterroot Mountains into western Montana. General John Gibbon later swept down on the Nez Percé camp on the Big Hole River and shot and bayoneted every Indian in sight. Miraculously, the Chief rallied his forces, beat off the attackers, and escaped. He then continued in a general eastward direction through Yellowstone Park and eventually reached the Bear Paw Mountains, where the feeble remnants of the tribe were captured only thirty miles from its goal, the Canadian border.

When Chief Joseph began his retreat, his followers numbered 750 persons, including women, children, and sick and old people. In what remains the most remarkable feat in the annals of Indian warfare, the Nez Percé traveled some 1700 miles over mountains and plains with all their baggage and a large herd of ponies. Throughout the retreat they engaged in eighteen battles, including four major ones, and altogether faced some 2000 army regulars and another 3000 Indian auxiliaries. They lost 120 people, of whom 65 were men and 55 were women and children. The army suffered 180 killed and another 150 wounded.[19] When Chief Joseph accepted the harsh peace terms from General O. O. Howard and other officers on October 5, 1877, he seemed to speak for all his race: "I am tired; my heart is sick and sad. From where the sun now stands, I will fight no more forever." [20]

No tribes fought harder for their lands than the Hunkpapa, Miniconjou, Brule, and Oglala Sioux of the Northern Plains. In 1868 they forced the army to acknowledge that their sacred land in the Black Hills would forever belong to the Sioux. But when gold miners poured into the Dakota country after 1874 and the government tried to force the Indians to accept a new treaty, war broke out anew. In June 1876, the Crow and Shoshoni joined the soldiers under General George Crook to fight their ancient enemies, the Sioux, in the Battle of the Rosebud. Warriors under Crazy Horse and Sitting Bull then moved further west to the Little Big Horn, where they combined with other Sioux and Cheyenne warriors to constitute a force estimated by the army at approximately 15,000. (The Indians probably were more accurate in their estimate—3000 warriors.) The so-called "Custer Massacre" that followed shocked the na-

INDIAN GHOST DANCE
BEFORE BATTLE AT
WOUNDED KNEE
1891

The army became alarmed as the Ghost Dance spread throughout
the West. Suspicion that Sitting Bull planned a Ghost Dance uprising resulted in his assassination. But the real climax came at
Wounded Knee, South Dakota, in late December 1890.

tion, which was then in the midst of celebrating the centennial of its independence.

The Sioux eventually lost the Black Hills for having disgraced the army. With the nation's honor at stake, it could be expected that thousands of soldiers would chase them all over the Plains until they were killed, driven into Canada, or rounded up on reservations. After years of intermittent fighting, the Plains and mountains were finally made safe for miners, cowboys, and farmers. Meanwhile, the Indians were never paid justly for the Black Hills. They saw the end long before it came, their ponies having been killed off or stolen, their supplies depleted, and their rifles no match for the Hotchkiss guns and other superior weapons of the white soldiers.

For all practical purposes the reservations were prisons, and when individuals or groups tried to escape their miserable surroundings, the soldiers were quick to punish them. Their only hope was a messiah, and one appeared before the end of the century. He was a Paiute named Wovoka, and he preached that the ghosts of dead Indians would return to drive out the whites and that the vanished buffalo would reappear. Soon the Plains and mountains and deserts would belong to the original owners, and the old way of life would be restored. The army became alarmed as the Ghost Dance spread throughout the West. Suspicions that Sitting Bull planned an uprising by the Ghost Dancers resulted in his assassination. But the real climax came in late December 1890, in South Dakota, where a band of half-starved Miniconjou Sioux under their aged chief, Big Foot, appeared to have resisted arrest. After the smoke from the Hotchkiss guns had cleared, more than half the band of 350 men, women, and children lay dead in the snow. Some sixty soldiers, caught in their own crossfire, were killed or severely wounded.[21]

For the army the event was hardly an honorable one, although it represented a significant victory in the dreary history of Plains warfare. The Indian's spirit by now was completely

When the smoke from the Hotchkiss guns had cleared, more than half the band of Miniconjou Sioux lay dead in the snow at Wounded Knee. This photograph was taken a few days after the massacre.

broken, and all hope that he could live out his life in his own way was gone. Warfare and disease already had reduced the red man's population to approximately 250,000—less than one-third of the number that had inhabited the continent three centuries earlier.[22]

The Sioux who fell at Wounded Knee died in the same year that the census bureau announced that there no longer was an American frontier. By this time the Western tribes had lost three-fifths of the land that had been granted to them by treaty since 1851. What they have managed to keep to this date is largely sand and rock, but that is another story. By the mid-twentieth century the white man had developed a tremendous sense of guilt over the physical violence and cultural genocide practiced against the Indian. It is one reason that Dee Brown's *Bury My Heart at Wounded Knee*, published in 1970, remained on the best-seller list for more than fifty-two consecutive weeks.

In his emotion-packed book, Brown glorifies the Indian, but he stacks the cards heavily against the whites. Thus, his work could hardly be called an objective treatment of the subject of Indian-white relations between 1860 and 1890. Yet thousands of readers, conditioned as they are to generations of Indian hating, probably agree with the following comment, made by one of the reviewers: "Nothing I have ever read has saddened and shamed me as this book has. Because the experience of reading it has made me realize for once and all that we really don't know who we are or where we came from, or what we have done, or why." [23]

VIII
The Northern Plains Frontier

No nation in the history of the world has had at its disposal a public domain of wealth and size comparable to that of the United States. And none has been more generous and more wasteful in the manner and speed with which it allowed so great a birthright to be spirited away. European peasants could only hope to acquire a small plot of land after countless generations of waiting, and then they often hoped in vain. But upon arriving in the New World they looked forward to acquiring a 160- or 320-acre homestead within a few weeks or months. They expected the government not only to provide land for them, but to protect it, increase its value, and to come to their aid during economic distress.

"We hear less about the Land Rush today," Daniel J. Boorstin wrote in *The Americans*, "because it is only another name for much of American history." It was directly related to our struggle for independence, our Indian campaigns, Manifest Destiny and the Mexican War, slavery and the Civil War, the development of transportation, public schools, and state universities. And it shaped many of our political and economic institutions. In the nineteenth century, the availability of good land provided a form of government relief which differed only in substance from the early welfare programs of the New Deal. It has consistently remained the principal source of speculation, profiteering, and corruption throughout almost four centuries of Anglo-American history. Legislation relating to land has absorbed the energies of our politicians and fostered endless debates in the Congress. Yet land laws have been openly flouted whenever and wherever they have stood in the path of settlers and speculators.

The notion that "free land" left the average American self-dependent hardly accords with the fact. In actual practice, there was no such thing as "free land for the landless," even after the passage of the Homestead Act of 1862. Most of the public domain west of the ninety-eighth meridian went to the swift and to the strong. This frequently resulted in violent confrontation among cattlemen, nesters, and sheepmen, between miners and road agents, and between vigilante committees and outlaws and rustlers. The law was often far away, and justice was usually on the side of the most heavily armed. Courage and cowardice existed in equal quantities, and greed, murder, thievery, and cruelty were facts of life, like the harshness of the climate and the scarceness of water.

Under the circumstances, the early settlers of Montana and Wyoming often took the law into their own hands, just as the people had done earlier on the raw Texas frontier or in the mining camps of California. One of the most dramatic and efficient vigilante movements in the West took place in the vicinity of Bannock, in present Montana, during the 1860's. The principal character in this drama was a refugee road agent from California and Nevada, the dark and dapper Henry Plummer. Thanks to a carefully written little book by an Oxford-educated Englishman who lived in Montana at the time, we have an accurate and detailed account of Plummer's activities following his arrival in the mining town of Bannock in 1862.[1] If the story reads like a movie or a TV script, it is because it has served as a model for literally hundreds of westerns in which the crooked sheriff is finally exposed and brought to justice by the decent, law-abiding citizens of the community.

When Plummer arrived in Bannock as a young man in his twenties, he already had accumulated considerable experience as a professional gambler—and as the leader of a band of road agents which had formerly operated in Lewiston, Idaho. In 1862, Bannock was enjoying a profitable business from the diggings, but it also had an unparalleled number of robberies, shootings, and killings. Something had to be done, but the local sheriff and his deputies proved totally inept in their efforts to enforce the law. Plummer's good looks and ingratiating personality quickly won him a host of friends, and within a few months he had chased the unpopular sheriff out of town and gotten himself elected as the chief law-enforcement officer of the only organized county in Montana Territory.

The new sheriff wasted little time in putting his considerable executive ability to work, and he soon formed the most efficient organization of highway robbers in the history of the frontier. The gang numbered somewhere between fifty and a hundred men, all recruited from the worst elements of the region. But they operated in a well-disciplined and secretive manner, identifiable to one another by the special sailor's knot in their neckties or kerchiefs. Plummer planted an "Innocent," as his men were called, in each mining camp of the far-flung district, to keep him informed about gold shipments and individuals who might have struck it rich. The Innocents met regularly at various hideouts and passed along their information. And they developed a system of marking those stagecoaches carrying gold, so that other members of the gang would know which ones to stop. In less than eighteen months the Innocents had committed numerous robberies, killed some two dozen travelers, and shot at least three friendly Bannock Indians "just for the hell of it."

Some of Plummer's men became rich almost overnight, purchased ranches, and stocked them with stolen cattle. When one member of the gang who served as a deputy warned a wealthy friend that he was to be ambushed, Plummer became suspicious and assigned three Innocents "to take care of him." On June 30, 1863, they caught the deputy on the outskirts of a public meeting and "blew him to kingdom come." In spite of the fact that there were several witnesses to the event, the sheriff made no attempt to arrest the three men, nor did any of the local citizens dare challenge him for his failure to do so. This kind of success made Plummer bolder, and he was soon taking a hand in some of the highway robberies himself. A few people had already begun to suspect the double role that the sheriff was playing, and one acquaintance later recognized him among four horsemen who robbed him on a lonely road. The youth reported the incident to his uncle, a prominent citizen of Bannock, and the two agreed to keep the matter to themselves for the time being.

A few days later George Ives, one of Plummer's men, robbed and killed a local businessman and was quickly captured and tried by a mob of angry miners. After due deliberation they found Ives guilty and summarily hanged him to a ridgepole. Various leaders of the same group then organized themselves into secret vigilante committees, and a few days later they hanged two other members of the gang. One of the victims, in the hope of being spared, gave a detailed description of how Plummer operated, whereupon the vigilantes arrested the sheriff and two of his deputies just as they were planning their escape. The deputies shouted curses at their captors and fought every inch of the way to the scaffold, but the once suave, cool Plummer "broke down and whined like a whipped cur." He was, one witness remarked, "loathsome in his abject and abandoned cowardice." [2]

The vigilantes did not stop with the hanging of Plummer, but soon went after other members of his gang with speed and efficiency. In a six-week operation they executed twenty-two of the worst outlaws in the territory, banished several others, and frightened the rest away. Meanwhile, a conservative estimate, based on bodies actually discovered and confessions made, placed the number of men murdered between May 1863 and January 1864 at 102. The bodies of several dozen more men who had disappeared were never discovered.[3] Although the reign of terror in the Montana mining camps ended by 1865, informal executions occasionally took place outside the regular courts of law even after that year. The leaders of the various vigilante committees usually came from the class that Easterners would call "gentlemen of property and standing." Between 1865 and 1880 they hanged more than sixty men throughout Montana, including the infamous Joseph A. Slade.

Slade worked for the Overland Stage Company for several years. As Dimsdale wrote, "He was feared a great deal more, generally, than the Almighty, from Kearny, west."[4] In his classic *Roughing It*, Mark Twain observed that fully two-thirds of the talk of drivers and conductors from one end of the Overland Stage route to the other was "about this man Slade."[5] His reputation as a natural-born killer probably was exaggerated, but there is no doubt that he was a truly mean man, especially when drunk. In 1863 the company transferred him to Virginia City, Montana, and made him superintendent of its local division there. Several months earlier he had quarreled with another employee of the company, René Jules, and received what was thought to be a mortal wound from a load of buckshot. Somehow he survived, and after his transfer to Montana he made good his oath to find Jules, torture him to death, and cut off both of his ears. He carried the ghastly trophies in his pockets during the last months of his life and delighted in tossing them across a bar in mock payment for a drink. His general hell-raising and shooting up the town soon became more than the people of Virginia City could stand.

"It had become quite common, when Slade was on a spree," Dimsdale wrote, "for the shopkeepers and citizens to close the stores and put out all the lights; being fearful of some outrage at his hands."[6] Later, when he sobered up and had the money, he was always ready to pay for the damages, but merchants and saloon operators more and more regarded these payments as small satisfaction for the outrages he committed. The local vigilantes invited him to leave town on several occasions, but Slade refused to take them seriously until it was too late. On March 10, 1864, he "stood on nothing looking up a rope," in the old slaughter pen behind the hotel in Virginia City.[7] According to an eyewitness to the event, Slade so completely exhausted himself by tears, prayers, and lamentations before his execution that he scarcely had strength left to stand under the fatal beam.[8]

Elsewhere on the northern frontier, vigilante groups and "people's courts" were equally busy. Much of their action has been glossed over or explained away by citing the truism that the West was untamed, that it was a raw frontier, and that the people had no recourse but to take the law into their own hands. These trite phrases may be true, but they do not mitigate the violence that characterized the struggle over who was to control the vast grasslands of Wyoming—cattlemen, sheepmen, nesters, or rustlers. The big cattlemen, who got there first, vociferously maintained that the public domain belonged to them by prior appropriation. They hated the nesters, or grangers, who took up homesteads throughout the Northern Plains, "busted" the sod with their moldboard plows, and fenced off the water holes for their own use.

Farmers from Illinois, Iowa, and Nebraska believed that they had as much right to the land as the cattlemen did. The sheepmen, who followed in the wake of the grangers, felt the same. In time the cattle ranchers would detest the sheepmen even more than they did the farmers, for they maintained that cattle would not drink where sheep had watered and that the sheep ate the grass down to the roots and destroyed the ground cover. Newcomers who otherwise were honest men saw no harm in butchering an occasional calf or putting their brand on a maverick that belonged to one of the large outfits. On the

other hand, many cattlemen lost the power to distinguish between the bona fide settler and the professional cow thief and
were soon lumping them all together as "rustlers."

There was enough truth to the charge that the cattlemen
were oppressive and that the settlers rustled cattle on the side
to make understandable the intolerance that followed. The cattle barons generally had the unqualified support of state and
federal officials, while the grangers and small stockmen would
frequently capture control of the county courts and sheriff's
offices. Thus, rustlers often escaped arrest, for local juries
would simply refuse to convict them for alleged crimes against
the big cattlemen. The conflict between the various factions
reached a climax in Johnson County, Wyoming, where the
ranchers declared war upon the settlers. At first they did their
own dirty work and hanged a couple of suspected rustlers.
Later, they brought in a small army of hired gunmen from
Texas to help finish the job.

More than any other outbreak on the Western frontier, the
Johnson County War provided the basic plot for the conflict
between the good cowboys and the villains, the powerful big
cattle ranchers and the "little fellers," the underdogs. In "the
great American morality play," the villain may be the greedy
rancher or a hard-bitten rustler, while the hero is a lonely
settler. Or the roles may be reversed and the rancher may be
so hard pressed by the decimation of his herds by cattle rustlers and horse thieves that he is forced to take personal retribution to protect the sacred right of property. In the fictional
accounts, virtue always triumphs, but in real-life situations such
as Johnson County, everybody lost.

The first and most significant book written on the Johnson
County War, A. S. Mercer's *The Banditti of the Plains*, has
almost as interesting a story itself as the events described. The
author accused some of Wyoming's most powerful men of
crimes ranging from genocide to perjury, and he named names
and supplied details. His little book was thoroughly and ruth-

lessly suppressed, the plates destroyed, and the author jailed for
sending obscene matter through the mail. Yet a few copies survived, and in 1954 the University of Oklahoma Press reprinted
the original narrative and restored it to the shelves of hundreds
of libraries throughout the United States. The motion picture
Shane (1953) was straight out of *The Banditti of the Plains.*

The violence that erupted along the Powder River in Johnson County during the latter part of the nineteenth century
was not a war in the sense of pitched battles between masses
of men. Rather, it was an ugly, savage confrontation between
the few who virtually monopolized the public domain and
those who wanted their share. "It was the war of the shot in
the back from ambush on a lonely road under the pitiless sky,
of the sudden descent by a little party of armed men and a
body left dangling from a tree; a war in which the other side
fought back with the rustler's weapons, the rope and the running iron, and the snarling dispute over who began it will never
be settled." [9]

The era of the cattle barons began in Wyoming in the summer of 1879, and no section of the territory was more ideal for
grazing than the Powder River Country of Johnson County.
For the next six or seven years, "grass was king" throughout
the Northern Plains, but by 1888 granger families were arriving in Wyoming an average of fifteen per day.[10] By then the
range was already overstocked, cattle prices were declining,
and a cycle of brutal winters and dry summers had set in. As
the grass withered and disappeared, unemployment arose and
hundreds of cowboys joined the grangers in homesteading.
Since horses and cattle were the only thing they knew, they
put their brand on every stray cow and calf they could find.
The big stockmen were soon claiming that the rustlers were
driving them into bankruptcy, and they were determined to do
something about it. Moreover, they possessed the power to do
the job. Most of them belonged to the Wyoming Livestock
Association, an organization of about a hundred members

whose combined holdings totaled more than two million cattle
and whose roster included the Governor, two United States
Senators, and the State Livestock Commissioners.

The Commissioners possessed unlimited power to seize and
sell the cattle of suspected rustlers, retain the proceeds for the
expense of the operation, and even execute alleged cattle thieves
without serious inconvenience. But their power in Johnson
County was considerably limited by the fact that the local
grangers and small stockholders had elected one of their own
as sheriff and were so completely in control of the county government that conviction of a suspected rustler was almost impossible. Here, more than in any other section of the state, the
settlers had filed on lush grass and hay lands along the creek
and river banks and shut the big ranchers off from the choice
watering holes. Since grass and water were natural resources
that cattle ranchers had long considered their own, the way
was paved for a violent showdown.

Three years before the 1892 invasion of Johnson County by
an army of local cattle ranchers and their hired gunmen from
Texas, one of the most blatant incidents of frontier violence
had taken place on the Sweetwater River, in Carbon County in
south central Wyoming. There, on July 20, 1889, a lynch mob
of prominent cattlemen arrested Jim Averell and his neighbor
and former mistress, Ella Watson. They charged the two with
possessing stolen cattle and condemned them to death by stran-
gulation. Twenty-eight-year-old Ella, unquestionably a prostitute, frequently accepted yearlings for the services she ren-
dered to the sex-starved cowboys of the Sweetwater Valley.
She operated what was commonly called a "hog ranch" about
a mile from Averell's store and saloon, which was located at
the crossing of the Rawlins-Lander stage line and the Old Oregon Trail. In addition to running a store and saloon, Jim served
as postmaster and justice of the peace and owned a so-called
road ranch, although in 1889 he possessed not a single cow or
calf. He and Ella ("Cattle Kate") apparently remained close

friends after she moved down the road to a cabin that the local cowboys had constructed for her on her own claim.

The adjoining homesteads lay in the center of a large cattle range operated by Albert J. Bothwell, a wealthy member of the Wyoming Livestock Association. Jim Averell had never been accused of rustling, but he was outspoken in his denunciation of "land-grabbing," arrogant cattle barons like Bothwell, over whom he had recently won a court battle for clear title to his small ranch. As for Ella, she might have been careless in accepting stolen calves from her customers, but regardless of what she had done, the punishment hardly fit the crime. Once she and Jim were taken into custody, their captors forced them into a buckboard and drove them to Spring Creek Canyon, approximately five miles away. Members of the lynching party tied a noose around Jim's neck, threw the rope over the limb of a stunted pine tree, and tied the other end taut around Ella's neck. They then drove the buckboard away, causing the two to drop about two feet in the air. The victims kicked and struggled for several minutes before death released them. Their bodies were left hanging side by side until neighbors cut them down two days later. By that time their faces had swollen and were discolored almost beyond recognition.

The hanging created great excitement throughout the territory. Four persons had witnessed the abduction, but before the grand jury met three months later, one of them had died under mysterious circumstances, another had fled the country, and the other two had vanished without a trace. Six prominent cattle ranchers were later arrested and taken to Rawlins for arraignment. There they were allowed to sign each other's bond for $5000 and were released. Since no witnesses were ever called, a jury eventually handed down the verdict that "James Averell and Ella Watson met their death at the hands of unknown parties." [11]

Bothwell later got what he wanted—possession of the land that had legally belonged to Ella and Jim. He then had Ella's small cabin moved near his ranch headquarters and converted into an icehouse. Meanwhile, "the very best people of Wyoming" apparently approved of the hanging as an effective and justifiable method of range control. "The success of the 'enterprise,' and the failure to successfully prosecute the perpetrators of the outrage," A. C. Mercer wrote a few years after the incident, "gave special encouragement to the stock growers and they determined to 'continue the good work.' " [12]

On June 4, 1891, three men rode up to the cabin of Thomas Waggoner, near Newcastle, in the northeast corner of the state, and took him from his home. His wife, a mental defective, failed to report the incident for several days, but friends finally found his body dangling from the limb of a cottonwood about two miles from the house. Several theories still exist as to why Waggoner, who seems to have had a good reputation in the community, was lynched. According to Helena Huntington Smith, the only explanation that has any credence is that Waggoner's ranch served as a relay station for a band of horse thieves operating out of Montana and Nebraska. Several stockmen claimed to have identified some of the horses among Waggoner's herd a few days after the recovery of the body.

Circumstances clearly pointed to the men responsible for the lynching, but the cattlemen so thoroughly controlled the community that no arrests were ever made. Several months later two professional gunmen were apprehended for the attempted assassination of two cowboys asleep in their cabin on the Powder River, but they were quickly released. The intended victims were suspected of being cattle rustlers, but, interestingly enough, their would-be murderers turned out to have been involved in the lynching of Waggoner, and one of them had gotten himself named administrator of the dead man's estate. It is suspected that the gunmen were involved in the ambushing of two or three other men in Johnson County later that year, but there is no proof.

A group of insiders who dominated the Wyoming Livestock Association, and who were generally referred to as "the Cheyenne ring," soon became convinced that Johnson County was made up of two classes of people—ranchers who rustled on the side, and rustlers who ranched on the side. "The whole question at issue is whether the rustlers, which is another name for thieves, shall be allowed to set up business for themselves with cattle stolen from their rightful owners," *The New York Times* editorialized on May 14, 1892. "There can be but one answer to this question. The cattlemen were forced either to submit to these depredations or to take law into their own hands." They took the law into their own hands.

Most authorities on the Johnson County War declare that by early 1892 the ranchers were determined to terrorize the small ranchers and farmers and to wipe out the rustlers entirely. The political power of the ring was so great that it completely controlled the Wyoming Livestock Commission. It ordered the Commission's inspectors to seize all cattle shipped from Johnson County by suspected rustlers. The inspectors carried out their orders most zealously and impounded five carloads of cattle. More than anything else, their seizure of a man's property on suspicion that he was a rustler was responsible for the war that followed. Meanwhile, the immediate reaction was an outburst of cattle stealing such as Wyoming had never known. "It was more than range thievery undertaken for gain: it was rebellion; the oppressed striking back at its oppressors." [13]

In the struggle in Johnson County, there was no neutral ground between the cattle barons and the rustlers—the latter term being applied not only to those who stole cattle, but to all who otherwise abetted or sympathized with them. Preparations for a well-organized and generously financed invasion began in January 1892. In that month, one of the Association members went to Texas and recruited a number of professional gunmen. The men were promised five dollars a day and a bonus for each man killed, plus expenses. They were to be deputized, furnished a list of approximately seventy rustlers, and given blank warrants that could be filled out with the dead man's name, whom they could then claim had been shot while resisting arrest. Even the most partisan defender of the cattlemen later admitted that this plan of sending an army of mercenaries through the country to burn property and murder citizens was inexcusable.

The cattlemen chartered a special train to haul the army of men and their horses, tents, ammunition, dynamite—and strychnine—as far as Casper. The train reached its destination on April 6, 1892, and the twenty-two hired gunfighters, along with some thirty ranchers, detectives, and teamsters, and two newspaper reporters, were on their way northward by noon the next day. John Clay, one of the most prominent ranchers in Wyoming, was in Europe in 1892. Thirty-one years later, he wrote that, at the time of the war, he had thoroughly disapproved of the rash action by his fellow cattle raisers. Even so, he asserted that every man involved, with the exception of some of the hired gunmen from Texas, had been "of the best, bravest men who ever lived." [14] The invasion was not only backed by virtually every wealthy rancher in the state, but also by Acting Governor Amos W. Barker, both United States Senators in Washington, and the Adjutant General of the Wyoming National Guard.

The news of the arrival of the special train at Casper reached Buffalo, the county seat of Johnson County, and the small communities, ranches, and farms throughout northern Wyoming within twenty-four hours. On April 9 the ranchers and mercenaries surrounded a lonely cabin belonging to Nick Ray and Nate Champion, two of the men on the wanted list. In addition to the suspected rustlers, two trappers also were inside the cabin at the time, and both were captured when they ventured forth to fetch some water. Ray stepped out a few minutes later and was immediately brought down with a bullet in the head. Nate darted through the door and dragged his companion inside with one hand while firing his pistol with the other. The wounded man died a few hours later, as the attackers kept up a steady drumbeat of rifle shots through the cabin door and windows. Throughout the morning, as he held them off, Champion, a truly brave man, made brief entries in a diary that would later make him into a martyred hero. After a siege of more than twelve hours, the attackers rigged up a wagon load of hay, set it ablaze, and pushed it against the cabin. When Champion finally rushed out through the flames, he was brought down by an avalanche of bullets, twenty-eight of which found their mark.[15]

By daybreak the next day the residents of Buffalo had learned of the attack. They had also learned that the invaders were moving northward in their direction. The townspeople and near-by settlers responded as the embattled farmers at Lexington and Concord had, and soon parties of well-armed men were on their way to intercept the invaders. When the ranchers and Texas gunmen learned that they were about to encounter more trouble than they had bargained for, they halted and barricaded themselves at the TA ranch headquarters, about fourteen miles south of Buffalo. The main building, made of squared logs twelve inches thick, was ideal for withstanding attack by rifle fire. By the morning of April 11 some 250 Johnson County men had surrounded the main house and outlying buildings. It now became obvious to those inside that their situation was desperate, especially when most of their supplies of food, ammunition, and dynamite fell into the hands of the enemy. Although the invaders had previously forted up the main building by piling logs against the windows, leaving loopholes at the top, and by digging trenches around the outside, the long-range advantages were all on the other side.

Two days went by before the Johnson County men decided to blow up the main building. They lashed two wagons together, loaded them with bales of hay and dynamite, and started inching the contraption forward. The going was torturously slow, and before the "Go Devil" could be brought into effective use, three companies of the Sixth Cavalry arrived from near-by Fort McKinney. It seems that, two nights before, one of the beleaguered men had slipped out of the main building and through the lines. He had ridden the hundred miles to Gillette to send a telegram to Governor Barker. This official in turn had sent frantic messages to both of Wyoming's Senators and to President Benjamin Harrison, urging that federal troops be dispatched to the scene of the insurrection to protect the lives and property of the large number of persons involved.

After a brief conference with the commander of the troops, the leaders of the Johnson County men agreed to lift the siege, provided that the cattlemen and their hired gunmen would be turned over to civil authorities for trial. Completion of the formalities took about two hours, during which time the military captured 45 men, 46 horses, 45 rifles, 50 revolvers, and 5000 rounds of ammunition.[16] The prisoners were marched off to Fort Fetterman and then were sent by special train to Cheyenne. Eventually they were lodged in a wing of their own at the state penitentiary in Laramie, where they were treated as guests. Previously, on April 15, the people of Buffalo had turned out 500 strong for the funeral for Nate Champion and Nick Ray. It was the most elaborate affair of its kind that Wyoming had yet experienced.

Nine months passed before the defendants came to trial. By then the hired gunmen had already been released and allowed to return to Texas, and the Wyoming cattlemen had been freed without bail on their own recognizance. They were allowed to move about at will, carry arms, and patronize the local saloons. The principal witnesses for the state, the two trappers who had been captured shortly before the death of Champion and Ray, were bribed (ironically, with bad checks) and left the territory. To no one's surprise, the trial, which began in January 1893, turned out to be a farce. The people of Wyoming had long since become bored with the whole business. No witnesses could be called to testify, and the twenty-three remaining defendants were acquitted without a single question being asked.

The New York Times gave extensive coverage to the events connected with the Johnson County War, from the time of the invasion in April 1892 through the so-called trial in Cheyenne, nine months later. The editor left little doubt as to which side he was on; he regularly extolled the virtue of each of the defendants. Their leader, and the man behind the whole operation, was Major Frank Wolcott, a wealthy rancher from Converse County. Some of his colleagues in the Cheyenne Club considered him a hothead, but the *Times* virtually conferred sainthood upon him. "He has wonderful determination, and is a stranger to fear," a reporter wrote on January 5, 1893. "Before going on the raid he sent his wife and daughter to Paris, made his will and was ready for anything. He wears a little badge of the Loyal Legion, earned his rank on the field, is a polished, educated gentleman, likes good living, is an excellent whist and chess player, a judge of wines, and is at the club regularly. He is a Kentuckian."

The Johnson County War cost the cattlemen $100,000 and greatly tarnished their reputations. What is more, it contributed considerably to the popular conviction that the code of the West often involved cold-blooded murder as well as good manners, the writings of Owen Wister in *The Virginian* notwithstanding. It split the state of Wyoming from one end to the other, weakened the position of the courts, stimulated distrust of wealth and power, and created hatred and feuds that kept the people divided for generations. The county in which most of the violence had taken place remained in debt for many years because of the heavy cost of the fruitless court action. While they were defending themselves against the invaders, the local residents had won considerable public sympathy throughout the nation. Unfortunately, they turned around and destroyed their own reputations by failing to stop the looting, disorder, and murder committed by local bullies, two-bit bad-men, and cattle rustlers, who now felt free to operate openly.

Only four people were killed in the war itself—two residents of Johnson County and two Texans who died of accidental gunshot wounds. These statistics of violence are relatively minor compared to those of the Routt War of the 1890's in Colorado, during which thousands of sheep were driven off cliffs to their death, cattle were shot and poisoned, ranch houses and sheep camps attacked, barns and haystacks burned, and cowboys and sheepherders dry-gulched. The earlier turmoil in New Mexico during the Lincoln County War of the 1870's was even more severe. It was during that war that Billy the Kid alone killed somewhere between half a dozen to more than twenty men. In the Graham-Tewksbury Feud, or Tonto Basin War, which began in Arizona in 1887, twenty-nine men died of gunshot wounds.

But the events of April 1892 in Johnson County constitute *the* war of the range. According to Mrs. D. F. Baber, in *The Longest Rope*, its significance lies in the fact that it marked the dividing line between the Old West, ruled by the big cattle kings, and the New West of the pioneer homesteader. Perhaps so, but it obviously did not mark the end of violence on the northern grasslands. Indeed, the decade that followed produced a whole new crop of frontier-type outlaws—among them Butch Cassidy; Harry Longbaugh, alias the Sundance Kid; Harry Logan, alias Kid Curry; and Ben Kilpatrick, alias the Tall Texan. Cassidy, the leader of the gang of more than a dozen outlaws known as the Wild Bunch, is invariably de-scribed as a likeable scoundrel, in spite of the fact that his followers included some of the worst cutthroat thieves and cold-blooded murderers that the West ever saw.

The Wild Bunch specialized in robbing trains and express companies throughout Wyoming, Colorado, Utah, and Mon-tana. They also rustled cattle and occasionally held up a bank. After major robberies they often escaped to one of their far-flung hideouts, the most popular of which was an empty valley in northern Wyoming which is still known as Hole in the Wall. This spot lies approximately fifty miles south of Buffalo, not far from the excellent grazing lands of the Powder River country. Rustlers and horse thieves had used it as a rendezvous for many years.

The outlaws who came and went from Hole in the Wall and similar hideouts developed a unique way of getting rid of their stolen livestock. They would split up into small groups, each taking charge of a few cattle which they would drive to a rendezvous. The next day they would continue on to another small isolated ranch, or "station," subsidized by the gang, where the cattle could be held until they were sold. Thus, the rustlers would be gone from home for only a couple of days, and then, if caught driving a small herd of cattle, they could merely claim that they were moving some "strays" off their land.[17]

Pinkerton detectives in the employ of the Union Pacific Railroad and the Adams Express Company eventually broke up the Wild Bunch. Butch Cassidy and the Sundance Kid fled to Bolivia and continued their careers there until they were killed by federal troops near La Paz in 1909. All of the other members of the old gang sooner or later met death at the hands of a posse, or otherwise came to a violent end.

One Wyoming outlaw who is particularly remembered even today was Big Nose George Curry (George Parrott)—no relation to Kid Curry. Like other members of his profession, he considered killing, robbing, and violence as a way of life; he had the simple philosophy that if you wanted something, you should take it with a gun.[18] Big Nose participated in several train and bank robberies throughout the West, and from time to time he returned to the Hole in the Wall country to rustle cattle or to hide out from the law. He was captured in eastern Montana in July 1880 and sentenced to be hanged on April 3, 1882, in Rawlins, Wyoming. A week before that date he tried to break jail, but he was immediately captured by a mob and taken out on the street to be hanged. The mob forced him to climb a ladder set against a tall lamp post, put a rope around

Handsome "Black Jack" Ketchum began his outlaw career in Wyoming, stealing cattle. He ended it—literally head first—in Clayton, New Mexico, in 1901. The jerk proved considerably more terrific than the amateur hangman had anticipated, and Ketchum's head was wrenched from his shoulders.

his neck, and told him to jump. When he did, the rope broke, and rather than go through the ceremony again, some of the spectators shot him as he lay on the ground.

There are several versions of what happened next, each differing in detail, but not in substance. This much seems certain: the body fell into the hands of young Dr. J. E. Osborne, a local druggist who was also in the sheep business and who would later become Governor of the state. According to T. A. Larson, Research Professor of History at the University of Wyoming, Dr. Osborne performed an autopsy on Big Nose in the course of his duties as local coroner. In the process he helped himself to some of the victim's parts, peeled the hide off of his chest, tanned it, and made a pair of slippers which are still on display in a Rawlins bank. He also took George's pouch—on the assumption that he had no further use for it—and made it into a purse.[19]

Another Wyoming outlaw whose distinction rests primarily upon the bizarre events associated with his hanging was Tom Ketchum, better known as Black Jack Ketchum. Like Big Nose George, Ketchum worked with Butch Cassidy's gang from time to time, but he rarely remained in one place very long. He frequently operated on his own, and he hired some of Cassidy's Wild Bunch riders to rustle cattle for him in the Powder River country. When things got too warm for him in the Northern Plains region, he transferred his operations to the Southwest. He was finally captured in New Mexico in 1899, convicted of several local murders and robberies, and sentenced to be hanged. Because of his long record as a notorious outlaw, and also because of the many rumors that his gang planned to storm the jail at Folsom and rescue him, the authorities finally moved Black Jack to Clayton, New Mexico, where he was hanged in the spring of 1901.

A wedding, funeral, and camp meeting combined did not create as much excitement and entertainment nor draw as large a crowd as a public hanging on the frontier. Black Jack was equal to the occasion; he obviously relished every moment of being the center of attention. It is alleged that he called out from his cell window as the carpenters finished work on the scaffold: "Very good, boys, but why don't you tear down that stockade so the boys can see a man hang who never killed anyone?" When a priest came to his cell a few minutes before he was led out, Black Jack politely rejected his solicitations and prayers. He requested instead that someone play a fiddle during his final performance on the scaffold. According to *The New York Times* of April 25, 1901, Black Jack "leaped" up the gallows steps, joked with the hangman, and even assisted with the adjustment of the noose around his neck. "I'll be in Hell before you start breakfast, boys," he said cheerfully. He then called out: "Let 'em go."

The audience admired this kind of high drama, and they were even more delighted when the tall, handsome gunman dropped through the trap door with such force that his head was literally wrenched from his shoulders. It seems that the hangman, an amateur, had not adjusted the weights properly and that the jerk had proved considerably more terrific than anticipated. Fortunately for posterity, a photographer recorded the gruesome hanging in a sequence of shots taken immediately before and after the fatal drop. Judging from the number of prints still available in private collections and in various libraries and archives, profits from the sale of the photographs must have been considerable.

The macabre details of Black Jack Ketchum's hanging are indeed unusual. But there was nothing unique about the way he achieved fame throughout his long career as a professional outlaw. This was especially true during the post-Civil War years in the Southwest, where history and environment had combined to produce an even more tolerant attitude toward violence than that which existed on the northern grasslands near the end of its frontier period.

IX
Turmoil in the Southwest

Horses and cattle were directly related to general lawlessness throughout the Northern and Southern Plains, in somewhat the same way that automobiles and bootleg whiskey were associated with the gang wars of the 1920's. From early Colonial days, horse thieves and cattle rustlers acted as parasitic growths upon frontier life and as retarding forces to the development of the country by Anglo-American settlers. Since horses were the chief means of transportation, they were always in demand, and stolen animals, especially, found a ready market among newcomers. In many sections of the Southern Plains and Great Southwest, the buyer of a horse would neither ask embarrassing questions nor demand a bill of sale. Indeed, he was more than eager to purchase a good mount at one-third to one-half the market price. If the original owner successfully located and identified his property, he generally had to pay the sale price to recover it. But, unfortunately for the thief, if he were caught, a sure ticket to a public hanging awaited him.

Cattle, like horses, were a form of wealth in the ranching country. During the early years, when most of the land was open range, it was comparatively easy for thieves to separate a dozen or so yearlings from herds and drive them across the mountain or into a hidden valley until they could be sold. Rustlers could usually find ready markets at the various Indian agencies and military posts, where subcontractors sought the best bargain possible.[1] Some of the agents made huge profits for themselves, buying and selling stolen horses and cattle from rustlers and Indians. This was particularly true of the agents at Fort Sill, in present Oklahoma. Cattle stealing was reduced somewhat when various Western states and territories passed laws requiring the branding of animals and the registration of all brands. Barbed wire later made it less convenient for thieves to put their own brand on strays, or to slip into another man's range and drive off part of his herd.

There is an old saying that "barbed wire and Johnson grass sure played hell with Texas." There is another to the effect that "barbed wire and windmills made the settlement of the West possible." Undoubtedly, the new type of fencing helped make the Great Plains fit for settlement, but the introduction of barbed wire into the cattle country resulted in immediate outbursts of violence and vigilantism. Fence-cutting wars broke out in Texas in the early 1880's, and they soon spread north into Montana and as far west as Arizona. Feuds started that lasted for a generation or more, people were murdered, property was destroyed, and sheep and cattle were slaughtered.

In 1874, Joseph Glidden of De Kalb, Illinois, received a patent for barbed wire, and within a few years the new type of wire began arriving in Texas by the trainload. The three-million-acre XIT Ranch in the Panhandle was one of the first to enclose its vast grasslands, a job that required 6000 miles of single-wire strand. By 1885 most of the so-called Texas cattle empires in the Panhandle—such as the Frying Pan, the Spur, and the Matador, and, of course, in south Texas, the great King Ranch—had fenced their land and cattle in and the small ranchers and farmers out. Expensive though it was, the big outfits and many of the smaller ones accepted the fact that fencing was the only way to stop herds from drifting away or being driven off by rustlers.

In parts of the Plains, some of the large ranches at first co-operated in building drift fences across the open range to prevent their neighbor's cattle from encroaching on their territory, and also to keep their own herds from straying too far. Within a few years after barbed wire appeared in the West, cattlemen had constructed a series of east-west drift fences from Texas to Wyoming. The longest of these spanned the Panhandle for approximately 200 miles without a single gate. But such fences soon created disaster for men and animals, particularly during the winter months, when livestock were unable to escape beyond the reach of blizzards that roared down from the north. Thousands were trapped and frozen to death before legislation was finally passed outlawing or regulating fence construction on public lands.

As ranchers built fences around their holdings, they frequently enclosed choice pastures along streams that did not belong to them. They also built across public roads and made it difficult or impossible for children to ride to school or for people to get back and forth to town and to church services. As more and more fences went up, it became increasingly difficult for small ranchers and farmers to drive their livestock to market or to find enough grass and water on what was left of the open range. The drought of 1883 compounded the situation. The grass withered, the wells went dry, the earth cracked and turned brown. As some of the open-range cowmen moved further west or north, they discovered that several of the big outfits had tried to fence in the entire country. Consequently, they cut any barbed-wire construction that blocked their paths, gunned down the fence builders, and sometimes were gunned down themselves—along with their herds.

To some, barbed wire represented an instrument of the devil and a symbol of monopoly. In state after state, farmers and landless ranchers banded together, held public meetings, and sent letters and telegrams to members of the legislature and to the Governor. When all their legal protests came to naught, they moved out in small bands at night and destroyed fences that blocked roads or enclosed other people's land. As the war heated up, the cutters became less discriminate. They were soon wrecking fences that enclosed legitimately owned land and setting fire to the grass in pastures. Night after night the larger ranchers sent cowboys out to protect their fences, but there were too few of them, too many homesteaders and lawless cattlemen, and too many miles of fences to patrol.

Fence-cutting was reported in over half of the counties in Texas in 1883, and damage was estimated at more than $20 million. The *Fort Worth Gazette* declared that the trouble had caused tax valuation for the state to decrease by $30 million that year.[2] Sometimes the cutters left penciled notes warning the owner that if he rebuilt the fence without gates, "we will make them for you." Not infrequently a rancher would find a coffin nailed to a post or left on his porch with the warning that "This will be your end if you keep fencing." Wayne Gard, author of *Frontier Justice*, maintains that there was more shooting during three or four months of fence cutting in Texas than that which took place during several years of the Lincoln County War in near-by New Mexico. Literally dozens of men were shot, but probably no more than six or seven were actually killed as a direct result of the conflict. Finally, in January 1884, the Governor of Texas called a special session of the legislature for the purpose of finding a solution to the problem. After several weeks of debate, the legislature passed a law making fence-cutting and pasture-burning felonies, punishable by a term of from one to five years in prison. It also enacted legislation making it a misdemeanor to carry a "patented wire cutter" on one's person, to knowingly fence public land, to enclose another man's property without his consent, or to fail to provide a gate every three miles for fences that crossed public roads. The legislation had the desired effect, and, except for occasional outbreaks of nipping, especially during droughts, the war had ended in Texas by 1885.

Meanwhile, outlaws in New Mexico and Arizona were making life miserable for those who wanted to live in peace. Many young, rootless men drifted into Arizona soon after the close of the Civil War. Vigilante committees went to work in Yuma as early as 1866, and they took the law into their own hands at one time or the other in practically every settlement in the territory. Phoenix, Tucson, Globe, Tombstone, Bisbee—each had its vigilante groups who hanged Mexicans for stealing, desperadoes for knifing or shooting local citizens, and road agents for robbing express offices or holding up stagecoaches. Because of the menace of outlaws and Apaches, anyone who stirred a few hundred yards from town without being armed to the teeth was asking for trouble. "The great arid regions west of Texas produced rather more than their full quota of bad white men who took naturally to the gun," Emerson Hough wrote several decades ago.[3] With so many outlaws and guns around, it is small wonder that Arizona experienced so much violence—in both the towns and in the countryside.

Violence associated with the cattle industry on the Northern Plains was fairly tame stuff compared to what went on in New Mexico and Arizona in the 1870's and 1880's. Soon after the southwestern territories became part of the United States in 1848, adventurers moved in from all parts of the country. Many of the newcomers, particularly veterans of the Mexican War, brought their hatred of Latins and Indians with them. During the Gold Rush days, an estimated 50,000 men crossed the vast stretch of the Southwest en route to California. Of these, a few hundred decided not to go farther, and a few hundred more who failed to strike it rich in the gold fields later returned. The United States census of 1870 placed the population of Arizona Territory at 9658, a figure that in ten years quadrupled, to slightly more than 40,000.

The quality of the newcomers to Arizona apparently did not improve even after more than a generation of population growth, judging from the constant reference to violence, gunplay, mayhem, and thievery one finds in the reports, correspondence, and local newspapers of the time. In June 1881, the United States Attorney wrote from Tucson that the lawless elements in southern Arizona were "augmented by the exiled rangers from Texas, the hunted stage robbers from Montana, the murderers from Idaho, the desperate and criminal class from every place." [4]

John D. Tewksbury hardly seemed to fit the description of such individuals. He arrived at Globe, Arizona, in 1880 with his wife and five sons. The Tewksbury clan soon moved across the mountain to Pleasant Valley, in the Tonto Basin in central Arizona, where they built a cabin and established a ranch. Two years later Tom and John Graham, two brothers in their early twenties who had grown up on an Iowa farm and had later migrated to California, settled in Pleasant Valley, ten miles north of the Tewksbury cabin. Another brother joined them later, and the three occasionally worked with the Tewksbury boys for a neighboring rancher. The Grahams and the Tewksburys were soon stealing cattle and horses from their employer and quarreling over the loot. Bad blood began to develop. But the first victim in the most famous family feud in the history of the Western frontier was the foreman of the ranch, who was not a member of either family. People who knew Ed Tewksbury recognized that he had a mean, cruel streak, and the foreman should have had better judgment than to accuse him of stealing horses. Ed shot him on the spot.

The Tewksbury and Graham boys continued to build up their own herds by rustling cattle and horses from the ranches of their more prosperous neighbors until the fall of 1887. At that time the Daggs brothers employed the Tewksburys to move their sheep south of Flagstaff into the Tonto Basin. Even though it was public domain, the cattlemen of the region were determined that sheep would never be allowed in what they considered "cow country." On the other hand, the Daggs believed that they could count upon the Tewksbury brothers to protect their flocks and herders from the cattle ranchers, once they had moved into the forbidden territory. They were wrong. Cattle ranchers, led by the Grahams, systematically raided the flocks at night and slaughtered sheep by the hundreds or drove them into creeks or over bluffs. At least one Navajo herder was killed and beheaded before the Daggs withdrew from the valley.

The cattlemen had won their point, but the feuding between the Tewksburys and Grahams had only begun. Sooner or later almost every family in the Tonto Basin was forced to choose one side or the other, or leave the country. The conflict lasted five years. Men were ambushed on lonely trails, caught outside their cabins and gunned down, or overpowered by three or four opponents and hanged. Before it all ended, twenty-nine men had died, including every member of the Graham clan.[5] Ed Tewksbury, the only member of either family who escaped shooting or hanging, succumbed to tuberculosis in 1904. Ironically, no member of either group was ever convicted of murder by a legal court, and apparently the only one who really profited from the feud was Zane Grey. His popular novel, *To the Last Man*, sold several hundred thousand copies and provided the plot for an untold number of westerns. Meanwhile, ranchers throughout the West continued to contest with one another over the limited grass and water until the first decade of the twentieth century. By that time the cattlemen had learned to take advantage of some of the positive factors contributed by sheep, and to profit by raising them alongside of cattle.

Considerably more violent action took place in the frontier

cattle and mining towns than ordinarily occurred on the open range. Today it is difficult for the average American to hear the name Tombstone without thinking of the fight at the OK Corral in 1881, or of the Earp brothers and their friend Doc Holliday. The celebrated shoot-out was one of the most senseless acts of violence ever perpetrated on the frontier, which takes in a large catalogue of events. Tombstone, like so many other boom towns at one time or the other, had a reputation of being "the wickedest place in the West." The sudden development of silver mining in the southeastern corner of the territory in the late 1870's and early 1880's attracted the usual human scum: gunslingers, bums, gamblers, prostitutes, and fugitives from other parts of the West. Opportunities for ill-gotten gain were plentiful, since stagecoaches regularly moved silver bullion out of Tombstone to the railroad at Benson, twenty miles away. Also, subcontractors, hard pressed to satisfy the demand for beef for the near-by San Carlos Indian Agency, unhesitatingly purchased cattle from cowboys who rustled them from ranches on both sides of the international boundary.

The Acting Governor of the territory, John J. Gospen, reported to President Chester A. Arthur in 1882 that the difficulty in suppressing violence in Arizona arose from the fact that the local sheriffs were either intimidated or from personal motives desired to curry favor with the outlaws. "The people of Tombstone and Cochise County," the Governor wrote, "in their mad career after money, have grossly neglected local self-government until the more lazy and lawless elements of society have undertaken to prey upon the more industrious and honorable classes for their subsistence and gain. . . . The thoroughly abandoned class of men called highway robbers and cattle thieves called 'cowboys,' cunningly taking advantage of the favorable state of affairs for themselves, have robbed from the wealthier class, and when apprehended and detected by the officers of the law have in many cases, no doubt, purchased their liberty, or have paid well to be left unmolested." [6]

The most famous law officers in the history of Tombstone were the Earp brothers—Wyatt, Virgil, and Morgan. They arrived in southern Arizona in 1879, having migrated, via brief stops in Kansas, Texas, and Oklahoma, from their family farm in Illinois. They were soon joined by Bat Masterson and Doc Holliday, with whom they had formed close friendships in Dodge City. At one time or another the Earps and Masterson had worked both sides of the law, spent time in jail for disturbing the peace, and served brief terms as deputy marshals in various frontier towns. Their friend Doc Holliday was a dentist and professional gambler, with few redeeming characteristics other than an unswerving loyalty to his friends. The Earp brothers found it tough going at first, and, were it not for the money that their wives earned from sewing, they would have been destitute.

The reputation of the Earps as gamblers and former marshals was well known in Tombstone. Wyatt soon found work as a deputy sheriff, and a few months later he obtained employment as a guard and part owner in the town's largest gambling house. "There was no prejudice against a gunfighter working simultaneously as a town marshal or sheriff and as a house man in a gambling saloon, gambling being a respected profession almost equal in rank to medicine and a lot higher than dentistry or undertaking," Bat Masterson wrote years later, when he had become a respected New York newspaperman. "Gambling was not only the principal and best paying industry in town, but also was reckoned among its most respectable." [7]

Wyatt employed his brother Morgan as a faro dealer in the saloon where he kept order, while Virgil accepted an appointment as town marshal until an election could be held, in January 1881. For some reason Virgil did not run for the office, but when the incumbent was forced out a few months later because of numerous unsolved crimes in the area, he accepted the job once again. Wyatt and Morgan then became

A gambling hall in the 1890's. Gambling was not only the principal and best paying industry in a frontier town, according to Bat Masterson, it was "a respected profession almost equal in rank to medicine and a lot higher than dentistry and undertaking."

his deputies. The situation worked to Doc Holliday's considerable advantage, for soon thereafter he became a prime suspect in a Wells, Fargo stagecoach robbery in which the driver was killed. Holliday was arrested by the local county sheriff, who was no friend of the Earps, but Virgil managed his release from jail and later got the charge thrown out of court.

In October 1881 the Earps had trouble with a band of cowboys led by the Clanton brothers, Ike and Billy. The Clantons knew that Holliday had been involved in several stagecoach robberies in the region. They also had reason to dislike the Earps. On one occasion Virgil pistol-whipped Ike after a quarrel between him and Holliday, and a few days later Wyatt did the same to another member of the Clanton gang, Tom McLowry. The showdown came on October 26. The cowboys made the rounds of the local saloons that afternoon and boasted that they planned to wipe out the Earps. The three brothers and their friend Doc Holliday then gathered in front of Hafford's Saloon to watch the cowboys on their way to their horses, which they had left at the OK Corral earlier that day.

There are several versions of what happened next. John P. Gray, a witness to the event, wrote years later that the Earp brothers and Doc Holliday advanced to the rear entrance of the OK Corral just as the cowboys were preparing to leave town. After yelling "hands up," the four men began firing simultaneously. The whole episode looked like an obvious plan to shoot their enemies under the pretense of enforcing the law. According to Gray, one of the victims had his hands raised over his head when a load of buckshot cut him down. It was over in seconds. Three of the four cowboys lay dead, and the other was severely wounded. Wyatt Earp and Doc Holliday escaped without a scratch, but Virgil and Morgan received bullet wounds. Some of the townspeople later maintained that it had been a fair fight, but others called it cold-

blooded murder. Public opinion quickly turned against the
Earps, and all three were suspended from office. They, along
with Holliday, were arrested by the sheriff of Cochise County
and tried for murder, but they were eventually acquitted. In
December 1881, Virgil was shot from ambush. He never
completely recovered. Three months later Morgan was assassi-
nated.[8]

Wyatt Earp and Doc Holliday stayed around Tombstone
until the middle of 1883. By that time the local citizens had
had enough of them and "requested" that they leave the territory. Doc died in a Colorado sanatorium four years later, at the
age of thirty-five, but Wyatt moved on to Kansas, Wyoming,
Idaho, Texas, Alaska, and Nevada before settling down in California. He died at the age of eighty-one in Los Angeles, in
January 1929, and has since been the subject of more than a
dozen biographies. Like Billy the Kid, about whom an even
larger number of books has been written, the real Wyatt Earp
was poor material for an American folk hero, yet he and dozens
like him have managed somehow to survive both hero wor-
ship and debunking.

Four or five hundred miles northeast of Tombstone is the
relatively quiet, small university town of Las Vegas, New
Mexico. The modern visitor would hardly suspect that this
place was once a byword for frontier violence throughout
much of the country. According to Emerson Hough, "There
was no one part of the remote West which could claim any
monopoly in the product of hard citizens, but there can be
small challenge to the assertion that eastern New Mexico, for
thirty years after the Civil War, was without doubt, as dangerous a country as ever lay out of doors." [9]

Las Vegas was an important stop on the old Santa Fe Trail,
and five years after General Stephen Watts Kearny's 1846
"entrada" en route to the capital city of Santa Fe, the United
States army established near-by Fort Union. For several years,

until it was evacuated in 1891, this fort remained one of the most important military establishments in the Southwest. Many soldiers, upon being discharged or dismissed from the army, settled in the Las Vegas area, and when the tracks of the Santa Fe Railroad reached the town in the early 1870's, it brought in an even rougher element, along with the inevitable army of camp followers. Within a few years so many criminals and violent characters of all types had drifted into Las Vegas that the patience of the local citizens was exhausted. Like residents of the mining camps of California, Nevada, Colorado, and Montana, they took the law into their own hands. On March 24, 1882, the following warning appeared on posters throughout Las Vegas: [10]

NOTICE!

To Thieves, Thugs, Fakirs and Bunko-Steerers, Among whom are J. J. Harlin, alias "Off Wheeler;" Saw Dust Charlie, Wm. Hedges, Billy the Kid, Billy Mullin, Little Jack, The Cuter, Pock-Marked Kid, and about Twenty Others:

If Found within the Limits of this City after Ten O'clock P. M., this Night, you will be Invited to attend a Grand Neck-tie Party, The Expense of which will be borne by 100 Substantial Citizens.

Not far away, Lincoln County was just ending one of the most intense periods of violence that any frontier county ever experienced. Much has been written about the Lincoln County War, but few authorities are in complete agreement as to its specific causes and ramifications. Some have portrayed it as a land war growing out of cattle rustling and range rights, and others as a struggle for enormous power between newcomers from Texas and residents of long standing who controlled the officers of the law. The Mexican-American his-

Boredom and sheer loneliness were far more characteristic of the frontier than so-called romance and adventure. Thus, victims of "neck-tie parties" were left to hang for several days to provide excitement for the settlers. Professional photographers sold hundreds of macabre scenes such as these at one dollar each.

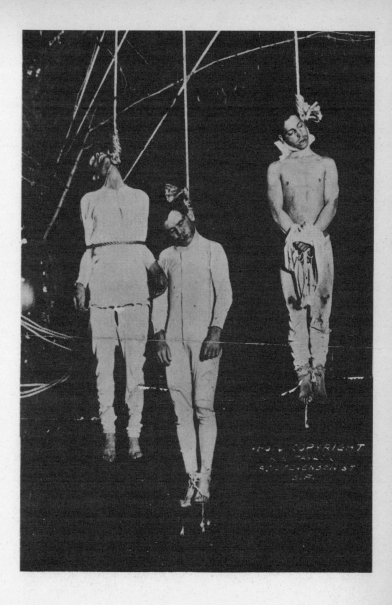

torian Rodolfo Acuña implies that the violence in Lincoln
County was primarily a racist war in which the losers were
the poor Mexican sheepherders and farmers.[11]

A *New York Times* editor wrote, on October 9, 1877, that
the trouble resulted from a conflict of jurisdiction among rival
county officials. "Under the benevolent rule of Gov. Axtell,
each small politician in the county was developed into a statesman. Each statesman was ambitious to rule, and, by some
hocus pocus never fully understood by persons outside of the
Territory, two or three claimants for each local office were
arrayed against one another."

Three things are certain about the war: It was bitter, it was
complex, and it was bloody. The New Mexican lawyer-his-
torian William A. Keleher has followed the strange bypaths
and ramifications of events in eastern New Mexico perhaps
more thoroughly than anyone else. He claims that Texans had
little or nothing to do with the war, rather, that it was fought
to the finish between young men from all parts of the country
—Vermont, Massachusetts, Kansas, Michigan, and even Canada and the British Isles. It involved men in high and low places
in civil and military life, ignorant men with malice and hatred
in their hearts who utterly disregarded the rights of others and
"blindly followed stupid leaders along trails of dishonor which
led to disaster." [12]

Among the leading cast of characters was Lawrence G.
Murphy, an aggressive man who controlled many ranching
and business enterprises in the area; Sheriff William Brady and
a small army of deputies, mostly hired gunslingers who were
wanted in half a dozen Western states and territories; Thomas
B. Catron, the United States District Attorney at Santa Fe,
political boss of the Territory, and future United States Senator from New Mexico; Governor Samuel Axtell, a political
hack who had once served as Governor of Utah Territory;
General Lew Wallace, of Civil War fame, who later wrote
Ben Hur; John Chisum, formerly of Texas, who was one of

the most ruthless and powerful cattle barons the industry ever produced; Alexander McSween, originally from Canada, a practicing lawyer and former Presbyterian minister who accumulated a vast empire in eastern New Mexico which included banking, general merchandising, and cattle ranching; John Henry Tunstall, scion of a wealthy English family who came to Lincoln County to make a fortune in the cattle business; buck-toothed William Antrim, later known as William Bonney, whose place of birth is uncertain but whom the world knows as Billy the Kid and New Mexicans simply call the Kid; and an assortment of cowboys, Spanish-American or Hispanic sheepherders, professional outlaws, beardless youths who were cold-blooded killers, Indians, soldiers, and cattle rustlers.

New Mexico was sparsely populated in the 1870's, but it is doubtful whether there has ever been another place in the United States where so many men were indicted for murder and so few convicted. If a lawyer could not win a case by bribing the judge or jury, escape for the criminal was relatively easy. Little wonder New Mexico won the reputation as the worst-governed place in the United States, a reputation that continued far into the twentieth century. And nowhere was that more apparent than in Lincoln County. Farmers and cattle ranchers began moving into that corner of the Southwest soon after the Civil War, and they staked out claims without benefit of legal patents or titles. The excellent grazing lands and many streams for irrigation made conflict among cattlemen, sheep ranchers, and farmers inevitable.

The famous Goodnight-Loving Trail ran through Lincoln County from Texas, and, as more and more cattle were driven into the Pecos River country, range thievery took place on an unprecedented scale. Even large ranchers in New Mexico bought livestock, which they knew to be stolen, without asking any questions. In fact, it often was easier to steal cattle or to purchase them from rustlers than to raise them yourself. As for markets, there were lucrative beef contracts for supplying near-by Fort Stanton and the Mescalero Apache Reservation.

The most prominent rancher in the region during the post-Civil War period was Colonel John Chisum. His empire in southeastern New Mexico at one time included hundreds of thousands of acres of public land and from 60,000 to 80,000 head of cattle. Chisum, later one of the storm centers of the Lincoln County War, employed as many as a hundred cowboys during busy seasons of the year. Many of his cowpunchers turned out to be ordinary cow thieves and fugitives from justice who welcomed involvement in the local war, a conflict that some estimate took as many as 200 lives between 1875 and 1881.[13] The Colonel did not hesitate to lead his men against Indians who slipped off the reservation to raid his herds, or to declare all-out war against rustlers who returned to his range to steal back the stolen cattle they had sold to him previously. But he reserved his greatest hatred for Mexicans. When a Mexican party robbed and beat up his invalid brother Jeff, the Colonel gave strict orders to his men to shoot any Mexican caught trespassing on his land.

Among the employees of the Chisum ranch in New Mexico were three Negro cowboys whom the Colonel had brought from Texas. The blacks seem to have been hardworking, dependable individuals who got along reasonably well with the white cowboys—as long as they "stayed in their place," of course. The story of what ultimately happened to them is told in a small book by a Texas cowboy who followed the Colonel to New Mexico soon after the Civil War. According to Ike Fridge, one Christmas the boss invited all of his hands to the ranch headquarters for dinner. After a few drinks, one of the blacks got "out of line," and several of the other cowboys immediately riddled him with bullets. The Colonel then detailed two men to bury the dead Negro, so Ike and a companion tied ropes around his legs and dragged the body behind their horses to the banks of the near-by Pecos River, dug a shallow grave, wrapped the dead man in a saddle blanket, and buried him with his boots on. A few months later one of the other blacks made the same mistake of "talking back" to a white cow puncher while the two were branding calves. Both went for their guns, but the Negro received a bullet between the eyes before he could get off a shot. His subsequent burial alongside his companion was carried out with similar informality.

The remaining Negro employee was more fortunate, doubtless because he was a good cook and therefore less expendable. Beaver Smith possessed an annoying habit, however, of shouting the praise of Abraham Lincoln every time he had one or two drinks of whiskey. One day Beaver got drunk and began yelling for Lincoln again, whereupon the white cowboys decided to hang him. "Since the Negro had really committed no crime, I didn't want to see him hanged," Ike later wrote matter-of-factly. He suggested instead that they merely brand Beaver with a hot spade. "As this was the last of the Negroes the Colonel had taken to New Mexico, I wanted to do the branding. We laid him on his stomach and I put the Chisum brand on his loin, then jingle-bobbed his right ear, as that was the Colonel's mark." [14]

Men who could so easily kill or torture others apparently made fit representatives of the vast majority of the white population of Lincoln County in the 1870's.

But let us return to the war itself. There were three or four factions in the Lincoln County conflict, one of which was headed by Lawrence G. Murphy and another by Alexander McSween. Murphy, in association with James J. Dolan and John H. Riley, controlled so many business and ranching activities in the county that without their approval few men could obtain work, credit, or justice, or, indeed, even remain in the county. They "owned" Sheriff William Brady and his army of hired gunslingers and maintained a close relationship with practically all of the territorial politicians at Santa Fe.

Allied with McSween in opposition to the Murphy-Dolan-
Riley faction were Colonel John Chisum and the young Englishman, John Henry Tunstall. McSween, who had ranching
and banking interests, opened a merchandising store at the town
of Lincoln. It is not clear what his relationship was with Chisum
and Tunstall relative to the store, but it was generally believed
that both men had a financial stake in the enterprise, and
various sources refer to it as Tunstall's store instead of Mc-
Sween's.[15] At any rate, the McSween-Chisum-Tunstall group
hoped to challenge the trade monopoly so long enjoyed by
the opposition.

Poor health caused Murphy to sell his interest in the mercantile firm to his partners and devote his attention primarily
to ranching. The inevitable clash between Dolan and Riley and
the McSween group was not long in coming to a head. Earlier,
Dolan and Riley had accused McSween of overcharging them
in a legal matter. They also were furious with Tunstall for
having outbid them on the purchase of 300 head of mature
cattle from the estate of another rancher who had been murdered. Although Tunstall was an honorable man, and free of
all debts, the Dolan-Riley crowd thrust him into a plot to
destroy McSween. Their lawyer, Tom Catron, persuaded a
territorial judge to issue an attachment on all of McSween's
property, including Tunstall's ranch. The sheriff's posse sent
out to serve legal papers against the Englishman met him and
five or six of his cowboys on the road en route to town. In
a senseless act of violence, the deputies immediately opened
fire and killed Tunstall. Among those who escaped was Billy
the Kid, who later swore that he would avenge the death of
his employer—who was probably the only real friend he ever
had in his life.

Tunstall's death created a sensation. Several hundred men
gathered at McSween's home a few days later to attend
funeral services and to plot the strategy of revenge. Richard
Brewer, a strong anti-Murphy man and friend of the deceased,

became leader of a small faction of those present. He later got himself appointed constable by a friendly justice of the peace and went after the guilty men, whose identities were well known. Brewer and some of his followers subsequently captured two members of the sheriff's posse and murdered them on the spot. A few days later a blast of gunfire directed from behind an adobe wall killed Sheriff Brady and one of his deputies. Other murders followed on both sides, until Lincoln County became an armed camp—unsafe for man, woman, or child. The new sheriff appointed by the territorial Governor soon put together a force of forty or fifty deputies, good men and bad—some were honest, others were professional killers. He was determined to harass the McSween-Chisum combination until he had driven every one of them out of the county.

John Chisum was an old man by then, so leadership of the forces allied against Dolan and Riley and their new sheriff fell to McSween. The former Canadian had never worn a gun, and, having been a man of peace, he found it difficult to control the actions of those who sided with him. Such allies included Billy the Kid and others who had worked for Tunstall, cowboys on Colonel Chisum's payroll, men who were more anti-Dolan-Riley than pro-McSween, and a few farmers and small ranchers. This motley crew numbered around forty or fifty, about equal the force under the sheriff's command.

In mid-July of 1878 McSween and his followers were besieged in Lincoln town by Sheriff George Peppin, and they were forced to barricade themselves in McSween's home and two adjoining houses. The sheriff was backed up by a detachment of troops from Fort Stanton, under the command of Colonel Nathan A. Dudley. (The Colonel was later charged with misconduct for having participated in the affair.) There was sporadic shooting between the sheriff's posse and McSween's men for three days, and finally, on July 19, the attackers set fire to the McSween home. Among those inside

who escaped through the bullets and flames via the back door
was Billy the Kid, who so far seemed to be living a charmed
life. McSween's wife had been allowed to leave, but her husband and three of his followers were brought down by rifle
fire as they stepped beyond the threshold of the front entrance. They and one of the deputies were the only men to
die during the three days of gunfire.

By the time the battle had ended, few people were left in
Lincoln County other than the actual participants in the war.
(During this same period a similar situation existed in nearby
Colfax County, where ranchers, sheepherders, and farmers were
caught up in full-scale range war.)[16] With both Tunstall and
McSween dead and the Dolan-Riley faction victorious, the Kid
became the most wanted and feared man in the Southwest.
Previously involved in several shooting scrapes, he now gathered a handful of followers and turned to outlawry as a full-
time occupation. To many of the McSween partisans Billy was
a popular hero, and before Sheriff Pat Garrett's pistol ended
his career in May 1881, he established a reputation for killing
twenty-one men—not counting Mexican and Indians, of
course.[17] Like his spiritual descendants—Lee Harvey Oswald,
Sirhan Sirhan, and Lieutenant William Calley—the New Mexican outlaw had few redeeming features. Yet there is no end
to the legends which his career set in motion.

Meanwhile, the situation in eastern New Mexico had become
outrageous enough to attract national attention. In August
1878, President Rutherford B. Hayes asked for Governor
Axtell's resignation and appointed in his stead the celebrated
General Lew Wallace. The General was far more interested
in pursuing his literary activities than in taming a wild frontier.
He had hoped for a better appointment, and for several months
after arriving in Santa Fe he devoted far more time to finishing
his novel than to the affairs of government. Although Mc-
Sween's death in a sense ended the war, it failed to end its
effects. Wallace finally rode down to Lincoln town, inter-

viewed several participants in the conflict, and promised
amnesty to all who would give testimony and desist from
further violence. He even had a personal conference with the
Kid and extracted from him a halfhearted pledge that he would
put away his gun—a pledge that Billy neither would nor could
keep.

For the most part, Wallace succeeded in restoring order,
and within a few years Lincoln County became a reasonably
safe place. On July 14, 1881, Sheriff Pat Garrett caught up
with the Kid at the home of Pete Maxwell, near Fort Sumner,
and ended his life with a well-placed bullet fired into a dark-
ened bedroom. Immediate reaction of the press throughout the
Southwest was one of general relief, although many people in
New Mexico found it difficult to believe that the young,
seemingly invincible killer was dead. Typical of the comments
at the time is the following observation, made on July 23 by
the editor of the Silver City *New Southwest and Grant
Herald*: "Despite the glamour of romance thrown about his
dare-devil life by sensational writers, the fact is, he was a low-
down vulgar cut-throat, with probably not one redeeming
quality." [18] The Kid's death created a flurry of dime novels
and newspaper and popular magazine articles about his outlaw
career. For the next generation, with rare exception, writers
treated him in much the same manner as the people of New
Mexico did. They knew him for what he was—a satanic killer.

"There are two Billy the Kids in legend," Kent Steckmesser
writes. "The first is a tough little thug, a coward, a thief, and
a cold-blooded murderer. The second is a romantic and senti-
mental hero, the brave and likeable leader of an outnumbered
band fighting for justice. The dominance of the second legend
in our day marks his significance as the personification of a
general type, the outlaw-hero." [19] According to that historian,
the transformation of the Satanic Billy to the Saintly Billy began with a play which opened on Broadway in 1906. For the
next dozen years *Billy the Kid* played in theaters across the

country and helped create a new and sympathetic image of the
New Mexican outlaw. The process has continued throughout
the twentieth century with the production of favorable articles,
books, and movies. In spite of the efforts made by a few serious scholars to set the record straight, the Kid's many acts of
violence have become less offensive and his qualities of character more attractive—as legend replaces reality.

Long before the Kid emerged as a Western Robin Hood,
the task of bringing law and order to every community in
New Mexico proved to be more than a few courageous individuals could accomplish. Men who had sufficient nerve to
serve as sheriff, or the legal and moral qualifications to be a
judge, were scarce indeed, and Governor Wallace eventually
resigned in disgust. Added to these conditions was the Santa Fe
Ring, perhaps the most corrupt political machine that ever existed in any region of the West for an extended period of time.

Among the many thieves and desperadoes that New Mexico
communities supported were a few ruthless killers who, to a
lesser degree, would become folk heroes like Billy the Kid.
They were men whose reputation for bravado matched their
legendary skill with a six-shooter or rifle, such worthies as Jim
Fowler, Clay Allison, and "Black Jack" Ketchum. (It will be
recalled that Black Jack began his outlaw career in Wyoming,
stealing cattle, and ended it—literally head first—in Clayton,
New Mexico, in 1901.) The Hispanos of New Mexico also had
their folk heroes, the two most famous of whom were Elfego
Baca and Juan Jose Herrera. Both resented the mistreatment
of Mexican farmers and sheepherders by Texans who moved
into the territory in the 1870's and 1880's and expropriated or
illegally purchased large tracts of land.

While campaigning for sheriff, Baca took it upon himself to
arrest a Texas cowboy who was shooting up the small town
of Frisco. He then started to Socorro with his prisoner, only
to be stopped by a mob of irate cowboys who demanded the
immediate release of their fellow Texan. When Baca refused,

shooting broke out and one of the cowboys was killed. The Hispano then took refuge in a small shed and exchanged shots with the Texans for several hours. Legend and fact relating to the battle have become so intermingled over the years that it is difficult to separate one from the other. Baca is said to have killed four of the Texans and wounded eight others without receiving a single scratch himself. If the legend bears any remote similarity to fact, the Hispano hero must have been well supplied with ammunition—he was said to have held off an army of eighty men for thirty-six hours. But, as New Mexico historian Warren A. Beck observed, "What people believe has far more influence than the truth anyway, and not only did Baca get off scot-free, but the fame attendant upon his deed propelled him into public life and earned him a reputation that continues to be exploited." [20]

The facts about Juan Jose Herrera have perhaps been less distorted by time. To the Anglos of New Mexico, he and Baca were no more than common outlaws, but to the poor Hispano farmers and sheepherders these men provided hope and admiration. Both had lived for a time outside of New Mexico, spoke excellent English, and had learned from the Anglo world how to respond to violence with violence. Herrera, for example, had witnessed some of the methods used by the unions against the railroads and mining companies in Colorado—among them, homicide and sabotage. Upon his return to eastern New Mexico in the late 1880's, he was determined to champion the cause of the poor paisano against the land-grabbing gringos. He deplored the fact that most of the millions of head of sheep and cattle belonged to "outsiders," and that a crop of ewes often brought the owners as much as $15,000, while the herder who actually cared for the flock could earn no more than $200 for a year's work.

During the first two decades after the Mexican War, the United States Congress confirmed various land grants that had been awarded to communities in New Mexico under Spanish and Mexican law. Among these was the Las Vegas Grant, a 500,000-acre tract of excellent farming, timber, and grazing land in San Miguel County in northern New Mexico. Herrera possessed some knowledge of law, and he maintained that the land known as the Las Vegas Grant belonged to the Mexican people who lived on it at the time, that they owned it in common, and that both law and tradition prohibited anyone from selling any part of it to anyone. Nevertheless, Anglos accustomed to taking what they wanted on the public domain moved in with their flocks and herds and either took what they wanted or bought land from families that had no legal right to sell it. By enclosing these holdings, some of which encompassed as much as 10,000 acres, the new owners denied the Mexicans access to timber, water, and grazing land that they had enjoyed for generations.

Sometime around 1888 Herrera organized his *Gorras Blancas*, or White Caps. This was a secret, vigilante type of society, not unlike many others that had operated throughout rural America since the Civil War. Membership was confined to Mexicans, and Herrera at one time claimed as many as 1500 followers. Professor Robert Larson maintains that the *Gorras Blancas* were not a revolutionary group, but that they represented an oppressed people fighting to preserve their traditional order from Anglo encroachers.[23] Nevertheless, they vented their frustration by cutting fences and destroying railroad property. Their activities soon spread beyond San Miguel into neighboring counties and frightened Anglos throughout the territory. The *Gorras Blancas* doubtless received the blame for much violence for which they were not responsible. Their ranks were eventually infiltrated by spies, several of their members were arrested on suspicion of fence-cutting, and, after Herrera and some of the other leaders defected to politics to further their own ambitions, their organization faded away.

Violence in New Mexico also found an outlet in the turbulent politics of the period, causing the territory to establish a record for political assassinations unmatched by any other frontier community. The most sensational murders, those of Colonel Albert Jennings Fountain and his eight-year-old son, occurred in January 1896, on the Tularosa-Las Crucas road. The bodies were discovered several days after the murders. There were no witnesses—at least, none who ever talked—and the mystery surrounding the event has never been solved. As a territorial judge, Colonel Fountain had sent a number of cattle rustlers to the penitentiary, and at the time of the murders, he was a key figure in a Lincoln County grand jury investigation of cattle rustling. He was also a political enemy of young Albert B. Fall, of future Teapot Dome fame, a man who had opposed Fountain many times in law, politics, and the territorial legislature. Suspicion exists to this day that Fall was somehow involved in the assassination of one of the few politicians of integrity in the territory.[24] "Truth will come to light; murder cannot be hid long," Shakespeare wrote in *The Merchant of Venice*. Yet, although several people were indicted, no convictions were ever secured in the Fountain case.

It would be an oversimplification to state that Colonel Fountain's assassination represented some sort of turning point in New Mexico's violent history. But it did not touch off a bloody frontier war, as had the murder of Tunstall in Lincoln County, eighteen years before. Maybe it was because the Southwest had finally reached the point in civilization where its people no longer would tolerate wholesale violence. And maybe too, in this corner of the vanishing frontier, the law had finally begun to arise over the ruin wrought by generations of lawlessness.

X
The Other Side of the Coin

The monumental report of the National Commission on the Causes and Prevention of Violence, published in 1969, reveals that violence in America has traditionally been an urban rather than a frontier problem. Moreover, no large city escaped one or more major riots in the nineteenth century. The urban historian Richard Wade emphasized the same thing in his *Violence in the Cities: A Historical View* (1969). John Hope Franklin, in *The Militant South* (1956), cites that region's greater use of firearms, dueling, vigilante groups, and public lynchings at the very time that the Western frontier was experiencing its most violent period. Why, then, has the theme of violence in the region beyond the Mississippi been so overplayed?

It should be remembered that the closing decades of the nineteenth century was the period of the Gilded Age, a time of such slogans as "dog eat dog," "rugged individualism," "Social Darwinism," and "root hog or die." These clichés applied alike to Eastern capitalists and Western outlaws. Gary L. Roberts has maintained in a recent article that the disillusionment of the Civil War, the rise of materialism and labor unions, the lack of concern for the plight of the poor, and the Indian wars on the frontier were primarily responsible for the absence of an effective social conscience. "Moreover, the rhetoric of the war, with its praise for physical courage and boldness, romanticized violence and produced a high respect for those virtues, even among criminals." [1]

To millions of people throughout the western world, the American frontier represented a combination of El Dorado, Zion, and Shangri-la. It offered adventure, excitement, and opportunity for wealth. The openness of the country, fertility of the soil, abundance of game, and lack of restrictions constituted the stuff that dreams are made of. Yet the frontier never quite lived up to this ideal, and many of those who went there found it better to keep the dream alive for others than to admit the truth. Perhaps this accounts for the tendency of some to exaggerate and to depict the good characteristics of the frontier as very good and the bad as very bad. The dime novels of Ned Buntline were pure fantasy, but so was much of the writing of Captain John Smith about the Virginia frontier three centuries earlier. What people believe to be true is often as important as reality, and generations of Americans have grown up accepting the idea that the frontier during the closing decades of the nineteenth century represented this country at its most adventurous as well as at its most violent.

Westerners themselves must share much of the blame for the image that the frontier came to represent. They have emphasized the more bizarre events, and they have developed a talent for taking something small and blowing it up to giant size. If one judged from the historical markers along the highways of central Wyoming, for example, it would appear that the most important event in that region's entire history was the hanging of "Cattle Kate" Watson and James Averell on the Sweetwater in 1889. The invasion of Johnson County, further north, two years later by Wyoming cattle ranchers and their hired guns from Texas is made to appear more extensive than the sacking of Rome by the Huns and Vandals.

The plain truth is that Westerners have had to make do with
what little historical material they have had to work with.

> They write of cowboys as if they were noble knights,
> and cowmen kings. They do biographies of bad men,
> Billy the Kid, the Plummer gang . . . Wyatt Earp
> and Wild Bill Hickok. . . . They blow up the aban-
> doned saloon into an art museum, the Boot Hill into
> a shrine for pilgrims. In Montana Charles Russell is
> better than Titian, and in the Black Hills Frederick
> Remington is greater than Michelangelo. Custer, who
> blundered to his death, taking better men with him,
> found a place in every saloon not already pre-empted
> to that travesty of justice, Judge Roy Bean.[2]

I once interviewed dozens of elderly people who had participated in the settlement of Oklahoma Territory in the late
1880's and early 1890's. When I asked them what they remembered most about the recent frontier, the answer that a great
majority gave was the wretched loneliness and almost total
lack of excitement in their lives. Sam Rayburn once reminisced
about his experiences in growing up on the frontier of northeastern Texas. He recalled the boredom that he could never
escape. Even though he worked in the fields all week, from
sunup to sundown, the worst time of all was Sunday afternoon,
when he had nothing to do. There were no newspapers to read
and no books other than the family Bible, there was no one
his age to talk with, and the nearest store was miles away.
He usually passed the entire afternoon sitting on the wooden
fence in front of the unpainted family house, gazing down
the country road in the hope that someone would ride by on
horseback, or, even more exciting, in a buggy.[3]

A few hundred miles north of Rayburn's birthplace, another future leader was growing into manhood just as the
last frontier was passing—Dwight D. Eisenhower of Abilene,
Kansas. Both Eisenhower and Rayburn admitted in later life

that their respective heroes were local boys who "made good." In Rayburn's case it was John Wesley Hardin, while Eisenhower's life-long admiration for Abilene's one-time town marshal, Wild Bill Hickok, is even better known. Without the Hardins and Hickoks, Raymond F. Adams wrote, the more or less orderly process of settlement would have been "as dull as neighborhood gossip in a country store. With them, the West was in ferment from the moment of its social emergence." [4]

The general public expected the frontier to be violent and would not have it any other way. Billy the Kid, for example, was, unquestionably, a psychopathic murderer, but it is highly doubtful that he killed half the number he is credited with. Authorities can only account for three men he killed for sure, and there were probably no more than three or four more.[5] Bat Masterson is also widely credited with killing between twenty and thirty men in gunfights, whereas the actual number was only three. Souvenir hunters constantly badgered Masterson to sell them "the gun you killed all those men with," until one day he picked up an old Colt .45 at a New York pawn shop, cut twenty-two notches in the handle, and sold it at a handsome price. The open-mouthed collector wanted assurance that it actually was the gun with which Masterson had killed twenty-two men. "I didn't tell him yes, and I didn't tell him no," Bat recalled, "and I didn't exactly lie to him. I simply said I hadn't counted Mexicans and Indians, and he went away tickled to death." [6] In reality, few of the top-notch frontier gunfighters ever resorted to violence unless they were forced to it, and then they did so only in self-defense.[7]

Most mining camps, cowtowns, and boom towns probably bore a close resemblance to Sodom and Gomorrah during their early days. Practically everyone wore sidearms, and the principal enterprises were saloons, gambling houses, and brothels. But, within a remarkably short time, schools and churches sprang up, and the various "dens of iniquity" were regulated

Most mining camps, cowtowns, and boom towns bore a close resemblance to Sodom and Gomorrah during their early days. But
within a remarkably short time schools and churches sprang up and
a reasonable degree of law and order was established. These are
street scenes of Helena, Montana, in 1865 and again a decade later.

or put out of business by blue laws. One repeatedly reads that
Dodge City, Abilene, and other Kansas cattle towns averaged
one or two killings each night during their heyday, but the
facts simply do not support the charge. In his quantitative
analysis of violence in five of the most important Kansas cattle
towns (Abilene, Dodge City, Ellsworth, Wichita, and Caldwell), Robert R. Dykstra could find no evidence that there
was ever a shoot-out on main street at high noon in any one
of these places—at least not in the fashion of the face-to-face
encounter presented thousands of times on television. His
study covered the period between 1870 and 1885, and the
statistics he compiled from local newspapers reveal that forty-
five homicides took place during that fifteen-year span—an
average of only 1.5 homicides per cattle-trading season.[8]

The number of killings never exceeded five in any one year,
and it reached that figure only in Ellsworth in 1873 and in
Dodge City in 1878. Most of the victims were law officers,
cowboys, and gamblers—several of whom were unarmed at
the time they received their fatal wounds. Although many of
the legendary gunfighters lived in the cattle towns at one time
or another, very few participated in any of the slayings. Among
those with clean records were Bat Masterson, Clay Allison,
Doc Holliday, and Ben Thompson. In 1871 the Texas outlaw
John Wesley Hardin killed one man accidentally, and Wild
Bill Hickok killed two men in Abilene the same year. One of
Hickok's victims was his deputy—shot by mistake by the any-
thing-but-cool swashbuckling town marshal. Wyatt Earp
shared credit with another Dodge City policeman for the
killing of a local law violator.[9]

Deadwood, South Dakota, has long been a favorite example of one of the most violent frontier mining towns that ever
existed. It was here, in 1876, that Hickok was shot in the back
while playing poker in a local saloon. Yet only three other
killings took place in Deadwood that year, and there was not

a single lynching—and 1876 was the most violent year in the town's history. Other crimes were committed, but the lawless aspect of the community's early history has been greatly over-emphasized, to the exclusion of other factors which made significant contributions to the town's stability and permanence.[10]

Tombstone is another famous example of a violent frontier mining town, primarily because of the celebrated fight at the OK Corral. Only five homicides occurred there in 1881, the most turbulent year of its existence, and three of the victims were killed by the Earps and Doc Holliday in the OK Corral fight. As the bodies were taken to the cemetery, local residents draped a banner over the caskets proclaiming "Murdered in the Streets of Tombstone." Moreover, a hastily organized "Citizens' Safety Committee" turned against the Earps and made it clear that any such future action on their part would result in an immediate public hanging.

By the end of 1883 the silver boom at Tombstone was over, and most of the population had drifted elsewhere. Those who remained behind searched desperately for a way to keep the community alive. They eventually cashed in on the tourist boom by inventing a myth about a town too tough to die. As Odie B. Faulk has shown in his recent history of Tombstone, the residents rediscovered the fight at the OK Corral and fashioned it into a great morality play about evil men and dark deeds. When myth ultimately blended with reality, Tombstone became known as one of the most famous—or infamous—towns in the American West.

Several hundred miles northeast of Tombstone, in Nevada, was another mining town with a well-established reputation for violence. Virginia City was still considered a lively place in 1876, when it was "one of the most thoroughly representative mining cities in America"—a collection of saloons, faro establishments, and brothels. But a foreign visitor that year expressed "disappointment" that he had failed to witness the legendary custom of a man being murdered before breakfast. Another admitted that while he was there he observed nothing but "the most perfect order and decorum." [11]

Several movies have been made and books written about the celebrated "runs" for land when Indian Territory—present Oklahoma—was opened for white settlement. With rare exception, the initial "run" of 1889 has been pictured as an orgy of claim jumping, quarreling, and murdering. It is true that some violated the rules and entered the territory and staked out claims before the legal entry date of April 22. Also, each of the 15,000 men who crowded into the boom town of Guthrie within the early hours of the opening day appeared armed to the teeth with six-shooters, knives, and perhaps a Winchester or shotgun. Contrary to "eyewitness" accounts by newspaper men—their stories having been written two or three days before the actual event and filed with a Guthrie dateline—not a single killing, gunshot wound, or fist fight took place. Disputed claims over lots frequently were settled by the flip of a coin, and those who found themselves in the middle of the street generally accepted their fate with good sportsmanship. As for the handful of "sooners" who had shaved the rules of the game and staked out choice corner lots beforehand, the majority ejected them by simple group action and without violence.

People from thirty-two states, three territories, and half a dozen foreign countries were represented at the first roll call in the late afternoon of April 22 in Guthrie. Hardly a man knew more than a dozen individuals present, outside of his immediate family. Yet within thirty-six hours after everyone had arrived at the "Magic City" on the Prairie, this heterogeneous mob had elected a mayor and a council of five members, adopted a city charter, and authorized the collection of a head tax. Within a week, Baptists, Methodists, and Presbyterians were holding church services in tents and planning the construction of permanent church buildings. The development of Oklahoma City, Edmond, Norman, and other towns that sprang up along the Santa Fe tracks on the same day paralleled that of Guthrie.[12]

Six months passed before Oklahoma Territory recorded its first homicide, a far cry from the general impression of unmitigated violence that the myth makers have created. "When youth and energy . . . and adventurers from every land under the sun joined in the famous gold-rush of 1849," a forty-niner wrote, "the marvel of marvels is, that mob-law and failure of justice were so infrequent, that society was so well and swiftly organized." [13] The same could be said about Oklahoma, or almost any other frontier boom settlement.

A standard prop in any TV western is the stage holdup by road agents, or the attack by a band of Indians. Yet during the three years that the famous Butterfield stage line operated between Missouri and California immediately before the Civil War, it was never stopped by highwaymen and it was interfered with only once by a band of Indians. For one thing, the Butterfield line, the first of the transcontinental stages, did not carry shipments of gold, as did the more famous Wells, Fargo and Company and other express and stage companies that operated before the railroads were completed. Even so, the actual cases on record of stagecoach robberies and the number of drivers and passengers killed or injured at the hands of road agents are relatively few—considering the hundreds of pack trains, expressmen, and stages that traveled the dusty roads of the West between 1848 and 1883.[14]

Another myth about frontier violence which refuses to die concerns the frequency and amount of bloodletting associated with the sheep-cattle wars of the late nineteenth century. Stories about the feuds between cattle ranchers and sheepmen are legend, but seldom do the writers get specific. Harry Sinclair Drago, who has done about as much investigating of the subject as anyone, declares that very few serious confrontations actually occurred, and that, with the possible ex-

Considering the hundreds of stages that traveled the dusty roads of the West between 1848 and 1883, the actual cases on record of robberies and murders of drivers and passengers by road agents and Indians are relatively few.

ception of the Pleasant Valley War in Arizona, none were serious enough to deserve the name of "war." And even in that celebrated affair, very few sheep were killed.[15] Another authority on the subject, C. L. Sonnichsen, author of *Ten Texas Feuds* and *I'll Die Before I'll Run*, recently observed that "Although there were fights and a few killings over barbed wire, I never knew of one of these 'difficulties' developing into a full-fledged feud between cattle ranchers and sheepmen." [16] A. S. Mercer, who had very few kind words to say about Western society of the 1880's and 1890's, nevertheless admitted that there was less stealing and lawlessness in the range country than in any other part of the world. He based his observation upon federal census statistics as well as upon personal experience.[17]

The recent attention given to the American Indian, and the guilt engendered by Dee Brown's *Bury My Heart at Wounded Knee* and Thomas Berger's *Little Big Man*, not to mention the activities of certain Indian leaders, is reversing the image of the Indian in the American mind. Indeed, he is in danger of becoming a twentieth-century noble savage who has a monopoly on understanding nature, a born conservationist possessed of a superior spirit.[18] However, as much as some modern critics may proclaim that the American people carried out a genocidal war against the original owners of the land, it is sheer fantasy to accept the notion held by some that the Indians fought according to the rules of the Geneva Convention. In the tragic conflict of which they were the chief victims, they were capable of striking terrible blows, of practicing sadistic cruelty upon their captives, and of maintaining utter contempt and hatred of white settlers. Anyone who survived a border raid or viewed the scalped body of a friend or relative was fairly certain to remain an "Indian hater" for life. The same principle applied in reverse to the Indian whose wife and children were shot down by soldiers, or who was cheated out of his land by a white man.

Writers have often left the impression that Indians and whites never really tried to understand one another because of a mutual, blind hatred. They have been fond of quoting the famous phrase attributed to General Sheridan that "The only good Indian is a dead Indian." Dee Brown, for example, has made a masterful job of selecting material that seems to fit a personal rather than a balanced view. As one reviewer wrote: "He scarcely hints at the serious concern for Indian rights on the part of the Indian Office and humanitarian reformers and the move for Indian welfare that they effected." [19] John C. Ewers, Senior Ethnologist at the Smithsonian Institution, believes that the generals who really won the Indian wars —the Crooks, Mileses, and Mackenzies—tried to understand the Indian and earn his respect: "I am impressed by the depth, the breadth, and the accuracy of the understanding of Indian life and cultures to be found in the writings of a number of army officers who served in the western Indian country before, during, and since the Indian wars," he stated in a paper presented at the Tenth Annual Western History Convention in Reno, Nevada, on October 9, 1970.[20]

Ewers points out that much of the research done by late-nineteenth-century army officers on Indians then living is still regarded as classic, and that several projects actually were the result of General Sheridan's encouragement. In addition, doctors of the Army Medical Corps stationed at the isolated frontier posts not only vaccinated Indians and cared for their wounds, but made extensive collections of Indian herbs and artifacts for the Army Medical Museum in Washington. In assessing the blame for the sorry state of Indians in the American West today, this ethnologist maintains that there is enough for all to have a share—the fur traders who introduced new and fatal diseases, misguided missionaries, aggressive soldiers, inept and dishonest Indian agents, and land-grabbing white settlers. The last group has become the most popular candidate for the scapegoat role, but Ewers bluntly states that the

Indians themselves must share some of the blame for their ill fortune, especially those who have been "the most vocal in passing the buck for their plight to the white man."

Among other authorities who have recently dared challenge the "devil theory" of American Indian policy is Father Paul Prucha of Marquette University. Prucha maintains that President Andrew Jackson, the symbol of Indian-hating Americans, has been unjustly maligned by historians for his removal of the Indians to the West. He claims that Jackson was not an Indian-hater, that his policy of removing all Eastern tribes to reservations beyond the Mississippi has to be weighed against the alternatives that faced the President in 1830. Those simply were either to destroy the Indian, or to rapidly assimilate him in white society, or to provide a standing army of sufficient strength to protect the large enclaves of Indian territories in the East from the encroachment of whites. Jackson had to deal with reality, not theory, and he sincerely believed that the policy he finally adopted would be in the best interests of the Indian himself.

The President established a reputation as an Indian fighter early in life, but Prucha presents impressive evidence that throughout his military and political career Jackson insisted upon justice and fairness toward both hostile and friendly tribes. "One of his first official acts as a major general of the Tennessee militia was to insist on the punishment of a militia officer who had instigated or at least permitted the murder of an Indian." On another occasion, when a group of Tennessee volunteers robbed a friendly Cherokee, the Commander became livid with rage and ordered that "the agents be promptly prosecuted and punished as robers [sic]." [21] Certainly, Jackson could not be classified as a great humanitarian, but he repeatedly demonstrated genuine concern for the well-being of the Indians and for their civilization. And who can argue that the Cherokees and Choctaws and other civilized tribes would have been better off today if they had been allowed to remain in Mississippi, Alabama, Georgia, and Florida?

The other side of the coin is considerably blurred when it comes to Orientals on the Western frontier. Without exception, the violence practiced against the Chinese was initiated by white Americans, whereas the Indians and Mexicans sometimes were the aggressors against the whites. And even when they were not, they were capable of answering violence with violence. Some of the worst oppressors of the Chinese in early California were Mexicans and recently arrived immigrants from Australia, Ireland, and Europe. Local sheriffs and other law officials frequently risked their lives and suffered the ridicule of friends and neighbors when they defended Chinese workers. And in no section of the country were the senseless acts of violence against Orientals more vociferously and courageously denounced than by newspaper editors and leading citizens of the communities in which the atrocities occurred.

Today, as one travels throughout the West and visits towns such as Laramie, Rock Springs, Boise, Evanston, Butte, San Francisco, and Los Angeles, it is difficult to believe that an "Oriental problem" once existed in these places. When questioned about the matter, the local editor, banker, judge, or motel operator almost invariably responds that "they are the least of our problems," or that "they are among our best citizens." Many Westerners a century ago evidently felt the same way, but it was sometimes dangerous to admit publicly that an Oriental deserved the same chance that other human beings enjoyed, or that he was even human. To a considerable extent the same was true of the attitude shown toward Mexicans.

It would be foolish to assert that racial prejudice on the part of both Anglos and Mexicans does not exist today in the former Mexican provinces of Texas, New Mexico, Arizona, and California. But most Anglos in this vast corner of the West now take considerable pride in their Spanish cultural heritage, and few would be so foolish as to claim any inherent superiority over people of Hispanic origin. They have adopted the food, architecture, crafts, words, and many of the Mexican customs as their own, and they have learned to appreciate the Latin temperament. They readily acknowledge that their ancestors were as much to blame as the Mexicans, and probably more so, for the shameful record of mutual hatred and violence that characterized so much of United States and Mexican relations.

There were few Negroes on the Western frontier, except in Texas, and fewer Jews. Two recent books reveal that many Negroes served with distinction as soldiers, and that many became exceptionally skilled as cowboys.[22] Considering the general intolerance associated with the Gilded Age, Negro soldiers and cowboys enjoyed a surprising degree of equality and prestige on the frontier. There were outstanding exceptions of course, as witness the case of the three blacks employed as cowboys on the Chisum Ranch in New Mexico. But in general, the frontier was far more tolerant of both Negroes and Jews than were the older regions in the South and Northeast.

The individualistic frontiersmen possessed many faults, but small-mindedness and petty thievery were rarely among them. A stranger was considered honest until he proved otherwise, and it was taken for granted that a traveler was welcome to help himself to a man's food and lodging if he were in need and no one was at home. (Obviously, this did not apply to a man's sluice box.) Locks symbolized an impeachment of public honesty and integrity, and frontier people frequently did not secure the door of their homes or even their places of business. A Texas historian declared that there was not one lock on a single store or office in the town of Colorado City through the 1880's:

In warm weather the merchant did not even close
the front door of his store before going home at night.
The next morning when he came to work, as apt as
not, he would find a group of freighters or cowboys
who had arrived in town during the night asleep on
the counters or floor, or perhaps someone passing
through during the night had helped himself to a pair
of California pants or a plug of chewing tobacco;
but if he did he left the price of the item where the
merchant could find it.[23]

A man's word on the frontier was in fact as good as his
bond. Doan's Store, at the Red River crossing a few miles
north of Vernon, Texas, was erected in 1874, and it was
eventually expanded to include a hotel, wagon yard, and
other enterprises. It has been estimated that more than six
million longhorns forded the river en route to Dodge City
and other cattle towns of Kansas and Nebraska during the
period of the great cattle drives. The owners of the store,
Corwin and Jonathan Doan, sold supplies and clothing on
credit and advanced money without collateral to literally
hundreds of drivers and cowboys—many of whom were complete strangers. According to J. Frank Dobie, over a period
of almost two decades the Doan brothers never lost a dime
from their customers, even though some of the cowboys often
had to ride several hundred miles out of their way to settle
their accounts.

Bancroft, in his two-volume work on violence in the California gold fields, concluded that, under the circumstances,
it was miraculous that mob law and failure of justice were
as infrequent as they were. And miners organized local society
swiftly and efficiently wherever they gathered:

In this respect the morals of the California miners
were far more pure than those of the Machiavellian

school. They would shoot their enemy, or hang the enemy of their camp, but they would not deceive him. They found a way to rule themselves and their little societies without Jesuitical cunning. They were the sons of their father Adam whose eyes had been opened to know good and evil, and when they saw wickedness coming into their camp, warned by the folly of their primogenitor, they lifted their heads and crushed it.[24]

Few were more revolted by the violence in the gold fields than Hinton Helper. At the same time, he believed that the miners displayed more real honesty and firmness than any other class of people in California did. "Taken as a body, they are a plain, straight-forward, hard working set of men, who attended to their own business without meddling in the affairs of others; and I have found as guileless hearts amongst them as ever throbbed in mortal bosom." [25] When a miner decided to quit his claim for a few days, he would stack his tools upon it, notify two or three adjoining neighbors of his intention, and go where he pleased. If he returned within the time prescribed by the rules of the camp, he was entitled to resume his claim. But if he remained absent a day longer, he had to step aside for whoever happened to find it. Miners frequently left their gold dust unguarded in their tents or cabins with little fear that it would be stolen by a neighbor.

Most frontier people were friendly, hard working, and fair-minded. But these simple virtues, along with hardships and general boredom, do not make good materials for exciting narrative. For every act of violence during the frontier period, there were thousands of examples of kindness, generosity, and sacrifice. More often than not, people worked together harmoniously for the good of the community. The majority literally practiced the biblical adage about being their "brother's keeper," and they devoted their time, money, and sometimes their lives to friends or total strangers in moments of misfortune or extreme danger.

Sir Rose Lambert Price, an Englishman who traveled extensively throughout the United States in the 1870's, observed that he had never met with more kindness, hospitality, and respect for the rights of others than in the American West: "Never once . . . in the meanest ranche [sic] or the most primitive mining camp did I ever experience the slightest discourtesy or lack of kindness." Another Englishman wrote that "Even the rough western men, the hardy sons of the Indian frontier, accustomed from boyhood to fighting for existence, were hospitable and generous to a degree hard to find in more civilized life." William Baillie-Grohman declared that when he arrived at a lonely cattle ranch it was unnecessary to make a request for accommodations. His horse was always given plenty of hay—often a scarce commodity in the West—while he received the best food available and the most comfortable bed in the house. "Many times I have extended my visit for two or three days, and yet not a penny would my host accept on parting." [26]

Professor Everett Dick, a social historian of the frontier, writes that neighborly helpfulness was manifested on every hand.

> If a prairie fire burnt a man's hay, a neighbor sent a load over to him. If he lost his crop by some accident, the neighbors each donated a few bushels to tide him over the winter. When sickness prevented the head of the house from putting in his crop, the whole neighborhood turned out with tools and in a day or two put the more unfortunate neighbor on the way toward economic stability and opportunity.[27]

In the early cattle towns, animosity invariably existed between townsmen and farmers. When the local farmers experienced a poor wheat crop in 1879, the more fortunate business and cattle men at Dodge City at first refused to lift a hand, but their womenfolk expressed anger over such indifference and soon organized a Benevolent Society to care for the needy in the immediate vicinity. Conditions worsened, and by the end of the year the Dodge City town leaders curbed their ill-feelings toward the farmers and authorized the county commissioners to purchase and distribute 7500 pounds of corn meal, 3000 pounds of flour, 500 pounds of bacon, and other staple food items. The aid undoubtedly kept many from starving, although it did not appreciably improve the mutual dislike that farmers and Dodge City residents held for one another. When the 1880 wheat crop turned out to be almost as disastrous as the previous one, urban leaders once again generously supported relief efforts for the rural people. Finally, in 1881, the Kansas state legislature established an official relief agency to handle the frontier problem. Bountiful rains later that spring ensured a good crop, and the bitter contention between the two groups in Ford County came to an end.[28]

Diaries and letters in manuscript collections provide considerable insight into the character of most frontier people. An outstanding example is found in the journal kept by John Udall, aged sixty-three, from Missouri. He and his wife started out from Independence in 1859 and, after many hardships, finally made it to Albuquerque, New Mexico. There they found several other California-bound emigrants in desperate straits, like themselves. The townspeople raised a public subscription to buy supplies and hire a guide for the remaining 900 miles of the journey. Near the California-Arizona line, Indians attacked the company and destroyed the wagons, drove off the livestock, and killed half the people.

Udall's situation was desperate. His sixty-five-year-old wife was too feeble to walk, most of his provisions were gone, and water in the region was extremely scarce. Their chances of survival were almost nil until he learned that another train from Missouri was close by. Upon joining up with the others, Udall saw immediately that their situation was almost as bad as his own. But a man from Missouri whom he had barely known previously, and who himself had lost four of his five wagons and most of his livestock, took him in. Mrs. Udall was placed in the one available wagon, and the Udalls shared what little food and water was available—at the risk of the man's own family starving to death.

A few days later another company joined the group, bringing the total number to 200 men, women, and children. They soon decided that the scarcity of water and the hostility of the Indians left them no recourse but to turn back to Albuquerque, some 400 miles across the desert. One of the men had been driving several head of cattle to California, where he hoped to stock a ranch. Even though most of the members of the company were too poor to pay, he supplied them with meat and kept them alive until a supply train from one of the New Mexican forts on the Rio Grande rescued them. The people at Albuquerque took the survivors back in, gave them clothing and food, and, in Udall's case, provided employment for him for the remainder of the winter so that he could keep his wife in food and medicine.[29]

Violence has always functioned in America, in forms varying from the crude to the sophisticated. It has been a regular force for changing the status quo, as well as for preserving it. And almost everything that has been said about it in relation to our frontier heritage contains large elements of truth. Like its symbolic representative—the American cowboy—the frontier has been the source of much of our strength as well as much of our dilemma. It has lent respectability to certain kinds of violence and provided excuses for various groups—including the government—to parade their barbarities as righteousness.[30] It has served as a reflector of the national psyche and as a never-never land wherein we can play out our fantasies. It has preserved, refined, and passed on a heritage for violence that began when the first European set foot on American soil. And it deserves no more credit or blame for what we are today than does Cain, who killed his brother Abel and thereby started the whole process.

A unique and admirable characteristic of Americans has been their ability to organize themselves smoothly and swiftly into a body politic. But as the philosopher Josiah Royce wrote, "the very ease with which a town government could be formed on paper sometimes lulled to sleep the political conscience of the ordinary man, and from the outset gave too much self-confidence in the community." [31] Indeed, the simplicity of frontier government apparatus made it easier for lawless elements to seize what government there was. When this happened, vigilante groups were formed to apprehend and punish the guilty and to put their weak government back on the right track.

Throughout the latter half of the nineteenth century, literally millions of people from eastern states and foreign countries poured into the vast region between the Mississippi River and the Pacific Coast. They came to participate in what Vernon Parrington called "the great barbecue." At no other time in the history of the world were there so many spoils to be divided among the swift, the strong, and the oppressed: land, game, furs, minerals, timber, grass, and water. Everything considered, it is miraculous that the last and largest frontier region in the United States was settled in as orderly a fashion as it was. A California pioneer recalled that "there was very little law [in Nevada County], but a large amount of good order; no churches, but a great deal of religion; no politics, but a large number of politicians; no office, and strange to say from my countrymen, no office-seekers." [32]

Graham and Gurr wrote, in their "Report to the National Commission on the Causes and Prevention of Violence," that

"Americans have always been given to a kind of historical amnesia that masks much of their turbulent past," as well as a magnified "process of selective recollection." [33] One of the results has been a tendency to over-emphasize the violent side of the frontier, in comparison to that of the cities, and to give short shrift to the peaceful and orderly side. Not only have we romanticized the violent characteristics of frontier life, we have transformed them into virtues and then tried to apply them to the elimination of crime at home and communism abroad. Unfortunately, modern society is too complex, and its problems are too difficult, to be settled by the simple solutions and direct actions of a frontier mentality.

Notes

Notes to Preface

1. Gilbert Geis, "Violence in American Society," *Current History*, LII (June 1967), p. 357.
2. There are many concepts of violence, including psychological warfare and violence to someone's psyche or livelihood. But as herein used, the word "violence" generally refers to physical aggression, especially aggression against the body.
3. Walter Prescott Webb, "An Honest Preface," reprint from the Southwest *Review* (Dallas: Southern University Press, 1951).

Notes to Chapter 1

1. For generations it has been common practice for historians to put most of the blame for the witch-hunting practices in seventeenth-century New England upon the religious fanaticism and influence of clergymen such as Michael Wigglesworth, Increase Mather, and Cotton Mather. Modern specialists on Puritanism do not accept this idea. They maintain that such men did not promote the hysteria of the period; rather, they often spoke harshly of those who "defiled their hands with the blood of the poor innocents at Salem." Moreover, the ministers were the leaders in every field of intellectual advance, and many of their difficulties resulted from the belief by the mass of the people that the clergymen were too liberal, rather than too conservative.
2. According to Pauline Maier, early uprisings often carried differ-

ent connotations for American Revolutionaries than they do today. "Not all eighteenth-century mobs simply defied the law:
some used extra legal means to implement official demands or to
enforce laws not otherwise enforceable, others in effect extended
the law in urgent situations beyond its technical limits." On some
occasions mobs took on the defense of the public welfare with
the tacit approval of the Colonial authorities. *See* Pauline Maier,
"Popular Uprisings and Civil Authority in Eighteenth-Century
America," *The William and Mary Quarterly*, XXVII, 1 (Jan.
1970), p. 4.
3. Quoted in Morton and Penn Borden (eds.), *The American Tory*
   (Englewood Cliffs, N.J.: Prentice-Hall, 1972), pp. 105–6.
4. Schlesinger's article originally appeared in *Proceedings of the
   American Philosophical Society*, IC, 4, pp. 244–50. Quoted by
   Lloyd I. Rudolph, "The Eighteenth Century Mob in America
   and Europe," *American Quarterly*, XI (1959), pp. 458–59.

Notes to Chapter II

1. Richard Maxwell Brown, "Legal and Behavioral Perspectives on
   American Vigilantism," *Perspectives in American History*, V
   (1971), p. 101 (offprint).
2. Hubert Howe Bancroft, *Popular Tribunals* (2 vols.; San Francisco: History Publishing, 1887), I, p. 152.
3. Michael Wallace, "The Use of Violence in American History,"
   The American Scholar (Winter 1970–71), p. 82. The so-called
   "upward mobility" thesis associated with Jacksonian Democracy
   has recently been challenged by Edward Pessen, "The Egalitarian Myth and the American Social Reality," *American Historical Review* (Oct. 1971), pp. 989–1034. "The pursuit of
   wealth in Jacksonian America was marked not by fluidity but
   by stability if not rigidity," Pessen wrote. "The race was indeed to the swift, but unfortunately the requisite swiftness was
   beyond the power of ordinary men to attain."
4. Quoted from "Introduction" to Tocqueville's *Democracy in
   America* (New York: Oxford University Press, 1946), p. xviii.
5. *Ibid.* pp. xviii–xix.
6. Quoted in Charles N. Glaab (ed.), *The American City: A Documentary History* (Homewood, Ill.: Dorsey Press, 1963), p.
   55, from Henry Reeve's 1839 translation of Tocqueville, *Democracy in America*, p. 89.

7. Leonard L. Richards, *Gentleman of Property and Standing: Anti-Abolition Mobs in Jacksonian America* (New York: Oxford University Press, 1970), pp. 11–14.

In 1850 a boy from London, recently arrived in the United States, wrote to his mother that New York was a city that combined luxury, violence, and dirt, and that it was generally agreed that the police were of no practical value whatsoever. "Now I will tell you something about the country," he continued. "Provisions are very cheap; plenty of work to be had; clothes are dear, but men paid well for their work; house rent is very dear in New York; it is a very healthy place; guns and pistols are very cheap. . . ." Quoted in Terry Coleman, *Passage to America: A History of Emigrants from Great Britain and Ireland to America in Mid-nineteenth Century* (London: Hutchinson, 1972), p. 158.

8. Ray Allen Billington, *The Protestant Crusade, 1800–1860* (New York: Macmillan, 1938), p. 42.

9. Clement Eaton: "Mob Violence in the Old South," *Mississippi Valley Historical Review*, XXIX (Dec. 1942), pp. 351–70.

It is ironic that, on the one hand, Southerners could have so much reverence for the federal Constitution and the Bible, and yet, on the other, they could accept mob rule in lieu of legal courts and judges. Small wonder that during Reconstruction they turned so readily to lynch law and to organizations such as the Ku Klux Klan, and that this tendency would hold on long after urbanization and industrialization had established a firm foothold.

10. Quoted in Thomas Rose (ed.), *Violence in America: A Historical and Contemporary Reader* (New York: Vintage, 1970), p. 122.

11. Richards, *Gentlemen of Property and Standing*, p. 5.

12. Quoted in Melvin Steinfield, *Cracks in the Melting Pot: Racism and Discrimination in American History* (Beverly Hills, Calif.: Glencoe Press, 1970), p. 198.

13. *Ibid.* p. 175.

14. David Abrahamsen, *Our Violent Society* (New York: Funk & Wagnalls, 1970), p. 205.

15. Quoted in Steinfield, *Cracks in the Melting Pot*, p. 71.

16. Quoted in Irving J. Sloan, *Our Violent Past: An American Chronicle* (New York: Random House, 1970), p. 133.

17. Perhaps the most objective and scholarly account of the inci-

dent in southern Utah is by Juanita Brooks, *The Mountain Meadows Massacre* (Norman: University of Oklahoma Press, rev. ed., 1962).

18. Recent events have demonstrated more than ever that the cliché about the "melting pot" is less than fact. Indeed, some militant leaders are now comparing American society to "vegetable soup," the ingredients of which retain their separate identities regardless of how long the pot remains on the burner.

19. This is not to say that the settlement of Australia in the eighteenth and nineteenth centuries was carried out nonviolently. Rather, the violence there was directed much more exclusively against the Aborigines. Outright slaughter with guns and the decimation of thousands of the original owners of the land by epidemic diseases resembles in many respects the fate of the California Indians. On the large island of Tasmania, the white settlers conducted such an efficient campaign of genocide that by 1900 not a single native was left alive. See Wilbur R. Jacobs' scholarly essay, "The Price of Progress: Native People on the European Frontiers of Australia, New Guinea, and North America" [reprinted as Chapter XI in Jacobs, *Dispossessing the American Indian* (New York: Scribner's, 1972), pp. 126–50.]

The French and British settlers in Canada were much more dependent upon the Indians as a source of furs and as an outlet for their manufactured goods than the Americans were. Obviously, it did not make much sense to kill off the very people one depended upon for existence. White settlers of the American frontier wanted the Indian's land much more than they wanted his furs.

Notes to Chapter III

1. William Ransom Hogan, *The Texas Republic: A Social and Economic History* (Norman: University of Oklahoma Press, 1946), p. 298.

2. Rodolfo Acuña, *Occupied America: The Chicano's Struggle Toward Liberation* (San Francisco: Canfield Press, 1972), p. 7.

3. Quoted from General Teran's report, in Walter Prescott Webb, *The Texas Rangers: A Century of Defense* (Boston: Houghton Mifflin, 1935), p. 22.

4. The use of the terms "massacre" and "battle" frequently depends upon who won and who lost. For example, the Mexicans

considered the attack on the Alamo in 1836 as a great military victory, but the Texans referred to it as an outright massacre. The situation was reversed in respect to the engagement at San Jacinto a few weeks later, when the Mexicans suffered a humiliating defeat. " 'Remember the Alamo!' colored Anglo attitudes toward Mexicans, for it served to stereotype the Mexican eternally as the enemy and the Texas patriots as the stalwarts of freedom and domocracy." Acuña, *Occupied America,* p. 10.

5. Carey McWilliams, *North from Mexico: The Spanish-speaking People of the United States* (New York: Greenwood Press, 1968), p. 103.

6. Quoted from *Green's Journal of the Expedition Against Mier,* in Leonard Pitt, *The Decline of the Californios: A Social History of the Spanish Speaking Californians, 1846–1890* (Berkeley: University of California Press, 1971), p. 60.

7. Samuel E. Chamberlin, "My Confessions," Part I, *Life* (July 23, 1956), p. 75.

8. Ben Proctor, "The Modern Texas Ranger: A Law Enforcement Dilemma in the Rio Grande Valley" (unpublished article), p. 1.

9. *Ibid.* (Comments on Proctor's manuscript are by Philip D. Jordan.)

10. *The Handbook of Texas* (2 vols; Austin: The Texas Historical Association, 1952), I, p. 424.

11. W. Eugene Hollon (ed.), *William Bollaert's Texas* (Norman: University of Oklahoma Press, 1956), p. 272.

12. Rupert N. Richardson, Earnest Wallace, and Adrian N. Anderson, *Texas: The Lone Star State* (Englewood Cliffs, N. J.: Prentice-Hall, 1970), p. 149.

13. Hollon (ed.), *William Bollaert's Texas,* p. 271.

14. Richard Hofstadter and Michael Wallace (eds.), *American Violence: A Documentary History* (New York: Knopf, 1970), pp. 202–3.

15. William W. White, "The Texas Slave Insurrection of 1860," *The Southwestern Historical Quarterly,* LII, 3 (Jan. 1949), pp. 259–85.

16. William L. Katz (ed.), *Eyewitness: The Negro in American History* (New York: Pitman, 1968), pp. 253–54.

17. The Special Committee on Lawlessness and Violence was appointed by Davis on June 6, 1868. The crime statistics subsequently submitted to the convention were generally accepted

as valid by both radical and conservative members. A printed copy of the committee's report is in the Thomas W. Streeter Texas Collection, Yale University Library.

18. Billy Bob Lightfoot, "The Negro Exodus from Comanche County, Texas," *The Southwestern Historical Quarterly*, LVI, 3 (Jan. 1953), pp. 407–16.

19. Greenville, the county seat of Hunt County, in northeast Texas where I grew up, was famous for many decades because of the large electric sign spanning Main Street, which read as follows: "Greenville, Home of the Blackest Land and the Whitest People." Until the mid-1950's, when the sign was removed, the city fathers were unaware, or unconcerned, that it represented an affront to the large black population of the area.

20. *Thirty Years of Lynching in the United States, 1889–1918* (New York: National Association for the Advancement of Colored People, 1919), p. 7. Several studies have been made of lynchings in the United States for the period between the 1880's and late 1920's. Discrepancies exist, but the various statistics compiled are all based upon cases that could be verified. Unquestionably, there were some lynchings that never got reported in newspapers and thus do not show up in statistical tables.

21. Walter F. White, *Rope & Faggot: A Biography of Judge Lynch* (New York: Knopf, 1929), pp. 21–22.

22. *Thirty Years of Lynching in the United States, 1889–1918*, p. 12.

23. *See* note 17, above, "Report of Special Committee on Lawlessness and Violence in Texas," p. 9.

24. Ann Patton Baenzinger, "The Texas State Police During Reconstruction: A Reexamination," *Southwest Historical Quarterly*, LXXII, No. 4, (April 1969), p. 473; Carl Coke Rister, "Outlaws and Vigilantes of the Southern Plains, 1865–1885," *Mississippi Valley Historical Review*, XIX (1932–33), p. 544.

25. Hugh David Graham and Ted Robert Gurr (eds.), *The History of Violence in America: Historical and Comparative Perspectives. (Report to the National Commission on the Causes and Prevention of Violence)* (New York: Praeger, 1969), p. 162.

26. *Ibid.* pp. 187–88.

27. *Ibid.* p. 143.

28. Quoted in Lewis Nordyke, *John Wesley Hardin: Texas Gunman* (New York: William Morrow, 1957), p. i.

29. Floyd Benjamin Streeter, *Ben Thompson: Man with a Gun* (New York: Frederick Fell, 1957), pp. 9–16.

Notes to Chapter IV

1. Quoted in Robert F. Heizer and Allen F. Almquist, *The Other Californians* (Berkeley: University of California Press, 1971), p. 201, from G. F. Parsons, *The Life and Adventures of James W. Marshall* (1870).

2. This statement may sound naïve in view of recent events at Kent State and Jackson State universities, not to mention the Vietnam War itself. But never again will the people of this country tolerate the mass killing or enslavement of Indians or Chinese for the crime of belonging to a minority group. The conscience of America is now answering for the racial misdeeds of the eighteenth and nineteenth centuries, just as future generations will have to answer for the violence of the 1960's and 1970's.

3. Quoted in Heizer and Almquist, *The Other Californians*, p. 4.

4. T. H. Hittell, *History of California* (4 vols; San Francisco: Pacific Press Publishing House, 1885) I, p. 563.

5. Zenas Leonard, *The Adventures of Zenas Leonard, Fur Trader and Trapper, 1831–1836* (Cleveland: Burrows Bros., 1904, p. 222.

6. C. L. Camp (ed.), *James Clayman, American Frontiersman, 1792–1881: the Adventures of a Trapper and Covered Wagon Emigrant as Told in His Own Reminiscences and Diaries* (Los Angeles: California Historical Society, 1928), pp. 173–74.

7. "Among the Diggers of Thirty Years Ago," *The Overland Monthly*, XVI, 2nd Series (July–Dec. 1890), p. 392.

8. Dale L. Morgan and James R. Scobie (eds.), *William Perkins' Journal of Life at Sonora, 1849–1852* (Berkeley: University of California Press, 1964), p. 123.

9. Quoted in Alvin M. Josephy, Jr., *et al.* (eds.), *The American Heritage Book of Indians* (New York: American Heritage, 1961), p. 305.

10. *George C. Yount and His Chronicles of the West, Comprising Extracts from His "Memoirs" and From the Orange Clark "Narrative"* (Denver: Old West Publishing, 1966), p. 155.

11. Morgan and Scobie (eds.), *William Perkins' Journal*, p. 124.

12. Leonard Pitt, *The Decline of the Californios: A Social History*

of the Spanish-speaking Californians, 1846–1890 (Berkeley: University of California Press, 1966).

13. The California Foreign Miners' Tax Law was passed by the state's first legislature on April 13, 1850. It was repealed the next year, but re-enacted in 1853, with the rate then fixed at the more reasonable sum of four dollars per month. *See* Hittell, *History of California,* III, pp. 251–71.

14. Charles Howard Shinn, *Mining Camps: A Study in American Frontier Government,* ed. by Rodman Wilson Paul (New York: Harper & Row, 1965), p. 218.

15. Pitt, *The Decline of the Californios,* p. 62.

16. Quoted by Heizer and Almquist, *The Other Californians,* p. 148, from Clarence King, *Mountaineering in the Sierra Nevada* (1872).

17. *Ibid.*

18. Morgan and Scobie (eds.), *William Perkins' Journal,* pp. 143–44.

19. *Ibid.* p. 237.

20. *Ibid.* pp. 167–68.

21. Robert Glass Clelend, *Cattle on a Thousand Hills: Southern California, 1850–80* (San Marino, Calif.: Huntington Library, 1969), p. 58.

22. Sweetser's original letter, addressed to "Dear Friend" and dated February 26, 1851, is in the Manuscripts Collection of the Huntington Library.

23. Hinton P. Helper, *Land of Gold* (Baltimore: H. Taylor, 1855), pp. 172–74.

24. Richard Maxwell Brown, "American Regulators and Vigilance: An Hypothesis," paper read at the annual meeting of the Mississippi Valley Historical Association, Cleveland, Ohio, May 1, 1964. *See also* Barton C. Olsen, "Vigilantes in the West: A Second Look," paper read at the annual meeting of the Western Historical Association, Tucson, Ariz.: Oct. 12, 1968.

25. Elizabeth Margo, *Taming the Forty-niner* (New York: Rinehart, 1955), p. 139.

26. Hubert Howe Bancroft, *Popular Tribunals* (2 vols; San Francisco: History Company, Publishers, 1887), I, p. 747.

27. *Ibid.* pp. 131–32.

28. Henry J. Labatt, "Jewish Business Interest in California," *True Pacific Messenger* (San Francisco, May 24, 1861), reprinted in *A Documentary History of the Jews in the United States, 1654–*

1875, ed. by Morris U. Schappes (New York: Citadel, 1950),
p. 442.

29. Robert Levinson to author, Aug. 30, 1972.
30. Labatt, "Jewish Business Interest in California," in Schappes
    (ed.), *Documentary History of the Jews in the United States,*
    p. 443.

Notes to Chapter V

1. David DuFault, "The Chinese in the Mining Camps of California: 1848–1870," *The Historical Society of Southern California Quarterly,* XLI, 2 (July 1959), p. 155.
2. Quoted from a reprint article in a long series published in the
   Sacramento Bee, Jan. 21, 1886, under the title, "Chinese in Early
   Days."
3. *Ibid.*
4. *Ibid.*
5. Hinton Helper, *Land of Gold* (Baltimore: H. Taylor, 1855),
   pp. 172–74.
6. Richard Dillon, *The Hatchet Men: The Story of the Tong
   Wars in San Francisco's Chinatown* (New York: Coward-
   McCann, 1962), pp. 75–76.
7. Quoted in Melvin Steinfield, *Cracks in the Melting Pot: Racism
   and Discrimination in American History* (Beverly Hills, Calif.:
   Glencoe Press, 1970), p. 126.
8. DuFault, "The Chinese in the Mining Camps of California," pp.
   159–60.
9. There are several versions of the tong wars in the mining camps
   in 1854 and 1856. The brief accounts herein described of the engagement are presented by Gunther Barth, *Bitter Strength,
   1850–1870* (Cambridge: Harvard University Press, 1964), pp.
   94–95.
10. Robert Louis Stevenson, *Across the Plains* (London: Chatto &
    Windus, 1905), pp. 41–45.
11. Quoted from the *Eighteenth Annual Report of the Women's
    Union Mission of San Francisco to Chinese Women and Chil-
    dren for the Year 1887* (San Francisco, 1888), in Robert Seager
    II, "Some Denominational Reaction to Chinese Immigration to
    California, 1856–1892," *Pacific Coast Historical Review,* XXVIII
    (1959), pp. 49–66.

12. *Ibid.*

13. Quoted in Elmer Sandmeyer, *The Anti-Chinese Movement in California* (Urbana, Ill.: University of Illinois Press, 1939), p. 25. These charges were repeated in so many speeches, reports, editorials, and articles that they obviously were believed by a majority of Californians. For the most recent interpretation of the causes of hatred of the Chinese, see Alexander P. Saxton, *The Indispensable Enemy: Labor and the Anti-Chinese Movement in California* (Berkeley: University of California Press, 1971).

14. *Copper Camp: Stories of the World's Greatest Mining Town, Butte, Montana,* compiled by the Members of Writers Program of the Works Projects Administration in State of Montana (New York: Hastings House, 1943), p. 108.

15. In 1878 the city council changed the name of "Nigger Alley" to "Los Angeles Street."

16. This incident has been described in many books and articles, and, except for minor details, the stories are essentially the same. However, one finds the amount of money which Dr. Gene Tong offered for his life varying from $1000 to $15,000.

17. C. P. Dorland, "The Chinese Massacre at Los Angeles in 1871," *Historical Society of Southern California Annual,* III (Los Angeles, 1894), p. 25.

18. Paul M. De Falla, "Lanterns in the Western Sky," *Historical Society of Southern California Quarterly,* XLII, 1 (1960), p. 58.

19. David G. Thomas, "Memories of the Chinese Riot," *Annals of Wyoming,* XIX–XX (1947–48), p. 105–11.

20. See Isaac Hill Bromley, *The Chinese Massacre at Rock Springs, Wyoming Territory, September 2, 1885* (Boston: Franklin Press, 1886), for the most complete and objective account published during the period. Primary sources for the "Rock Springs Massacre" are contained in the *Report of the Governor of Wyoming,* Nov. 25, 1885, 49th Cong., 1st sess., House Exec. Doc. 12, No. 1, part 5, II (serial 2379).

21. *Overland Monthly* (San Francisco), VI, 34, 2nd Series (Oct. 1885), p. 442.

22. Perhaps the most concise and objective account of this movement is W. P. Wilcox, "Anti-Chinese Riots in Washington," *The Washington Historical Quarterly,* XX, 3 (July 1929), pp. 204–12. *See also* George Kinnear, *Anti-Chinese Riots at Seattle, Wn., February 8th, 1886* (Seattle, Wash., privately printed, Feb.

8, 1911); and Clinton A. Snowden, *History of Washington* (4 vols., New York: Century History, 1909), IV, pp. 319–45.

23. Kenneth Owens, "Pierce City Incident, 1885–1886," *Idaho Yesterdays*, III, 3 (Fall 1959), p. 9.

24. *Ibid.* p. 10.

25. "Report of Governor Stevenson to Secretary of State Bayard," Aug. 2, 1886, Idaho Territorial Papers, Interior Department. (*See also* Owens, "Pierce City Incident.")

26. For a recent account of the Japanese story, see Roger Daniels, *The Politics of Prejudice: The Anti-Japanese Movement in California and the Struggle for Japanese Exclusion* (Berkeley: University of California Publications in History, 1962).

Notes to Chapter VI

1. Richard Hofstadter and Michael Wallace (eds.), *American Violence: A Documentary History* (New York: Knopf, 1970), p. 14.

2. Hofstadter, "America as a Gun Culture," *American Heritage*, XXI, 6 (Oct. 1970), p. 10.

3. Senator Joseph Tydings, "Americans and the Gun," *Playboy*, XVI, 3 (March 1969), p. 208.

4. Stanley Vestal, *Queen of Cowtowns Dodge City: The Wickedest Little City in America, 1872–1886* (New York: Harper & Brothers, 1952), pp. 7–8.

5. Walter Prescott Webb, *The Great Plains* (Boston: Ginn, 1931), p. 179.

6. Joseph G. Rosa, *The Gunfighter: Man or Myth?* (Norman: University of Oklahoma Press, 1968), p. 167.

7. In 1835, Samuel Colt of Hartford, Connecticut, received a patent in England on a percussion "revolving breech pistol." The next year he patented it in the United States. During the next twenty-five years his revolver underwent numerous modifications and became the model for many imitations.

8. *Time*, June 21, 1968, p. 18. In June 1971, Art Buchwald wrote, in his usual satirical style, the following observation about the gun as a phallic symbol: "Most American men who own guns have virility problems. The gun is an extension of their manhood. If you take the gun away from a man in this country you've emasculated him. . . . Every American child, from the day he can watch westerns on television, knows that guns and

virility go together, and you can't have one without the other.
So when you talk about disarming the people of this country,
you're dealing with a Freudian problem which no gun owner
will face up to."

9. Hofstadter, "America as a Gun Culture," p. 82.
10. Hubert Howe Bancroft, *Popular Tribunals*, I (San Francisco:
History Company, Publishers, 1887), p. 121.
11. *Ibid.* pp. 120–21.
12. This term was used by the proslavery people to mean "thief,"
and in time all of Free-State people of Kansas came to be called
Jayhawkers. Today the football team of the University of Kansas is affectionately called the Jayhawkers by their fans, while
the near-by Oklahoma team is known as the Sooners. Both
words were originally used in a derisive sense in reference to
those who disregarded the law.
13. George D. Hendricks, *The Bad Man of the West* (San Antonio: Naylor, 1959), p. 10.
14. Carl W. Breiham, *Quantrill and His Civil War Guerrillas* (Denver: Sage Books, 1959), pp. 168–74.
15. Paul I. Wellman, *A Dynasty of Western Outlaws* (Garden
City, N.Y.: Doubleday, 1961), p. 13.
16. Quoted from Michael Antonio Otero, *My Life on the Frontier,
1864–1882*, in Joe B. Frantz and Julian Ernest Choate, Jr., *The
American Cowboy: The Myth and the Reality* (Norman: University of Oklahoma Press, 1955), p. 90.
17. Estimates of the number of Billy's victims, like those of Lieutenant Calley, vary greatly. Calley admitted shooting twenty-
two men, women, and children at a distance of five feet with a
submachine gun. This is about the same number that generally
is attributed to Billy the Kid. However, one authority states
that Billy only killed three men for certain, and probably three
or four more. *See* Frantz and Choate, *The American Cowboy*,
p. 95n.
18. Webb, *The Great Plains*, pp. 495–96.
19. *Time*, June 21, 1968, p. 13.
20. Paul Good, "Blam! Blam! Blam! Not Gun Nuts, but Pistol Enthusiasts," *New York Times Magazine* (Sept. 18, 1972), p. 28.

Notes to Chapter VII

1. Quoted in Francis Paul Prucha (ed.), *The Indian in American
History* (New York: Holt, Rinehart, & Winston, 1971), p. 10.

2. *Bradford's History of Plymouth Plantation, from Governor William Bradford's Original Manuscript* (Boston: Wright and Potter, 1899), pp. 33–34.

3. Quoted in Dee Brown, *Bury My Heart at Wounded Knee: An Indian History of the American West* (New York: Holt, Rinehart, & Winston, 1970), p. 1.

4. Quoted in Alvin M. Josephy Jr., "The Custer Myth," *Life* (July 2, 1971), p. 56.

5. The phrase was first used by John L. O'Sullivan, the fighting Irish editor of the *Democratic Review*, in various editorials written during the summer of 1845 in an attempt to justify the annexation of Texas.

6. Herman Melville, *The Confidence Man: His Masquerade* (New York: Grove Press, 1955), p. 172.

7. *Ibid.* p. 174.

8. Wilbur R. Jacobs, *Dispossessing the American Indian* (New York: Scribner's, 1972), p. 108

9. *Bradford's History of Plymouth Plantation*, pp. 425–26.

10. Alvin M. Josephy Jr., *The Patriot Chiefs: A Chronicle of Indian Resistance* (New York: Viking, 1969), p. 159.

11. Quoted in Jacobs, *Dispossessing the American Indian*, p. 59.

12. Helen Hunt Jackson, *A Century of Dishonor: A Sketch of the United States Government's Dealing with Some of the Indian Tribes* (New York: Harper & Brothers, 1881), p. 29.

13. Stanley Vestal, *Warpath and Council Fire* (New York: Random House, 1948), p. 118.

14. Don Russell, "The Indians and Soldiers of the American West," in Jay Monaghan, *The Book of the American West* (New York: Julian Messner, 1963), p. 130.

15. George Bird Grinnell, *The Fighting Cheyenne* (Norman: University of Oklahoma Press, 1956), p. 180.

16. According to Donald J. Berthrong, Custer's figures are greatly exaggerated. Bethrong cites different sources which range from 9 to 20 Indian men killed, along with 18 to 40 women and children. *See* Berthrong, *The Southern Cheyenne* (Norman: University of Oklahoma Press, 1963), p. 328.

17. Quoted in Thomas Clark, *Frontier America: The Story of the Westward Movement* (New York: Scribner's, 1959), p. 627.

18. The events at Sand Creek and Washita were realistically presented in the movie *Little Big Man*. But in the Little Big Horn battle scene Custer was caricatured as a half-crazed buffoon. Even the General's defenders can hardly deny the man's arro-

gance, but few detractors go so far as to proclaim that Custer was a madman—as the movie implied.

19. These figures are based upon official army records and quoted in Alvin Josephy Jr., *The Nez Percé Indians and the Opening of the Northwest* (New Haven: Yale University Press, 1965), pp. 632–33. They are fairly consistent with other sources.

20. These words from Chief Joseph's speech are generally considered to be among the most memorable ever uttered by an American Indian. However, some authorities, notably Professor Paul Prucha, have suggested that the closing sentence was paraphrased from a Protestant missionary's sermon and was by no means original with Chief Joseph.

21. Estimates of the number of Indians killed at Wounded Knee vary considerably. Dee Brown claims that 153 were known dead, and that many of the wounded that crawled away died shortly thereafter. Alvin Josephy, Jr., puts the total number of Indians killed at approximately 300.

22. According to the United States Census, in 1970 there were 793,-000 Indians in the United States, including Alaska. More than 400,000 of these currently reside on 277 reservations which vary in size from tiny settlements in California of only a few acres to the 11 million-acre Navajo Reservation in Arizona, New Mexico, and Utah. The life expectancy of the average Indian in 1970 was 47 years; it was 70.8 for the United States as a whole. The median Indian family income in 1971 was $4000, while the national median was $9867; infant mortality among Indians was 30.9 per 1000, while nationwide it was 21.8; and the unemployment rate of Indians in 1972 was estimated to be 45 per cent, while it was 5.8 per cent for the entire United States. There is little wonder that the rate of Indian suicide was exactly twice that of the United States population, or 32 per 100,000. *See New York Times*, Nov. 12, 1972.

23. *Newsweek* (Feb. 1, 1971), p. 69.

Notes to Chapter VIII

1. Professor Thomas J. Dimsdale, *The Vigilantes of Montana* (reprinted from the 1866 original edition by the University of Oklahoma Press, 1953, as Volume I of The Western Frontier Library).

2. Hoffman Birney, *Vigilantes* (Philadelphia: Penn Publishing, 1929), p. 251.

3. Daniel J. Boorstin, *The Americans: The National Experience* (New York: Random House, 1965), p. 88.

4. Dimsdale, *The Vigilantes of Montana*, p. 204.

5. Mark Twain, *Roughing It* (Hartford, Conn.: American Publishing, 1872), p. 80.

6. Dimsdale, *The Vigilantes of Montana*, p. 196.

7. Birney, *Vigilantes*, p. 309.

8. Dimsdale, *The Vigilantes of Montana*, p. 200.

9. Helena Huntington Smith, *The War on Powder River* (New York: McGraw-Hill, 1966), p. xii.

10. Maurice Fink, W. Turrentine Jackson, and Agnes Wright Spring, *When Grass Was King* (Boulder: University of Colorado Press, 1956), p. 104.

11. Smith, *War on Powder River*, p. 130.

12. A. C. Mercer, *The Banditti of the Plains, or The Cattlemen's Invasion of Wyoming, 1892* (reprinted from the original 1894 edition by the University of Oklahoma Press, 1954, as Volume II of The Western Frontier Library), p. 20.

13. Harry Sinclair Drago, *The Great Range Wars: Violence on the Grasslands* (New York: Dodd, Mead, 1970), p. 275.

14. John Clay, *My Life on the Range* (New York: Antiquarian Press, 1961), p. 277.

15. Champion's diary was recovered from his blood-stained body and transcribed by one of the newspaper reporters who had gone with the invaders. The narrative was later published in the *Chicago Herald* and the Cheyenne *Leader*, but the original has long since disappeared.

16. Two Texans died during the invasion as a result of shooting themselves accidentally in the thigh. Another escaped detection, but he later surrendered to the sheriff at Buffalo and wrote a detailed description of the whole affair. *See* "The Confessions of George Dunning," in A. C. Mercer, *The Banditti of the Plains*, Appendix.

17. James D. Horan and Paul Sann, *Pictorial History of the Wild West* (New York: Crown, 1954), p. 205.

18. Joseph G. Rosa, *The Gunfighter: Man or Myth?* (Norman: University of Oklahoma Press, 1968), p. 43.

19. Letter from T. A. Larson, Laramie, Wyo., to the author, Feb. 2, 1973. Professor Larson claims that Big Nose was hanged in

1881, not 1882. Also, he is not positive whether Dr. Osborne relieved the victim of some of his parts at the time of the autopsy, or whether he exhumed the body several weeks later. Charles Kelley, in *The Outlaw Trail: A History of Butch Cassidy and his Wild Bunch*, states that the good doctor dug up the body "for medical purposes" several months after the lynching.

Notes to Chapter IX

1. Henry P. Walker, "Retire Peaceably to Your Homes: Arizona Faces Martial Law, 1882" (unpublished manuscript), p. 4.
2. Walter Prescott Webb (ed.), *The Handbook of Texas* (Austin: Texas Historical Association, 1952), I, p. 590.
3. Emerson Hough, *The Story of the Outlaw: A Study of the Western Desperado* (New York: Outing Publishing, 1907), p. 256.
4. Walker, "Retire Peaceably to Your Homes," p. 1.
5. This figure varies slightly from source to source. Joe B. Frantz states that within five years all peaceable ranchers had been driven from the country, and that 26 cattlemen and 6 sheepmen had been killed ("The Frontier Tradition: An Invitation to Violence," Chapter IV, *The History of Violence in America*, op. cit., p. 136). For brief and popular accounts of the Tewksbury-Graham feud, see Odie B. Faulk, *Arizona: A Short History* (Norman: University of Oklahoma Press, 1970) and Harry Sinclair Drago, *The Great Range Wars*, op. cit.
6. *New York Times*, Feb. 8, 1882.
7. Quoted in Richard O'Connor, *Bat Masterson: A Biography of One of the West's Most Famous Gunfighters and Marshals* (New York: Doubleday, 1957), p. 97.
8. Odie B. Faulk, *Tombstone: Myth and Reality* (New York: Oxford University Press, 1972), pp. 149–59.
9. Quoted in Ralph Emerson Twitchell, *The Leading Facts of New Mexican History* (Albuquerque: Horn & Wallace, 1963), II, p. 418n.
10. A facsimile reproduction of the poster is presented as a frontispiece in James D. Horan and Paul Sann, *Pictorial History of the Wild West* (New York: Crown Publishers, 1954).
11. Rodolfo Acuña, *Occupied America: The Chicano's Struggle Toward Liberation* (San Francisco: Canfield Press, 1972), p. 69.
12. William A. Keleher, *Violence in Lincoln County, 1869–1881* (Albuquerque: University of New Mexico Press, 1957), p. xiii.

13. New Mexican historian Ralph Emerson Twitchell believes that that figure represents a considerable exaggeration, although he himself offers no estimate of the total number killed in the Lincoln County War. Twitchell, *Leading Facts*, II, p. 418n.

14. *History of the Chisum War, or Life of Ike Ridge: Stirring Events of Cowboy Life on the Frontier*, p. 44 (original edition in the Huntington Library, San Marino, Calif.; no date; no publisher).

15. Warren A. Beck, *New Mexico: A History of Four Centuries* (Norman: University of Oklahoma Press, 1962), p. 165, p. 165n.

16. Colfax County and the Maxwell Land Grant region represented the coming together of three American frontiers in one place: mining, ranching, and transportation. "Colfax County, then, was in essence the scene of a fight between men who held an American or public domain concept of the frontier and an organization which insisted that the region, because of its Spanish-Mexican origins, was private property." Howard Robert Lamar, *The Far Southwest, 1846–1912: A Territorial History* (New Haven: Yale University Press, 1966), p. 155.

17. See Chapter III, note 17, for what is perhaps a more realistic figure of the number of men the Kid killed during his twenty-one years of life.

18. Quoted in Kent Ladd Steckmesser, *The Western Hero in History and Legend* (Norman: University of Oklahoma Press, 1965), p. 70.

19. *Ibid.* p. 57.

20. Beck, *New Mexico*, p. 173.

21. Acuña, *Occupied America*, p. 73.

22. *Ibid.* p. 74.

23. Robert W. Larson: "The 'White Caps' of New Mexico: The Political and Ethnic Origins of Western Violence" (unpublished manuscript), pp. 9–10.

24. For a recent, detailed account of the murder, see A. M. Gibson, *The Life and Death of Colonel Albert Jennings Fountain* (Norman: University of Oklahoma Press, 1965). Gibson utilizes previously unavailable documents in the Fountain murder case.

Notes to Chapter X

1. Gary L. Roberts, "The West's Gunmen," *The American West*, VIII, 2 (March 1971), p. 61.

2. Walter Prescott Webb, "The American West, Perpetual Mirage," *Harper's*, 214, 1284 (May 1957), p. 31.

3. *Life*, LI (Oct. 20, 1961), p. 4.

4. Quoted in Roberts, "The West's Gunmen," p. 61.

5. See Chapter VI, note 17.

6. Quoted in Joseph G. Rosa, *The Gunfighter: Man or Myth?* (Norman: University of Oklahoma Press, 1968), p. 122.

7. Kent Ladd Steckmesser, *The Western Hero in History and Legend* (Norman: University of Oklahoma Press, 1965), p. 139.

8. Robert R. Dykstra, *The Cattle Towns: A Social History of the Kansas Cattle Trading Centers* (New York: Knopf, 1968), pp. 144–46.

9. *Ibid.* p. 143.

10. *Montana: The Magazine of Western History*, XX, 1 (Winter, 1970), p. 47.

11. Robert Athearn, *Westward the Briton* (New York: Scribner's, 1953), pp. 59–60.

12. See W. Eugene Hollon, "Rushing for Land: Oklahoma 1889," *The American West*, III, 4 (Fall 1966), for a brief account of the first land rush and settlement of Guthrie. The article is based upon primary sources, particularly those in the Fred L. Wenner Collection, Manuscripts Division, University of Oklahoma.

13. Charles Howard Shinn, *Mining Camps: A Study of American Frontier Government*, ed. by Rodman W. Paul (New York: Harper & Row, 1965), p. 230.

14. Oscar O. Winther, *Via Western Express & Stagecoach* (Lincoln: University of Nebraska Press, 1968), pp. 81, 98.

15. Harry Sinclair Drago, *The Great Range Wars: Violence on the Grasslands* (New York: Dodd, Mead, 1970), p. v.

16. C. L. Sonnichsen to author, March 12, 1973.

17. A. S. Mercer, *The Banditti of the Plains* (Cheyenne, Wyo., 1894, privately printed; reprinted by the University of Oklahoma Press, 1954), pp. 6–7.

18. Howard R. Lamar, "The New Old West," *Yale Alumni Magazine* (Oct. 1972), pp. 9–10.

19. *American Historical Review*, LXXVII, 2 (April 1972), p. 589.

20. Ewer's paper was published as an article entitled "When Red and White Men Met," *Western Historical Quarterly*, II, 2 (April 1971), pp. 133–50.

21. Francis Paul Prucha, "Andrew Jackson's Indian Policy," *The*

Indians in American History (New York: Holt, Rinehart, & Winston, 1971), pp. 67–74.

22. William H. Leckie, *The Buffalo Soldier: A Narrative of the Negro Cavalry in the West* (Norman: University of Oklahoma Press, 1967); Philip Durham and Everett L. Jones, *The Negro Cowboy* (New York: Dodd, Mead, 1965).

23. William C. Holden, "Law and Lawlessness on the Texas Frontier 1875–1890," *The Southwestern Historical Quarterly*, XLIV (Oct. 1940), pp. 202–3.

24. *The Works of Hubert Howe Bancroft*, XXXVI, *Popular Tribunals* (San Francisco: History Publishing, 1887), I, pp. 142–43.

25. Hinton Helper, *Land of Gold* (Baltimore: H. Taylor, 1885), p. 153.

26. Athearn, *Westward the Briton*, pp. 62–63.

27. Everett Dick, *The Sod-House Frontier 1854–1890: A Social History of the Northern Plains from the Creation of Kansas and Nebraska to the Admission of the Dakotas* (New York: D. Appleton Century, 1937), pp. 248–49.

28. Robert R. Dykstra, *The Cattle Towns* (New York: Knopf, 1968), pp. 201–6.

29. "John Udall's Journal," photostatic copy, Huntington Library, San Marino, Calif.

30. Robert V. Hine, *The American West: An Interpretive History* (Boston: Little, Brown, 1973), p. 315.

31. Quoted in Daniel J. Boorstin, *The Americans: The National Experience* (New York: Vintage Press, 1965), p. 83.

32. *Ibid.* p. 84.

33. Hugh Davis Graham and Ted Robert Gurr (eds.), *The History of Violence in America, a Report to the National Commission on the Causes and Prevention of Violence* (New York: Praeger, 1970), p. xiv.

Bibliography

Literally millions of pages have been written on various aspects of violence in the American frontier. Books and articles about outlaws and gunfighters have been especially popular, although some are based upon pure fantasy and may properly be classified as literary trash. Popular writers and serious scholars have paid an extraordinary amount of attention to fur trappers, Indians, miners, military commanders, and ranchers—and violence has frequently gone hand in hand with the activities and institutions associated with all of them.

Since the 1960's, dozens of scholarly papers, books, and monographs have appeared which examine particular events, groups, and individuals associated with frontier violence. Few of these works attempt an analysis of psychological causes beyond superficial explanations.

So far, no major synthesis of general violence in the American West during the frontier period has been published. In the massive report submitted to the National Commission on the Causes and Prevention of Violence (1970), only one of the twenty-five chapters deals specifically with frontier aggression.

I have obtained copies of ten or twelve papers delivered at recent historical conventions during sessions on frontier violence; they are listed here under the heading of "Manuscripts and Miscellaneous Sources." Books, scholarly articles, manuscripts, newspaper and magazine articles, letters, and private journals which either touch upon or deal exclusively with the theme of frontier violence form the major body of the sources I examined.

Much information of an historical nature has also been published in current newspapers and popular magazines. Particularly useful were *The New York Times, Los Angeles Times, Toledo Blade, Toledo Times, Life* and *Look* (before they suspended publication), *Harper's, Atlantic, American Heritage, Newsweek, Time, Sunset Magazine,* and *Playboy.* Practically every current historical journal has from time to time published articles on events relating to frontier violence. Among those I consulted were *Mississippi Valley Historical Review, Journal of American History, American Historical Review, American Scholar, The American West, The Journal of the West, Arizona and the West, The Southwestern Historical Quarterly, Great Plains Journal, Southwest Review, Montana Magazine of History, Pacific Northwest Quarterly, Pacific Coast Historical Review, Southwestern Studies, Kansas State Historical Association Collection, Historical Society of Southern California Quarterly, American Jewish Archives, Colorado Magazine, New Mexico Historical Review, William and Mary Quarterly, Idaho Yesterdays,* and *Annals of Wyoming.*

Among the nineteenth-century newspaper and magazines that were indispensable to this study were *The Atlantic Monthly, The Overland Monthly, Outlook, Harper's New Monthly Magazine, Harper's Weekly, The Nation, Historical Society of Southern California Annual, Munsey's Magazine, Scribner's Magazine, Frank Leslie's Illustrated Newspaper, Police Gazette, San Francisco Post, San Francisco Call, San Francisco Examiner, Sacramento Bee, San Francisco Chronicle, Philadelphia Gazette, Arkansas Gazette,* and *Missouri Gazette.*

The following list of sources is not intended to be a complete bibliography of works on frontier violence. Rather, it represents what I found essential to the research and writing of this book. In addition, I have omitted listing considerable material on violence which was not especially relative to my approach to the subject.

Books

David Abrahamsen, *Our Violent Society* (New York: Funk & Wagnalls, 1970).

Rodolfo Acuña, *Occupied America: The Chicano's Struggle Toward Liberation* (San Francisco: Canfield Press, 1972).

Alexander B. Adams, *Geronimo* (New York: Berkeley Medallion Books, 1971).

James Truslow Adams, *Revolutionary New England 1691–1776* (New York: Cooper Square Publications, 1968).

A. C. Appler, *The Younger Brothers: Their Life and Character* (New York: Frederick Fell, 1955).

Herbert Aptheker (ed.), *A Documentary History of Negro People in the United States* (New York: Citadel Press, 1951).

Robert G. Athearn, *High Country Empire: The High Plains and Rockies* (New York: McGraw-Hill, 1960).

———, *Westward The Briton* (New York: Scribner's, 1953).

Lewis Atherton, *The Cattle Kings* (Bloomington: University of Indiana Press, 1961).

Carl Bakal, *The Right to Bear Arms* (New York: McGraw-Hill, 1966).

Leland D. Baldwin, *Whiskey Rebels: The Story of a Frontier Uprising* (Pittsburgh: University of Pittsburgh Press, 1939).

Hubert Howe Bancroft, *History of California* (7 vols., San Francisco: History Company, Publishers, 1886–90).

———, *History of Utah* (San Francisco: History Company, Publishers, 1890).

———, *Popular Tribunals* (2 vols., San Francisco: History Company, Publishers, 1887).

Eugene C. Barker (ed.), *Texas History* (Dallas: Southwest Press, 1929).

Gunther Barth, *Bitter Strength: A History of the Chinese in the United States, 1850–1870* (Cambridge: Harvard University Press, 1964).

Ed Bartholomew, *Cullen Baker: Premier Texas Gunfighter* (Houston: Frontier Press of Texas, 1954).

Keith H. Basso (ed.), *Western Apache Raiding and Warfare: From the Notes of Grenville Goodwin* (Tucson: University of Arizona Press, 1971).

Edwin C. Bearss and Arrell M. Gibson, *Fort Smith: Little Gibraltar on the Arkansas* (Norman: University of Oklahoma Press, 1969).

Delilah L. Beasley, *The Negro Trail Blazers of California* (Los Angeles: privately published, 1919).

Warren A. Beck, *New Mexico: A History of Four Centuries* (Norman: University of Oklahoma Press, 1962).

I. J. Benjamin, *Three Years in America, 1859–1862*, trans. by Charles

Reznikoff (Philadelphia: Jewish Publication Society of America, 1956).

Estelline Bennett, *Old Deadwood Days* (New York: J. H. Sears & Co., 1928).

Donald J. Berthrong, *The Southern Cheyennes* (Norman: University of Oklahoma Press, 1963).

Donald J. Berthrong and Odessa Davenport (eds.), *Joseph Reddeford Walker and the Arizona Adventure* (Norman: University of Oklahoma Press, 1956).

Henry Bienen, *Violence and Social Change: A Review of Current Literature* (Chicago: University of Chicago Press, 1968).

Alfred Hoyt Bill, *Rehearsal For Conflict: The Story of Our War with Mexico, 1846–1848* (New York: Knopf, 1947).

Ray Allen Billington, *The Far Western Frontier 1830–1860* (New York: Harper & Brothers, 1956).

———, *The Protestant Crusade, 1800–1860: A Study of the Origins of American Nativism* (New York: Rinehart, 1952).

———, *Westward Expansion: A History of the American Frontier* (New York: Macmillan, 1967).

Harrison Bird, *War for the West 1790–1813* (New York: Oxford University Press, 1971).

Hoffman Birney, *Vigilantes: A Chronicle of the Rise and Fall of the Plummer Gang of Outlaws in and about Virginia City Montana in the early '60's* (Philadelphia: Penn Publishing, 1929).

Daniel Boorstin, *The Americans: The Democratic Experience* (New York: Random House, 1973).

———, *The Americans: The National Experience* (New York: Random House, 1965).

Morton and Penn Borden (eds.), *The American Tory* (Englewood Cliffs, N.J.: Prentice-Hall, 1972).

Bradford's History of Plymouth Plantation, from Governor William Bradford's Original Manuscript (Boston: Wright and Potter, 1899).

Cyrus Townsend Brady, *Indian Fights and Fighters* (Lincoln: University of Nebraska Press, 1971).

Carl W. Breihan, *Quantrill and His Civil War Guerrillas* (Denver: Sage Books, 1959).

George Douglas Brewerton, *The War in Kansas* (New York: Derby and Jackson, 1856).

Isaac Hill Bromley, *The Chinese Massacre at Rock Springs, Wy-*

oming Territory, September 2, 1885 (Boston: Franklin Press: Rand, Avery, & Co., 1886).

Edgar Beecher Bronson, *Reminiscences of a Ranchman* (Lincoln: University of Nebraska Press, 1962).

Juanita Brooks, *The Mountain Meadows Massacre* (Norman: University of Oklahoma Press, rev. ed., 1962).

Dee Brown, *Bury My Heart at Wounded Knee: An Indian History of the American West* (New York: Holt, Rinehart & Winston, 1970).

Richard Maxwell Brown (ed.), *American Violence* (Englewood Cliffs, N.J.: Prentice-Hall, 1970).

Robert V. Bruce, *1877: Year of Violence* (Chicago: Quadrangle, 1970).

Walter Noble Burns, *The Saga of Billy the Kid* (Garden City, N.Y.: Doubleday, 1926).

Jeff Burton, *Black Jack Christian: Outlaw* (Santa Fe: Press of the Territorian, 1967).

C. L. Camp (ed.), *James Clyman, American Frontiersman, 1792–1881: The Adventures of a Trapper and Covered Wagon Emigrant as Told in His Own Reminiscences and Diaries* (Los Angeles: California Historical Society, 1928).

Harry Carr, *The West is Still Wild* (Cambridge: Houghton Mifflin, 1932).

Joseph H. Cash and Herbert T. Hoover (eds.), *To Be an Indian: An Oral History* (New York: Holt, Rinehart & Winston, 1971).

John Walton Caughey (ed.), *The Indians of Southern California in 1852: The B. D. Wilson Report and a Selection of Contemporary Comment* (San Marino, Calif.: Huntington Library, 1952).

———, *Their Majesties the Mob* (Chicago: University of Chicago Press, 1960).

David M. Chalmers, *Hooded Americanism: The First Century of the Ku Klux Klan; 1865 to the Present* (Garden City, N.Y.: Doubleday, 1965).

Thomas D. Clark, *Frontier America: The Story of the Westward Movement* (New York: Scribner's, 1959).

———, *The Rampaging Frontier* (Bloomington: Indiana University Press, 1964).

John Clay, *My Life on the Range* (New York: Antiquarian Press, 1961).

Robert Glass Cleland, *The Cattle on a Thousand Hills: Southern California, 1850–80* (San Marino, Calif.: Huntington Library, 1969).

Clarence C. Clendenen, *Blood on the Border: The United States Army and the Mexican Irregulars* (Toronto: Macmillan, 1969).

Stanton A. Coblentz, *Villains and Vigilantes: The Story of James King of William and Pioneer Justice in California* (New York: Wilson-Erickson, 1936).

Hamilton Cochran, *Noted American Duels and Hostile Encounters* (Philadelphia: Chilton Books, 1963).

Terry Coleman, *Passage to America: A History of Emigrants from Great Britain and Ireland to America in Mid-nineteenth Century* (London: Hutchinson, 1972).

Ray C. Colton, *The Civil War in the Western Territories: Arizona, Colorado, New Mexico, and Utah* (Norman: University of Oklahoma Press, 1959).

Robert H. Connery (ed.), *Urban Riots: Violence and Social Change* (New York: Random House, 1969).

Copper Camp: Stories of the World's Greatest Mining Town: Butte, Montana, comp. by Workers of the Writers' Program of the Works Projects Administration in the State of Montana (New York: Hastings House, 1943).

The Crimes of the Latter Day Saints in Utah, by a Mormon of 1831 (San Francisco: A. J. Leary, 1884).

George Crook, *General George Crook, His Autobiography*, ed. by Martin F. Schmitt (Norman: University of Oklahoma Press, 1960).

Homer Croy, *Last of the Great Outlaws: The Story of Cole Younger* (New York: Duell, Sloan and Pearce, 1956).

George Armstrong Custer, *My Life on the Plains or, Personal Experiences with Indians* (Norman: University of Oklahoma Press [1874], 1962).

James Elbert Cutler, *Lynch-Law: An Investigation into the History of Lynching in the United States* (London: Longmans, Green, 1905).

Edward Everett Dale, *The Indians of the Southwest: A Century of Development under the United States* (Norman: University of Oklahoma Press, 1949).

Edward Everett Dale and James D. Morrison, *Pioneer Judge: The Life of Robert Lee Williams* (Cedar Rapids: Torch Press, 1958).

———, *The Range Cattle Industry: Ranching on the Great Plains from 1865 to 1925* (Norman: University of Oklahoma Press, 1960).

Roger Daniels, *The Politics of Prejudice: The Anti-Japanese Movement in California and the Struggle for Japanese Exclusion* (Berkeley: University of California Publications in History, 1962).

Philip Davidson, *Propaganda and the American Revolution 1763–1783* (Chapel Hill: University of North Carolina Press, 1941).

David Brion Davis, *Homicide in American Fiction, 1798–1860: A Study in Social Values* (Ithaca: Cornell University Press, 1957).

———, *The Slave Power Conspiracy and the Paranoid Style* (Baton Rouge: Louisiana State University Press, 1969).

Angie Debo, *The Cowman's Southwest: The Reminiscences of Oliver Nelson* (Glendale, Calif.: Arthur H. Clark, 1953).

———, *The Road to Disappearance* (Norman: University of Oklahoma Press, 1941).

Ovid Demaris, *America the Violent* (New York: Cowles Book Co., 1970).

Chester McArthur Destler, *American Radicalism 1865–1901* (Chicago: Quadrangle, 1966).

Bernard DeVoto, *The Year of Decision 1846* (Boston: Little, Brown, 1943).

Everett Dick, *The Sod-House Frontier 1854–1890: A Social History of the Northern Plains from the Creation of Kansas and Nebraska to the Admission of the Dakotas* (New York: Appleton Century, 1937).

John P. Diggins, *The American Left in the Twentieth Century* (New York: Harcourt Brace Jovanovich, 1973).

Richard Dillon, *Burnt-Out Fires: California's Modoc Indian Wars* (Englewood Cliffs, N.J.: Prentice-Hall, 1973).

———, *The Hatchet Men: The Story of the Tong Wars in San Francisco's Chinatown* (New York: Coward-McCann, 1962).

Thomas J. Dimsdale, *The Vigilantes of Montana* (Norman: University of Oklahoma Press, 1953 reprint).

Randolph C. Downes, *The Rise of Warren Gamaliel Harding, 1865–1920* (Columbus: Ohio State University Press, 1970).

Harry Sinclair Drago, *The Great Range Wars: Violence on the Grasslands* (New York: Dodd, Mead, 1970).

John B. Duff and Peter M. Mitchell (eds.), *The Nat Turner Re-*

bellion: *The Historical Event and the Modern Controversy* (New York: Harper & Row, 1971).

Cordia Sloan Duke and Joe B. Frantz, *6,000 Miles of Fence: Life on the XIT Ranch of Texas* (Austin: University of Texas Press, 1961).

Philip Durham and Everett L. Jones, *The Negro Cowboy* (New York: Dodd, Mead, 1965).

Robert R. Dykstra, *The Cattle Towns* (New York: Knopf, 1968).

Allen A. Erwin, *The Southwest of John H. Slaughter 1841–1922: Pioneer Cattlemen and Trail-Driver of Texas, the Pecos, and Arizona and Sheriff of Tombstone* (Glendale, Calif.: Arthur H. Clark, 1965).

Odie B. Faulk, *The Geronimo Campaign* (New York: Oxford University Press, 1969).

———, *Land of Many Frontiers: A History of the American Southwest* (New York: Oxford University Press, 1968).

———, *Tombstone: Myth and Reality* (New York: Oxford University Press, 1972).

Esther Forbes, *Paul Revere and the World He Lived In* (Boston: Houghton Mifflin, 1942).

Jack D. Forbes, *Apache, Navaho, and Spaniard* (Norman: University of Oklahoma Press, 1960).

Arnold Forster and Benjamin R. Epstein, *Danger on the Right* (New York: Random House, 1964).

John Hope Franklin, *From Slavery to Freedom: A History of Negro Americans* (New York: Knopf, 1967).

———, *The Militant South, 1800–1861* (Cambridge: Harvard University Press, 1956).

Joe B. Frantz and Julian Ernest Choate, Jr., *The American Cowboy: The Myth and the Reality* (Norman: University of Oklahoma Press, 1955).

Joseph Lewis French (ed.), *A Gallery of Old Rogues* (New York: Alfred H. King, 1931).

Ike Fridge, *History of the Chisum War, or Life of Ike Fridge: Stirring Events of Cowboy Life on the Frontier* (no date, no publisher; copy, Rare Book Collection, Huntington Library).

Maurice Frink, W. Turrentine Jackson, and Agnes Wright Spring, *When Grass Was King* (Boulder: University of Colorado Press, 1956).

Gordon H. Frost and John H. Jenkins, *"I'm Frank Hamer": The Life of a Texas Peace Officer* (Austin: Pemberton Press, 1968).

Wayne Gard, *The Chisholm Trail* (Norman: University of Oklahoma Press, 1954).

———, *Frontier Justice* (Norman: University of Oklahoma Press, 1949).

George C. Yount and His Chronicles of the West, Comprising Extracts from His "Memoirs" and From the Orange Clark "Narrative" (Denver: Old West Publishing, 1966).

A. M. Gibson, *The Kickapoos: Lords of the Middle Border* (Norman: University of Oklahoma Press, 1963).

———, *The Chickasaws* (Norman: University of Oklahoma Press, 1971).

———, *The Life and Death of Colonel Albert Jennings Fall* (Norman: University of Oklahoma Press, 1965).

Fred Gibson, *Cowhand: The True Story of a Working Cowboy* (New York: Harper & Brothers, 1953).

Charles N. Glaab (ed.), *The American City: A Documentary History* (Homewood, Ill.: Dorsey Press, 1963).

Dr. Rudolf Glanz, *The Jews of California: From the Discovery of Gold Until 1880* (New York: published with the help of the Southern California Jewish Historical Society, 1960).

William H. Goetzmann, *Exploration and Empire: The Explorer and Scientist in the Winning of the American West* (New York: Vintage Books, Random House, 1966).

Lewis L. Gould, *Wyoming: A Political History, 1886–1896* (New Haven: Yale University Press, 1968).

Hugh Davis Graham and Ted Robert Gurr (eds.), *The History of Violence in America: Historical and Comparative Perspectives. (Report to the National Commission on the Causes & Prevention of Violence)* (New York: Praeger, 1969).

Samuel A. Green, *The Boston Massacre, March 5, 1770* (Worcester, Mass.: Charles Hamilton, 1900).

James Kimmins Greer, *Colonel Jack Hays: Texas Frontier Leader and California Builder* (New York: E. P. Dutton, 1952).

Josiah Gregg, *Commerce of the Prairies,* ed. by Max L. Moorhead (Norman: University of Oklahoma Press, 1954).

George Bird Grinnell, *The Fighting Cheyennes* (Norman: University of Oklahoma Press, 1956).

Don L. and Jean Harvey Griswold, *The Carbonate Camp Called Leadville* (Denver: University of Denver Press, 1951).

J. Evetts Haley, *Jeff Milton: A Good Man with a Gun* (Norman: University of Oklahoma Press, 1948).

Francis Hardman, *Frontier Life; or, Tales of the South-Western Border* (Philadelphia: Porter & Coates, n.d.).

Fred Harvey Harrington, *Hanging Judge* (Caldwell, Idado: Caxton Printers, 1951).

Richard Harris, *The Fear of Crime* (New York: Praeger, 1968).

Theodore D. Harris (ed.), *Negro Frontiersman: The Western Memoirs of Henry O. Flipper, First Negro Graduate of West Point* (El Paso: Texas Western College Press, 1963).

Willard A. Heaps, *Riots, U. S. A., 1765–1965* (New York: Seabury Press, 1966).

Robert F. Heizer and Alan F. Almquist, *The Other Californians: Prejudice and Discrimination under Spain, Mexico, and the United States to 1920* (Berkeley: University of California Press, 1971).

Hinton Helper, *Land of Gold* (Baltimore: H. Taylor, 1955).

George D. Hendricks, *The Bad Men of the West* (San Antonio: Naylor, 1941).

Stuart Henry, *Conquering Our Great American Plains: A Historical Development* (New York: E. P. Dutton, 1930).

John Higham, *Strangers in the Land: Patterns of American Nativism 1860–1925* (New York: Atheneum, 1971).

Robert V. Hine, *The American West: An Interpretative History* (Boston: Little, Brown, 1973).

———, *California's Utopian Colonies* (New Haven: Yale University Press, 1966).

The History of Bacon's and Ingram's Rebellion in Virginia, in 1675 and 1676 (Cambridge, Mass.: Press of John Wilson and Son, 1867).

T. H. Hittell, *History of California* (San Francisco: Pacific Press Publishing House, 1885).

Richard Hofstadter, *Anti-Intellectualism in American Life* (New York: Knopf, 1963).

———, *The Paranoid Style In American Politics* (New York: Knopf, 1965).

Richard Hofstadter and Michael Wallace (eds.): *American Violence: A Documentary History* (New York: Knopf, 1970).

William Ransom Hogan, *The Texas Republic: A Social and Economic History* (Norman: University of Oklahoma Press, 1946).

W. Eugene Hollon, *The Southwest: Old and New* (New York: Knopf, 1961).

———— (ed.), *William Bollaert's Texas* (Norman: University of Oklahoma Press, 1956).

James D. Horan, *Desperate Women* (New York: G. P. Putnam's, 1952).

James D. Horan and Paul Sann, *Pictorial History of the Wild West: A True Account of the Bad Men, Desperadoes, Rustlers and Outlaws of the Old West—and the Men Who Fought Them To Establish Law and Order* (New York: Crown Publishers, 1954).

Emerson Hough, *The Story of the Outlaw: A Study of the Western Desperado with Historical Narratives of Famous Outlaws; the Stories of Noted Border Wars; Vigilante Movements and Armed Conflicts on the Frontier* (New York: Outing Publishing, 1907).

W. H. Hutchinson, *California: Two Centuries of Man, Land, & Growth in the Gold State* (Palo Alto, Calif.: American West Publishing, 1969).

George E. Hyde, *Indians of the High Plains: From the Prehistoric Period to the Coming of Europeans* (Norman: University of Oklahoma Press, 1959).

Irwin Isenberg (ed.), *The City in Crisis* (New York: H. W. Wilson, 1968).

Helen Hunt Jackson, *A Century of Dishonor: A Sketch of the United States Government's Dealing with Some of the Indian Tribes* (New York: Harper & Brothers, 1881).

Joseph Henry Jackson, *Bad Company: The Story of California's Legendary and Actual Stage-Robbers, Bandits, Highwaymen and Outlaws from the Fifties to the Eighties* (New York: Harcourt, Brace, 1939).

————, *Tintypes in Gold: Four Studies in Robbery* (New York, Macmillan, 1939).

Wilbur R. Jacobs (ed.), *The Appalachian Indian Frontier: The Edmond Atkin Report and Plan of 1755* (Lincoln: University of Nebraska Press, 1967).

————, *Indians of the Southern Colonial Frontier: The Edmond Atkin Report and Plan of 1755* (Columbia: University of South Carolina Press, 1954).

Pat Jahns, *The Frontier World of Doc Holliday: Faro Dealer from Dallas to Deadwood* (New York: Hastings House, 1957).

Oakah L. Jones, Jr., *Pueblo Warriors and Spanish Conquest* (Norman: University of Oklahoma Press, 1966).

Philip D. Jordan, *Frontier Law & Order: Ten Essays* (Lincoln: University of Nebraska Press, 1970).

Winthrop D. Jordan, *White over Black: American Attitudes Toward the Negro 1550–1812* (Baltimore: Penguin Books, 1961).

Alvin M. Josephy, Jr., *The Nez Percé Indians and the Opening of the Northwest* (New Haven: Yale University Press, 1965).

———, *The Patriot Chiefs: A Chronicle of American Indian Resistance* (New York: Viking, 1958).

———, *Red Power: The American Indians' Fight for Freedom* (New York: McGraw-Hill, 1971).

Alvin M. Josephy, Jr., *et al.* (eds.), *The American Heritage Book of Indians* (New York: American Heritage, 1961).

William Loren Katz, *Eyewitness: The Negro in American History* (New York: Pitman, 1967).

William A. Keleher, *Violence in Lincoln County 1869–1881* (Albuquerque: University of New Mexico Press, 1957).

Charles Kelley, *The Outlaw Trail: A History of Butch Cassidy and His Wild Bunch* (New York: Devin-Adair, 1959).

Jack Temple Kirby, *Darkness at the Dawning: Race and Reform in the Progressive South* (Philadelphia: Lippincott, 1972).

Lily Klasner, *My Girlhood Among Outlaws*, ed. by Eve Ball (Tucson: University of Arizona Press, 1972).

Oliver Knight, *Following the Indian Wars: The Story of the Newspaper Correspondents Among the Indian Campaigners* (Norman: University of Oklahoma Press, 1960).

Arthur Kopit, *Indians* (New York: Bantam Books, 1971).

Howard Lamar, *The Far Southwest, 1846–1912: A Territorial History* (New Haven: Yale University Press, 1966).

Nathaniel P. Langford, *Vigilante Days and Ways*, Introduction by Dorothy M. Johnson (Missoula: Montana State University Press, 1957).

Robert W. Larson, *New Mexico's Quest for Statehood 1846–1912* (Albuquerque: University of New Mexico Press, 1968).

David Lavender, *Bent's Fort* (Lincoln: University of Nebraska Press, 1972).

David Lavender *et al.* (eds.), *The American Heritage History of the Great West* (New York: American Heritage, 1965).

Gustave LeBon, *The Crowd: A Study of the Popular Mind* (London: Ernest Benn, 1952).

William H. Leckie, *The Buffalo Soldiers: A Narrative of the Negro*

Cavalry in the West (Norman: University of Oklahoma Press, 1967).

Zenas Leonard, *The Adventures of Zenas Leonard, Fur Trader and Trapper, 1831–1836* (Cleveland: Burrows Bros., 1904).

John Lord, *Frontier Dust,* ed. by Natalie Shipman (Hartford: Edwin Valentine Mitchell, 1926).

James McCague, *The Second Rebellion: The Story of the New York City Draft Riots of 1863* (New York: Dial Press, 1968).

Jim McIntire, *Early Days in Texas: A Trip to Hell and Heaven* (Kansas City, Mo.: McIntire Publishing, 1902).

Edwin C. McReynolds, *Missouri: A History of the Crossroads State* (Norman: University of Oklahoma Press, 1962).

Carey McWilliams, *North from Mexico: The Spanish-Speaking People of the United States* (New York: Greenwood Press, 1968).

Raymond W. Mack (ed.), *Prejudice and Race Relations* (Chicago: Quadrangle, 1970).

Jacob Rader Marcus (ed.), *Memoirs of American Jews, 1775–1865,* I–III (Philadelphia: Jewish Publication Society of America, 1955).

Elizabeth Margo, *Taming the Forty-Niner* (New York: Rinehart, 1955).

Douglas D. Martin, *Yuma Crossing* (Albuquerque: University of New Mexico Press, 1954).

Everett Dean Martin, *The Behavior of Crowds: A Psychological Study* (New York: Harper & Brothers, 1920).

Merrill J. Mattes, *Indians, Infants and Infantry: Andrew and Elizabeth Burt on the Frontier* (Denver: Old West Publishing, 1960).

Samuel May, *The Fugitive Slave Law and Its Victims* (New York: American Anti-Slavery Society, 1861).

Mildred Mayhall, *The Kiowas* (Norman: University of Oklahoma Press, 1971).

Herman Melville, *The Confidence Man: His Masquerade* (New York: Grove Press, 1955).

A. S. Mercer, *The Banditti of the Plains or The Cattlemen's Invasion of Wyoming in 1892: The Crowning Infamy of the Ages* (Norman: University of Oklahoma Press, 1954).

Frederick Merk, *Manifest Destiny and Mission in American History: A Reinterpretation* (New York: Random House, 1963).

Nyle H. Miller and Joseph W. Snell, *Great Gunfighters of the*

FRONTIER VIOLENCE

Kansas Cowtowns, 1867–1886 (Lincoln: University of Nebraska Press, 1963).

Perry Miller, *The New England Mind: From Colony to Province* (Cambridge: Harvard University Press, 1953).

James I. Mitchell, *Colt: The Man, the Arms, the Company* (Harrisburg, Pa.: Stackpole, 1959).

J. Paul Mitchell (ed.), *Race Riots in Black and White* (Englewood Cliffs, N.J.: Prentice-Hall, 1970).

Jay Monaghan (ed.), *The Book of the American West* (New York: Julian Messner, 1963).

———, *Civil War on the Western Border, 1854–1865* (Boston: Little, Brown, 1955).

Dale L. Morgan, *Jedediah Smith and the Opening of the West* (Lincoln: University of Nebraska Press, 1964).

Dale L. Morgan and James R. Scobie (eds.), *William Perkins' Journal of Life at Sonora, 1849–1852* (Berkeley: University of California Press, 1964).

Mormons and Mormonism: Inside History of the Present Anti-Mormon Crusade, by a Non-Mormon ten years in Utah (Salt Lake City, Utah: 1899); original edition, Huntington Library, San Marino, Calif., Xerox copy in possession of the author).

Gustavus Myers, *History of Bigotry in the United States* (New York: Capricorn, 1960).

John H. Nankivell, *History of the Military Organizations of the State of Colorado, 1860–1935* (Denver: W. H. Kistler Stationery, 1935).

Maurice H. and Marco R. Newmark (eds.), *Sixty Years in Southern California, 1853–1913 Containing the Reminiscences of Harris Newmark* (New York: Knickerbocker Press, 1916).

Edward J. Nichols, *Zach Taylor's Little Army* (Garden City, N.Y.: Doubleday, 1963).

Lewis Nordyke, *John Wesley Hardin: Texas Gunman* (New York: William Morrow, 1957).

Richard O'Connor, *Bat Masterson: The Biography of One of the West's Most Famous Gunfighters and Marshals* (Garden City, N.Y.: Doubleday, 1957).

Ralph Hedrick Ogle, *Federal Control of the Western Apaches 1848–1886* (Albuquerque: University of New Mexico Press, 1970).

Watson Parker, *Gold in the Black Hills* (Norman: University of Oklahoma Press, 1966).

Rodman Wilson Paul, *Mining Frontiers of the Far West 1848–1880* (New York: Holt, Rinehart & Winston, 1963).

Jim Berry Pearson, *The Maxwell Land Grant* (Norman: University of Oklahoma Press, 1961).

Lynn I. Perrigo, *The American Southwest: Its People and Cultures* (New York: Holt, Rinehart & Winston, 1971).

Edward Pessen, *Jacksonian America: Society, Personality, and Politics* (Homewood, Ill.: Dorsey Press, 1969).

Leonard Pitt, *The Decline of the Californios: A Social History of the Spanish-Speaking Californians, 1846–1890* (Berkeley: University of California Press, 1971).

Richard Polenberg, *War and Society: The United States, 1941–1945* (Philadelphia: Lippincott, 1972).

Earl Pomeroy, *The Pacific Slope: A History of California, Oregon, Washington, Idaho, Utah, and Nevada* (New York: Knopf, 1965).

Austin L. Porterfield, *Cultures of Violence: A Study of the Tragic Man in Society* (Fort Worth: Texas Christian University Press, 1964).

Francis Paul Prucha, *Broadax and Bayonet: The Role of the United States Army in the Development of the Northwest, 1815–1860* (Lincoln: University of Nebraska Press, 1967).

———, *The Sword of the Republic: The United States Army on the Frontier, 1783–1846* (London: Macmillan, 1969).

——— (ed.), *The Indian in American History* (New York: Holt, Rinehart & Winston, 1971).

Richard Reinhardt, *Out West on the Overland Train: Across-the-Continent with Leslie's Magazine in 1877 and the Overland Trip in 1967* (Palo Alto, Calif.: American West Publishing, 1967).

Leonard L. Richards, *Gentlemen of Property and Standing: Anti-Abolition Mobs in Jacksonian America* (New York: Oxford University Press, 1970).

Rupert Norval Richardson, *The Frontier of Northwest Texas 1846–76: Advance and Defense by the Pioneer Settlers of the Cross Timbers and Prairies* (Glendale, Calif.: Arthur H. Clark, 1963).

Rupert Norval Richardson, Ernest Wallace, and Adrian N. Anderson, *Texas: The Lone Star State* (Englewood Cliffs, N.J.: Prentice-Hall, 1970).

Don Rickey, Jr., *Forty Miles a Day on Beans and Hay* (Norman: University of Oklahoma Press, 1963).

————, *War in the West—The Indian Campaigns* (Crow Agency, Mont.: Custer Battlefield Historical and Museum Association, 1956).

Robert E. Riegel and Robert G. Athearn, *America Moves West* (New York: Holt, Rinehart & Winston, 1971).

Carl Coke Rister, *Fort Griffin on the Texas Frontier* (Norman: University of Oklahoma Press, 1956).

————, *No Man's Land* (Norman: University of Oklahoma Press, 1948).

————, *Robert E. Lee in Texas* (Norman: University of Oklahoma Press, 1946).

————, *Southern Plainsmen* (Norman: University of Oklahoma Press, 1938).

Joe T. Roff, *A Brief History of Early Days in North Texas and the Indian Territory* (Roff, Okla.: privately printed, 1930).

Joseph G. Rosa, *The Gunfighter: Man or Myth?* (Norman: University of Oklahoma Press, 1969).

Arnold Rose, *The Roots of Prejudice: The Race Question in Modern Society* (Paris: UNESCO, 1958).

Thomas Rose (ed.), *Violence in America: A Historical and Contemporary Reader* (New York: Random House, 1970).

Elliott M. Rudwick, *Race Riot at East St. Louis, July 2, 1917* (Cleveland: World Publishing, 1966).

Budge Ruffner, *All Hell Needs Is Water* (Tucson: University of Arizona Press, 1972).

Don Russell, *The Lives and Legends of Buffalo Bill* (Norman: University of Oklahoma Press, 1960).

Kent Ruth, *Great Day in the West: Forts, Posts, and Rendezvous Beyond the Mississippi* (Norman: University of Oklahoma Press, 1963).

Elmer Clarence Sandmeyer, *The Anti-Chinese Movement in California* (Urbana, Ill.: University of Illinois Press, 1939).

Morris U. Schappes (ed.), *A Documentary History of the Jews in the United States, 1654–1875* (New York: Citadel Press, 1952).

Don Schellie, *Vast Domain of Blood: The Story of the Camp Grant Massacre* (Los Angeles: Westernlore Press, 1968).

Arthur Schlesinger, Jr., *Violence: America in the Sixties* (New York: New American Library, 1968).

Henry Blackman Sell and Victor Weybright, *Buffalo Bill and the Wild West* (New York: Oxford University Press, 1955).

William A. Settle, Jr., *Jesse James Was His Name* (Columbia, Mo.: University of Missouri Press, 1966).

Paul F. Sharp, *Whoop-up Country: The Canadian American West, 1865–1885* (Minneapolis: University of Minnesota Press, 1955).

Charles Howard Shinn, *Mining Camps: A Study in American Frontier Government*, ed. by Rodman Wilson Paul (New York: Harper & Row, 1965).

Glenn Shirley, *Law West of Fort Smith* (New York: Henry Holt & Co., 1957).

Charles A. Siringo, *A Cowboy Detective: A True Story of Twenty-Two Years with a World-Famous Detective Agency* (Chicago: W. B. Conky, 1912).

Irving J. Sloan, *Our Violent Past: An American Chronicle* (New York: Random House, 1970).

Richard Slotkin, *Regeneration Through Violence: The Mythology of the American Frontier, 1600–1860* (Middletown, Conn.: Wesleyan University Press, 1973).

Frank Meriweather Smith (ed.), *San Francisco Vigilance Committee of '56* (San Francisco: Barry, Baird, 1875).

Helena Huntington Smith, *The War on Powder River* (New York: McGraw-Hill, 1966).

Clinton A. Snowden, *History of Washington* (4 vols., New York: Century History, 1909), IV.

C. L. Sonnichsen, *Pass of the North: Four Centuries on the Rio Grande* (El Paso: Texas Western Press, 1968).

———, *Roy Bean: Law West of the Pecos* (New York: Macmillan, 1943).

Edward H. Spicer, *Cycles of Conquest: The Impact of Spain, Mexico, and the United States on the Indians of the Southwest, 1533–1960* (Tucson: University of Arizona Press, 1962).

Kenneth M. Stampp, *The Peculiar Institution: Slavery in the Antebellum South* (New York: Knopf, 1956).

Kevin Starr, *Americans and the California Dream, 1850–1915* (New York, Oxford University Press, 1973).

Kent Ladd Steckmesser, *The Western Hero in History and Legend* (Norman: University of Oklahoma Press, 1965).

Melvin Steinfield, *Cracks in the Melting Pot: Racism and Discrimination in American History* (Beverly Hills, Calif.: Glencoe Press, 1970).

Floyd B. Streeter, *Ben Thompson: Man with a Gun* (New York: Frederick Fell, 1957).

Granville Stuart, *Forty Years on the Frontier* (Cleveland: Arthur H. Clark, 1925).

Fred E. Sutton and A. B. MacDonald, *Hands Up! Stories of the Six-Gun Fighters of the Old Wild West* (Indianapolis: Bobbs-Merrill, 1926).

Morris F. Taylor, *First Mail West* (Albuquerque: University of New Mexico Press, 1971).

Thirty Years of Lynching in the United States, 1889–1918 (New York: NAACP Publishers, 1919).

Zoe A. Tilghman, *Outlaw Days: A True History of Early-Day Oklahoma Characters* (Oklahoma City: Harlow Publishing, 1926).

Alexis de Tocqueville, *Democracy in America*, trans. by Henry Reeve, ed. by Henry Steele Commager (New York: Oxford University Press, 1946).

K. Ross Toole, *Montana: An Uncommon Land* (Norman: University of Oklahoma Press, 1959).

Frederick Jackson Turner, *The Frontier in American History* (New York: Holt, Rinehart & Winston [1920], 1963).

Mark Twain, *Roughing It* (New York: Harper & Row, 1871).

Ralph Emerson Twitchell, *The Leading Facts of New Mexican History* (2 vols., Albuquerque: Horn and Wallace, 1963).

Stanley Vestal, *Joe Meek: The Merry Mountain Man* (Caldwell, Idaho: Caxton Printers, 1952).

———, *Queen of Cowtowns: Dodge City "The Wickedest Little City in America" 1872–1886* (New York: Harper & Brothers, 1952).

———, *Warpath and Council Fire* (New York: Random House, 1948).

Orville J. Victor, *History of American Conspiracies . . . From 1760 to 1860* (New York: James D. Torrey, 1863).

Daniel Walker, *Rights in Conflict* (New York: New American Library, 1968).

Edward S. Wallace, *The Great Reconnaissance* (Boston: Little, Brown, 1955).

Ernest Wallace and E. Adamson Hoebel, *The Comanches: Lords of the South Plains* (Norman: University of Oklahoma Press, 1952).

Eugene Victor Walter, *Terror and Resistance: A Study of Political Violence with Case Studies of Some Primitive African Communities* (New York: Oxford University Press, 1969).

Capt. Eugene F. Ware, *The Indian War of 1864* (Lincoln: Bison Book, University of Nebraska Press, 1960).

Walter Prescott Webb, *The Great Plains* (Boston: Ginn, 1931).

———, *The Texas Rangers: A Century of Frontier Defense* (Boston: Houghton Mifflin, 1935).

——— (ed.), *The Handbook of Texas* (2 vols., Austin: Texas Historical Association, 1952).

Albert K. Weinburg, *Manifest Destiny: A Study of Nationalist Expansionism in American History* (Chicago: Quadrangle, 1963).

Paul I. Wellman, *Death on Horseback: Seventy Years of War for the American West* (Philadelphia: Lippincott, 1934).

———, *A Dynasty of Western Outlaws* (Garden City, N.Y.: Doubleday, 1961).

Walter F. White, *Rope & Faggot: A Biography of Judge Lynch* (New York: Knopf, 1929).

James Williams, *Life and Adventures of James Williams, a Fugitive Slave, With a Full Description of the Underground Railroad* (Saratoga, Calif.: R and E Research Associates, [1874], 1970).

Mary F. Williams, *History of the San Francisco Committee of Vigilance of 1851* (Berkeley: University of California Press, 1921).

George F. Willison, *Here They Dug the Gold* (New York: Reynal & Hitchcock, 1931).

———, *Saints and Strangers* (New York: Reynal & Hitchcock, 1945).

Oscar Osburn Winther, *Via Western Express and Stagecoach* (Lincoln: University of Nebraska Press, 1968).

C. Vann Woodward, *The Strange Career of Jim Crow* (New York: Oxford University Press, 1966).

Richard P. Young, *Roots of Rebellion: The Evolution of Black Politics and Protest since World War II* (New York: Harper & Row, 1970).

Articles

"Abe Goldbaum and the General: An Incident of the Old West," *American Jewish Archives*, XIX, 1 (April 1957).

James Truslow Adams, "Our Lawless Heritage," *Atlantic Monthly*, XLII (1928).

"Agitation against Chinese in West," *The Nation*, 1060 (Oct. 22, 1885).

"Amador Lynching. Bonita, California, 1852," *San Francisco Post* (Nov. 7, 1896).

"Among the Diggers of Thirty Years Ago," *The Overland Monthly*, XVI, 2nd Series (July–Dec. 1890).

Harry H. Anderson, "Deadwood, South Dakota: An Effort at Stability," *Montana, the Magazine of Western History*, XX, 1 (Jan. 1970).

"Anti-Catholic Riots of 1844," *Philadelphia Gazette* (May–July 1844).

"Anti-Chinese Riot in Seattle, W. T.," *The Nation*, 1055 (Sept. 17, 1885).

"Anti-Chinese Prejudice in the West," *The Nation*, 1057 (Oct. 1, 1885).

"Anti-Jewish Sentiment in California, 1855," *American Jewish Archives*, XII, 1 (April 1960).

Ann Patton Baenzinger, "The Texas State Police During Reconstruction: A Reexamination," *Southwestern Historical Quarterly*, LXXII, 4 (April 1969).

C. Barbour, "Two Vigilance Committees," *The Overland Monthly*, X (Sept. 1887).

Jack Barrows, "Ringo," *The American West*, VII, 1 (Jan. 1970).

Rex Mitchell Baxter, "A New Kind of Vigilante Committee," *The Arena*, XL (Dec. 1908).

William Gardner Bell, "Frontier Lawman," *The American West*, I, 3 (Summer 1964).

"Blood in the Streets: Subculture of Violence," cover story, *Time* (April 24, 1972).

J. T. Botkin, "Justice Was Swift and Sure In Early Kansas," *Kansas State Historical Collection*, XVI (1923–24).

S. S. Boynton, "The Miner's Vengeance," *The Overland Monthly*, XXII (Sept. 1893).

Richard Maxwell Brown, "Legal and Behavioral Perspectives on American Vigilantism," in Donald Fleming and Bernard Bailyn (eds.), *Prospectives in American History*, V; *Law and Order in American History* (Cambridge: Charles Warren Center of Studies in American History. Harvard University, 1971), pp. 95–144.

———, "The San Francisco Vigilante Committee of 1856," in John A. Carroll (ed.), *Reflections of Western Historians* (Tucson: University of Arizona Press, 1968).

Porter Emerson Browne, "The Vigilantes: Who and Why and What They Are," *Outlook*, CXIX (May 2, 1918).

Art Buchwald, "Drastic Action Needed to Promote Use of Hand-guns for Safer America," *Toledo Blade* (May 23, 1972).

Hamlin Cannon, "The Morriste War: Insurrection of a Self-styled Prophet," *The American West*, VII, 6 (Nov. 1970).

"Carrying Concealed Weapons in St. Louis," *Missouri Gazette* (Feb. 24, 1819).

John G. Cawelti, "Cowboys, Indians, and Outlaws," *The American West*, I, 2 (Spring 1964).

———, "The Gunfighter and Society," *The American West*, V, 2 (March 1968).

Samuel E. Chamberlin, "My Confession," Part I, *Life* (July 23, 1956).

"A Chapter on the Coolie Trade," *Harper's New Monthly Magazine*, XXIX (June 1864).

"Chinese Massacre at Rock Springs, Wyoming," *The Nation*, 1054 (Sept. 10, 1885).

"Chinese Massacre at Rock Springs, Wyoming," *The Nation*, 1056 (Sept. 24, 1885).

"The Connection of the Mormons with the Mountain Meadows Massacre," *San Francisco Call* (Jan. 29, 1882).

John L. Considine, "The Vigilantes of the Comstock: How the Mysterious 601 Cleaned up Virginia City," *Sunset Magazine* (June 1922).

Win. J. Davis, "Chinese in Early Days," *Sacramento Bee* (Jan. 21, 1886).

Paul M. De Falla, "Lantern in the Western Sky," *Historical Society of Southern California Quarterly*, XLII, 2 (1943).

Carl N. Degler, "Our Taste for Violence," *The Nation*, CXCI (Aug. 20, 1960).

"Democracy versus Demo-n-cracy," *Survey*, XL (Aug. 3, 1918).

C. P. Dorland, "The Chinese Massacre at Los Angeles in 1871," *Historical Society of Southern California Annual*, III (1894).

David DuFault, "These Chinese in the Mining Camps of California: 1848–1870," *The Historical Society of Southern California Quarterly*, XLI (July 1959).

"Early Days in the Mountains: A Pioneer's Quaint Relations of Personal Experience," *San Francisco Call* (July 21, 1889).

Clement Eaton, "Mob Violence in the Old South," *Mississippi Valley Historical Review*, XXIX (Dec. 1942).

John C. Ewers, "When Red and White Men Met," *The Western Historical Quarterly*, II, 2 (April 1971).

"Excerpts from National Panel's Statement on Violence in TV Entertainment," *New York Times* (Sept. 25, 1969).

Odie B. Faulk, "Law and the Land," *The American West*, VII, 1 (Jan. 1970).

Floyd S. Fierman, "Peddlers and Merchants on the Southwest Frontier, 1850–1880," *Password* of the El Paso County Historical Society, VIII, 2 (1963).

"The First Two Official Hangings in San Francisco," *San Francisco Examiner* (Oct. 2, 1887).

"A 'Forty-Niner," in *Jewish Pioneers and Patriots* (Philadelphia: Jewish Publication Society of America, 1948).

Joe B. Frantz, "The Frontier Tradition: An Invitation to Violence," in Hugh Davis Graham and Ted Robert Gurr (eds.), *The History of Violence in America* (New York: New York Times, 1970).

Erich Fromm, "The Erich Fromm Theory of Aggression," *New York Times Magazine* (March 27, 1972).

Wayne Gard, "The Law of the American West," in Jay Monaghan (ed.), *The Book of the American West* (New York: Julian Messner, 1963).

Gilbert Geis, "Violence in American Society," *Current History*, LII (June 1967).

Paul Good, "Blam! Blam! Blam! Not Gun Nuts, but Pistol Enthusiasts," *New York Times Magazine* (Sept. 18, 1972).

Mrs. J. H. Goodnough, "David G. Thomas' Memories of the Chinese Riot at Rock Springs," *Annals of Wyoming*, XIX–XX (1947–48).

Lewis L. Gould, "A. S. Mercer and the Johnson County War: A Reappraisal," *Arizona and the West*, VII (Spring 1965).

Calvin W. Gower, "Vigilantes," *Colorado Magazine*, XLI (Spring 1964).

J. M. Guinn, "The Sonoran Migration," *Annual Publications of The Historical Society of Southern California, 1909–1910*, VIII (Feb. 1891).

William T. Hagan, "Kiowas, Comanches, and Cattlemen: A Case Study of the Failure of U. S. Reservation Policy," *Pacific Historical Review*, XL, 3 (Aug. 1971).

Thomas W. Higginson, "Nat Turner's Insurrection," *The Atlantic Monthly*, VIII (Aug. 1861).

Ted C. Hinckley, "Prospectors, Profits & Prejudice," *The American West*, II, 2 (Spring 1965).

Richard Hofstadter, "America as a Gun Culture," *American Heritage*, XXI, 6 (Oct. 1970).

Stewart H. Holbrook, "Our Tradition of Violence," *The American Mercury*, LXVIII (Nov. 1939).

W. C. Holden, "Law and Lawlessness of the Texas Frontier," *The Southwestern Historical Quarterly*, XLIV (Oct. 1940).

W. Eugene Hollon, "Rushing for Land: Oklahoma, 1889," *The American West*, III, 4 (Fall 1966).

W. H. Hutchinson, "Law, Order, and Survival," *The American West*, VII, 1 (Jan. 1970).

"Is America by Nature a Violent Society?" series of articles by nine authorities on violence, *New York Times Magazine* (April 28, 1968).

Wilbur Jacobs, "The Fatal Confrontation: Early Native-White Relations on the Frontiers of Australia, New Guinea, and America—A Comparative Study," *Pacific Historical Review*, XL, 3 (Aug. 1971).

———, "Frontiersmen, Fur Traders and Other Varmints: An Ecological Appraisal of the Frontier in American History," AHA *Newsletter* (Nov. 1970).

"Jews in the Colorado Mining Camps," *American Jewish Archives*, XIII, 2 (Oct. 1956).

"Joaquin Murieta: The Truth About a Notorious Outlaw," *San Francisco Call* (March 14, 1894).

Alvin M. Josephy, Jr., "The Custer Myth," *Life* (July 2, 1971).

Joseph Nimmo Jun, "The American Cowboy," *Harper's New Monthly Magazine*, LXXIII (1886).

"Juan Batista Alvarado, Governor of California," *The Overland Monthly*, VI, 2nd series (Oct. 1885).

Earnest Kaiser, "American Indians and Mexican Americans: A Selected Bibliography," *Freedomways*, IX (Fall 1969).

Michael Kennedy, "Infernal Collector," *Montana Magazine of History*, V (Spring 1954).

"The Knights of Labor on the Chinese Labor Situation," *The Overland Monthly*, VII, 2nd series (March 1886).

Dr. N. D. Labadie, "Let Us Attack the Enemy and Give Them Hell! The Battle of San Jacinto," ed. by Stephen B. Oates, *The American West*, V, 3 (May 1968).

Howard R. Lamar, "The New Old West," *Yale Alumni Magazine*, XXXVI, 1 (Oct. 1972).

David Lavender, "The Mexican War: Climax of Manifest Destiny,"
    The American West, V, 3 (May 1968).

Billy Bob Lightfoot, "The Negro Exodus from Comanche County,
    Texas," *The Southwestern Historical Quarterly*, XVI, 3
    (Jan. 1953).

William H. Locklear, "The Celestials and the Angels: A Study of
    the Anti-Chinese Movement in Los Angeles to 1882," *The
    Historical Society of Southern California Quarterly*, XLII
    (Sept. 1960).

"London Safest of World's Major Cities," *Los Angeles Times*
    (Aug. 20, 1972).

"Lucky Bill's Hanging: Mormon Dislike for the Gentiles," *San
    Francisco Chronicle* (Oct. 9, 1892).

"Lynching of Irish Dick in the Spring of '50," *San Francisco Alta*
    (Aug. 23, 1885).

Don McLeod, "Massacres Part of the American Historical Record,"
    Toledo Blade (Nov. 15, 1970).

Pauline Maier, "Popular Uprisings and Civil Authority in Eight-
    eenth-Century America," *The William and Mary Quarterly*,
    XXVII, 1 (Jan. 1970).

Charles Michelson, "The Vigilantes of the West," *Munsey's Maga-
    zine*, XXV (1910).

"The Mining Troubles in Wyoming," *Frank Leslie's Illustrated
    Newspaper* (Oct. 3, 1885).

Jean Douglas Murphy, "Guns and Butter Life-Style—Rural Militant
    Version," *Los Angeles Times* (Aug. 22, 1972).

James Naughton, "Study of Violence Replacing Law in Protests,"
    Toledo Blade (Dec. 5, 1969).

Stephen B. Oates, "To Wash This Land in Blood: John Brown in
    Kansas," *The American West*, VI, 4; VI, 6 (July 1969; Nov.
    1969).

Roger Olmstead, "San Francisco and the Vigilante Style," *The
    American West*, VII, 1; VII, 2 (Jan. 1970; March 1970).

James O'Meara, "Concealed Weapons and Crimes," *The Overland
    Monthly*, XVI (July 1890).

———, "Early California: How Justice Was Often Administered,"
    Sacramento Bee (Dec. 21, 1881).

Kenneth Owens, "Pierce City Incident, 1885–1886," *Idaho Yester-
    days*, III, 3 (Fall 1959).

Drew Pearson, "Report of Violence Sober Reading," *Toledo Blade*
    (Jan. 1, 1969).

———, "TV Violence Quiz Handed Old Line," *Toledo Blade* (Jan. 12, 1969).

Lynn I. Perrigo, "Law and Order in Early Colorado Camps," *Mississippi Valley Historical Review*, XXVIII (June 1941).

Edward Pessen, "The Egalitarian Myth and the American Social Reality,"*American Historical Review*, LXXVIII, 4 (Oct. 1971).

James E. Pilcher, "Outlawry on the Mexican Border," *Scribner's Magazine*, X (July–Dec. 1891).

"The Pit River War: Joaquin Miller's Share in the Campaign," *San Francisco Chronicle* (April 1, 1883).

"Playing at 'Gun Control,' " *Toledo Blade* (May 23, 1972).

John Poppy, "Violence: We Can End It," *Look* (June 10, 1969).

Francis Paul Prucha, "Andrew Jackson's Indian Policy," *The Indians in American History* (New York: Holt, Rinehart & Winston, 1971).

———, Review of *Bury My Heart at Wounded Knee*, *American Historical Quarterly*, LXXVII, 2 (April 1972).

Edmund E. Radlowski, "Law and Order at Cripple Creek, 1890–1900," *Journal of the West*, IX (July 1970).

"The Right to Bear Arms," *Toledo Blade* (Sept. 15, 1968).

Carl Coke Rister, "Outlaws and Vigilantes of the Southern Plains, 1865–1885," *Mississippi Valley Historical Review*, XIX (1932–33).

Gary L. Roberts, "The West's Gunmen," *The American West*, VIII, 1; VIII, 2 (Jan. 1971; March 1971).

Henry Robinson, "Pioneer Days of California," *The Overland Monthly*, VIII (May 1872).

Lloyd I. Rudolph, "The Eighteenth Century Mob in America and Europe," *American Quarterly*, XI (1959).

Don Russell, "How Many Indians Were Killed," *The American West*, X, 4 (July 1973).

———, "The Indians and Soldiers of the American West," in Jay Monaghan (ed.), *The Book of the American West* (New York: Julian Messner, 1963).

"Sam Rayburn's Frontier Life," *Life*, LI (Oct. 20, 1961).

Arthur Schlesinger, Jr., "The Politics of Violence," *Harper's*, CCXXXVII, 1419 (Aug. 1968).

Robert Seager II, "Some Denominational Reaction to Chinese Immigration to California, 1856–1892," *Pacific Historical Review*, XXVIII (1959).

Helena Huntington Smith, "Sam Bass and the Myth Machine," *The American West*, VII, 1 (Jan. 1970).

J. W. Smurr, "Afterthoughts on the Vigilantes," *Montana Magazine of History*, VIII (April 1958).

C. L. Sonnichsen, "The Wyatt Earp Syndrome," *The American West*, VII, 3 (May 1970).

Robert Louis Stevenson, "Despised Races," *Across the Plains* (London: Chatto & Windus, [1892], 1905).

Lee Scott Theisen (ed.), "The Fight in Lincoln, N. M., 1878: The Testimony of Two Negro Participants," *Arizona and the West*, XII, 2 (Summer 1970).

"A Triple Hanging: An Event in Sonora in the Early Days," *San Francisco Chronicle* (March 25, 1883).

U. S. Senator Joseph Tydings, "Americans and the Gun," *Playboy*, XVI, 3 (March 1969).

Robert L. Tyler, "Violence at Centralia, 1919," *Pacific Northwest Quarterly*, XLV (Oct. 1954).

Robert M. Utley, "A Chained Dog: The Indian-Fighting Army," *The American West*, X, 4 (July 1973).

"Violence: Angry Heritage," *Time* (July 13, 1969).

"Violence Necessary to TV, Report Says," *Toledo Blade* (Feb. 1, 1972).

"Violence in U. S. Rooted in History," *Toledo Blade* (June 5, 1969).

Richard C. Wade, "Violence in the Cities: A Historical View," in Charles V. Daly (ed.), *Urban Violence* (Chicago: University of Chicago Center for Policy Study, 1969).

Michael Wallace, "The Uses of Violence in American History," *American Scholar*, XL (Winter 1970–71).

"War on the Willamette," *American Jewish Archives*, X, 2 (Oct. 1958).

Walter Prescott Webb, "An Honest Preface," reprinted from *Southwest Review* (Autumn 1951).

William W. White, "The Texas Slave Insurrection of 1860," *The Southwestern Historical Quarterly*, LII, 3 (Jan. 1949).

W. P. Wilcox, "Anti-Chinese Riots in Washington," *The Washington Historical Quarterly*, XX, 3 (July 1929).

"Wild Bunch—Violent Look at a Violent Breed," *Los Angeles Times* (June 15, 1969).

Geoffrey Wolff, Review of *Bury My Heart at Wounded Knee*, *Newsweek* (Feb. 1, 1971).

Manuscripts and Miscellaneous Sources

"A. C. Sweetser to Friends," seven-page letter written from Sacramento City, Feb. 26, 1861, commenting on several acts of violence. (Original, Huntington Library.)

"Anti-Chinese Riot in Seattle, Washington, February 7, 1886," unpublished one-page account of the event by an eyewitness, Col. G. O. Haller (?). (Original manuscript, Huntington Library.)

Richard M. Brown, "American Regulators and Vigilantes: An Hypothesis," paper read at the annual meeting of the Mississippi Valley Historical Association, Cleveland, Ohio, May 1964. (Copy in possession of the author.)

"Chinese Immigration," speech delivered by Hon. William W. Morrow of California, House of Representatives, Washington, D.C., June 28, 1886. (Printed copy, Manuscripts Division, Huntington Library.)

Robert W. Coakley, Paul J. Scheips, and Emma J. Portuondo, "Antiwar and Antimilitary Activities in the United States, 1846–1954," 148-page manuscript, written 1970. (Mimeographic copy, U. S. Army Military Research Collection, Carlisle Barracks, Pa.)

L. W. Coe, "The Cascade Massacre of March 26, 1856," 11-page unpublished manuscript. (Huntington Library.)

Melvyn Dubofsky, "The Role of Environment: The American West and Labor Radicalism," paper read at the Mississippi Valley Historical Association Convention, Cleveland, Ohio, April 1964. (Copy in possession of the author.)

Eighteenth Annual Report of the Women's Union Mission of San Francisco to Chinese Women and Children for the Year 1887 (San Francisco, 1888).

"An English Scrapbook: A Collection of Articles, Reviews, Items and Illustrations Relating to Early California," clipped from twenty-one English newspapers and magazines, 1850–51. (Manuscripts Division, Huntington Library.)

Patrick A. Folk, "The Cincinnati Courthouse Riot of 1884," 22-page unpublished manuscript. (Copy in possession of the author.)

Gerald N. Hallbert, "Bellingham, Washington's Anti-Hindu Riot," 16-page unpublished manuscript. (In possession of the author.)

"Inhuman Behavior of the Anti-Mormons in Illinois," 3-page un-
   published manuscript. (Huntington Library.)
Philip D. Jordan, "Comments on Professor Ben Proctor's "The
   Modern Texas Rangers: A Law Enforcement Dilemma in
   the Rio Grande Valley," 3-page unpublished manuscript.
   (In possession of the author.)
"The Journal of John Udall," photostatic copy of original. (Hunt-
   ington Library, n.d.)
"Journal of a Voyage from Newburyport, Mass. to San Francisco,
   Cal. In the Brig *Charlott*, By a Passenger Commencing Jan.
   23, 1849 and Ending July 23, 1849," unpublished manuscript.
   (Manuscript Division, Huntington Library.)
George Kinnear, "Anti-Chinese Riots at Seattle, Wn., 1886," 22-
   page booklet, privately printed, Seattle, Wash., Feb. 8, 1911.
   (Original copy, Huntington Library.)
Robert W. Larson, "The White Caps of New Mexico: The Political and Ethnic Origins of Western Violence," paper read
   at the annual meeting of the Western Historical Association,
   Tucson, Ariz., Oct. 1968. (Copy in possession of the author.)
Fred Lockley, *Vigilante Days at Virginia City: Personal Narrative
   of Col. Henry E. Dosch, Member of Frémont's Body Guard
   and One-Time Pony Express Rider*, 19-page booklet. (Published by Fred Lockley, Portland, Ore., n.d.)
"Newspaper Record of Jim Marshall of Cripple Creek Colorado,"
   extensive collection of newspaper clippings relative to the
   notorious exploits of the town marshal of Cripple Creek.
   (Huntington Library.)
Robert F. Oaks, "Rationalization for Violence in American History," paper read at the American Historical Convention,
   Pacific Coast Branch, Santa Barbara, Calif., Aug. 1972. (Copy
   in possession of the author.)
Barton C. Olsen, "Vigilantes in the West: A Second Look," unpub-
   lished manuscript. (Copy in possession of the author.)
F. Ross Peterson, "Rationalization for Violence in Contemporary
   America," paper read at the American Historical Convention,
   Pacific Coast Branch, Santa Barbara, Calif., Aug. 1972. (Copy
   in possession of the author.)
William V. Plummer, "Post-Vigilante San Francisco: Changing
   Interpretations," 25-page unpublished manuscript. (Xerox
   copy in possession of the author.)
Ben Proctor, "The Modern Texas Ranger: A Law Enforcement

Dilemma in the Rio Grande Valley," 23-page unpublished manuscript. (In possession of the author.)

Report of Governor Stevenson to Secretary of State Bayard, Aug. 2, 1886, Idaho Territorial Papers, Department of Interior.

Report of the Governor of Wyoming, Nov. 25, 1885, 49th Cong., 1st sess., House Exec. Doc. 12, No. 1, part 5, II (serial 2379).

Richard E. Rubenstein, "Mass Political Violence in the United States: The Wars of Group Liberation," 75-page manuscript, prepared at The Adlai Stevenson Institute, Chicago, Ill., 1967. (Xerox copy in possession of the author.)

Frank H. Smyrl, "Unionism, Abolitionism, and Vigilantism in Texas, 1856–1865." M. A. Thesis, University of Texas, 1961.

"To the President and Members of the Six Chinese Companies" [1876], unpublished, unsigned letter. (Manuscripts Division, Huntington Library.)

U. S. Adjutant General's Office, Federal Aid in Domestic Disturbances, 1787–1903, Sen. Doc. No. 209, 57th Cong., 2nd sess. (Washington, D.C.: Government Printing Office, 1903).

U. S. Congress. House. Joint Select Committee on the Condition of Affairs in the Late Insurrectionary States. *Affairs in the Late Insurrectionary States,* I–XIII. House Report No. 22, 42nd Cong., 2nd sess. (Washington, D.C.: Government Printing Office, 1872).

U. S. War Department, *Annual Report* (Washington, D.C.: Government Printing Office, 1822–1941).

Henry P. Walker, "Retire Peaceably to Your Homes; Arizona Faces Martial Law, 1882," twenty-page paper read at the annual meeting of the Western Historical Association, Tucson, Ariz., Oct. 1968. (Copy in possession of the author.)

Index

Abilene, Kans.: marshal of, 116–17; killings in, 200

abolitionists: violence against, 23, 25; in South, 26; in Kansas and Nebraska, 26–27; unpopularity of, 27; in Texas, 47

Abrahamsen, Dr. David, on Puritan influence, 3, 4

Acuña, Rodolfo, on Lincoln County violence, 182

Adams, Samuel, 10, 14

adultery, death for, 6

Alamo, massacre at, 39, 221

alcohol, effect of, on Indians, 124

Allegheny-Appalachian ridge, laws on land beyond, 9

Allen, Fred, on Indians, 124

Allison, Clay, lawlessness of, 190, 200

American Colonization Society, attacks on, 28

American Revolution, civil violence during, 11–13

Andros, Gov. Edmund, uprising against, 8

"Anti-Coolie Clubs," 95

Antrim, William, *see* Billy the Kid

Apache Indians: in Texas, 43; defeat of, 133; peace of, 139; menace of, 171

Appalachian Mountains, lynch law beyond, 18–19

Arapaho Indians: assigned to Oklahoma, 45; defeat of, 134, 135, 139; help of, at Washita, 136; treaties with, 136–37

Army Medical Corps, and Indians, 206

Army Medical Museum, Indian collections in, 206

Arizona: feuds in, 162; fence-cutting wars in, 168; population of, 172; outlaws in, 172–78; Mexicans in, 208

arson, death for, 6

Arthur, Pres. Chester A., 174

Articles of Confederation, defiance of, 12

assassinations, political, in New Mexico, 192–93

Australia: convicts from, 56; violence in, 220

Australians: in California, 73; and violence, 208

Averell, Jim, lynching of, 154–55, 195

Axtell, Gov. Sam: role of, in Lincoln County War, 182; resignation of, 188

267